THE POLITICS OF
SUCCESSION IN THE U.S.S.R.

Materials on Khrushchev's Rise to Leadership

Sovfoto

THE POLITICS OF SUCCESSION IN THE U.S.S.R.

Materials on Khrushchev's Rise to Leadership

HOWARD R. SWEARER

University of California, Los Angeles

with **MYRON RUSH**

Boston   *Toronto*
LITTLE, BROWN AND COMPANY

PREFACE

THE STUDENT of a foreign government is faced with the problem of a political culture gap. How can he develop an understanding of the dynamic reality of a political system beyond his personal experience — a system that exists behind organizational charts, statistics, and formal institutional structures and procedures? If the country under study is the U.S.S.R., the problem is compounded by the secrecy in which political processes and conflicts are shrouded. This book meets this problem with the idea that the student's perception of the realities of Soviet politics will be heightened by engaging him with Soviet materials organized in a systematic manner and focusing on a major political problem: the succession of political leadership.

Used carefully, this book may also help to answer a question that haunts most beginning students of the Soviet Union: If the nature of the Soviet political system is deliberately obscured and Soviet publications are controlled by the regime and used propagandistically to support its aims, how can we learn about the Soviet political process and how can we be reasonably certain that our perceptions approximate reality? The purpose of this volume is to present a range of Soviet materials on the post-Stalin succession struggle in an orderly way and with some commentary, but, at the same time, to permit the reader considerable latitude for independent interpretations. Thus, he will become sensitized to some of the possibilities and pitfalls in the analysis of the Soviet system through the official press.

The translations from the published speeches at the 20th, 21st, and 22nd Party Congresses used here have been reproduced, by permission, from *The Current Digest of the Soviet Press,* published weekly at Columbia University by the Joint Committee on Slavic Studies, appointed by the American Council of Learned Societies and the Social Science Research Council (copyright, 1956, 1959, and 1962).

Dr. Myron Rush provided valuable advice during the preparation of this book. He read the entire manuscript critically, made suggestions for the selections of Soviet materials, and helped in drafting a number of passages. His pioneering study of the early post-Stalin political struggle, *The Rise of Khrushchev,* provided a number of insights that were beneficial in constructing this volume. I am indebted to Richard Little, Peter Freiberg, and Lidia Savenkov, who provided help in locating materials and in translating sources. The ultimate responsibility for the selections and commentary, however, is mine.

HOWARD R. SWEARER
Pacific Palisades, California

CONTENTS

vii

INTRODUCTION

SPECULATION on the course of leadership politics in the Soviet Union, and the related impact on policy-making, has become since World War II a widespread activity among Western journalists, government analysts, and academic specialists. Although this is an elusive enterprise involving a substantial degree of deduction or even outright guesswork, it is nonetheless a legitimate and important — if oftentimes frustrating — exercise. Some writings of this genre, of course, have been rank speculation, based on flimsy evidence and catering to the sensational. These negative examples, however, should not overshadow those careful attempts to chart the murky course of Kremlin politics which have employed sometimes ingenious techniques to squeeze all possible information from Soviet sources and have woven together the resulting material into a reasonable representation of reality.

"Kremlinology," as the study of Soviet elite politics is sometimes designated in half jest, is stimulated not just by curiosity about the unknown, although the fascination of fitting together the pieces of a mystery is rarely absent. An appreciation of the nature and course of elite politics helps to shed light on Soviet policies, both domestic and foreign, which may be directly related to Western interests. For example, during 1954–55 the available evidence indicates that disagreements within the leadership centered in part on military strategy and its implications for Soviet foreign policy and domestic economic priorities. In a broader context Kremlinology contributes to fuller understanding of the Soviet socio-political system. Because political power is so highly concentrated and wielded so extensively and intensively by a small elite, and since the leadership attempts with varying degrees of success to control and direct all societal activities, to discuss the Soviet system without consideration of elite politics would be akin to flying an airplane without an instrument panel.

This book is not yet another interpretation of the course of Soviet elite politics after Stalin's death. Rather, it aims to present the reader with sufficient Soviet documents relevant to leadership activities between 1953 and 1958 that he may try his own hand at interpretation. Working through Soviet materials on the leadership struggle after Stalin's death should help to sensitize the reader to the possibilities and pitfalls of this type of analysis and enhance his ability to judge the validity of interpretations offered by specialists — interpretations that not infrequently differ at critical points. Merely first-hand engagement with Soviet sources should be an enlightening experience which makes more realistic and vivid to the reader his knowledge about the Soviet Union gleaned from secondary accounts. A number of collections of Soviet sources are now available in English translation but they are not selected and organized for the study of general problems of Soviet politics. By focusing on a particular facet of the Soviet system (i.e., the leadership struggle) and presenting all kinds of Soviet materials — speeches by various officials, newspaper editorials, articles from Party journals, Central Committee resolutions, and still others — bearing on this subject in sequence over a five-year period, the reader hopefully will come away with a deeper understanding of Soviet communications and how they reflect the realities of the system.

By being encouraged, indeed forced, to become intellectually engaged with the raw data, the reader should develop a firmer grasp of the techniques and tactics of Soviet leadership and the issues which occupy its attention. Since, as I believe, leadership is such a central component of the entire Soviet system, this book also sheds light on a number of other important questions about the Soviet Union. For the college or university instructor, the materials in this book might well serve as the basis for a wide range of student essays. Only a partial list of subjects which might be fruitfully examined are: the policy issues in contention after Stalin's death; Khrushchev's style of leadership; the role of ideology in decision-making and leadership conflict; the real or potential modifications in the Soviet system as a result of a succession crisis; and the use of the Soviet press to analyze Soviet politics.

The materials in this book cover the period from Stalin's death in March 1953 to March 1958. Sources published after March 1958 are presented in the last chapter, but they are concerned with the 1953–1958 period. This was a time of intense personal and factional struggle among the leaders who survived Stalin and the particular system of dictatorial rule now designated in the Soviet Union as "Stalinism." The terminal date was marked by Khrushchev's assumption of the Chairmanship of the Council of Ministers, in addition to his other two key positions: First Secretary of the Party Central Committee and Chairman of the Party Central Committee Bureau for the Russian Republic. With Khrushchev's defeat of the "anti-Party" group in June 1957 and his removal of Marshal Zhukov from the political scene the following October, a new phase of post-Stalin leadership commenced. Evidence about post-1958 elite politics is less plentiful and more obscure, and opinions by Western specialists based on this evidence more diverse and tentative than for the previous period. One thing is clear: by early 1958, if not earlier, Khrushchev was the most powerful political leader in the USSR. Whether he has continued to face serious opposition to his policies which limits his exercise of power, and, if so, the nature of this political opposition, cannot at this time be answered with any surety.

There will be a new succession problem facing the Soviet system before too long. At the time of writing, Khrushchev is 70 years old. Whether he dies in power, or, less likely, retires voluntarily or involuntarily, a period of leadership transition could occur at any time. This is a highly important event with potentially far-reaching domestic and international ramifications. No one can foretell what the next transitional period will be like. While it will most certainly not duplicate in detail previous succession crises, a knowledge of these is vital to any reasonable speculation on events in the next such period. A number of developments after Stalin's death were remarkably similar to those after Lenin's: the critical role of the Party machine being perhaps the most

egregious. Thus, by contributing to an understanding of leadership dynamics in the immediate post-Stalin period, this book may also provide
insights into the post-Khrushchev succession period.

As far as possible I have attempted to avoid interpretations when
introducing source materials. The purpose of the first chapter and the
connecting commentary in Chapters II–VII is to put the Soviet documents into context for the reader and to give him some pertinent background information. Of course, I do have my own opinions about the
events following Stalin's death and these cannot be entirely eliminated.
To some extent Soviet materials have had to be "pre-digested." Not all
conceivably relevant sources could be included and some material had
to be abridged. Nevertheless, an effort has been made to include a
representative sampling of materials which can support most reasonable
hypotheses. Although chapters are delimited chronologically, within
chapters sources are sometimes arranged topically so that their significance will be highlighted and the reader will find it easier to make connections among them.

Although this book is designed to stand by itself, the reader unfamiliar with Soviet government and politics may wish to consult
several of the excellent books readily available on the subject. For a
general treatment of the Soviet system, I recommend: Merle Fainsod,
How Russia Is Ruled (Cambridge: Harvard University Press, 1963).
The two studies prepared at the request of the Subcommittee on National Policy Machinery of the United States Senate Committee on
Government Operations and printed by the Government Printing Office, entitled *National Policy Machinery in the Soviet Union* (1960)
and *Staffing Procedures and Problems in the Soviet Union* (1963),
contain excellent, detailed analyses of the top policy-making bodies in
the Soviet Union and descriptions of the men who staff them. For examples of how various Western specialists have interpreted the post-
Stalin leadership struggle, see: Myron Rush, *The Rise of Khrushchev*
(Washington, D.C.: Public Affairs Press, 1958); Robert Conquest,
Power and Policy in the U.S.S.R. (New York: St. Martin's Press,
1961); and Leonhard Wolfgang, *The Kremlin Since Stalin* (New York:
Praeger, 1962). Two interesting analytic studies of the dynamics of lead-
ership succession in the Soviet Union are: Myron Rush, "The Khru-
shchev Succession Problem," *World Politics,* No. 2 (January 1962); and
Brohdan R. Bociurkiw, "The Problem of Succession in the Soviet
Political System: The Case of Khrushchev," *The Canadian Journal of
Economics and Political Science,* No. 4 (November 1960). *The Cur-*

rent Digest of the Soviet Press, published weekly by the Joint Committee on Slavic Studies (with offices at 405 West 117th Street, New York City), contains translations from a large number of Soviet newspapers and journals on a wide variety of subjects for the reader who is unfamiliar with Russian.

I · LEADERSHIP AND ELITE POLITICS

The Theory and Practice of Leadership

According to the classical Marxist concept of historical materialism, the patterns or "laws" of historical development can be scientifically derived and projected into the future through an analysis of the changing modes of economic production and resulting class conflicts. Leaders are the product of their environment, thrown up by a society to carry out particular, historically necessary functions. As Engels once put it, "if a Napoleon had been lacking, another would have filled his place. This is proved by the fact that the man has always been found as soon as he became necessary: Caesar, Augustus, Cromwell, etc."*

* For a discussion of the role of the leader in Marxism and contemporary Soviet ideology, see: Howard R. Swearer, "Bolshevism and the Individual Leader," *Problems of Communism*, No. 2 (March–April 1963).

Marx, to be sure, did not overlook the role a leader may play; moreover, in emphasizing the limits placed on political leadership by its economic and social environment, Marxism served as a useful counterweight to such concepts as Carlyle's overdrawn and romantic thesis that only great men are of consequence in historical development. On the other hand, by asserting that political leadership itself cannot in any fundamental sense alter the course of a society's development, Marxism denigrated unduly the role of leadership and the political realm, making them merely the direct product of economic and class forces and denying that politically organized human will can have a truly reciprocal influence on its milieu. To cite Marx, "it is not the consciousness of men that determines their being, but on the contrary, their being that determines their consciousness." If "great men" could alter the course of history, then an accidental or unique element would be introduced which would cut at the heart of Marxism's essence and appeal: that it can "scientifically" predict the future by fastening on the dialectical development of economic laws and the history-making role of socio-economic classes.

One of the great historical ironies is that the Soviet Union, professing to be guided by Marxist teachings, is a highly politicized society in which a small elite has attempted to reshape society according to its own vision. The nature and role of the Communist Party, the personality and style of a particular leader, and the political conflicts among the elite are all vital (though not the only necessary factors) to an understanding of the development and operation of the Soviet system. The great debate that has stirred the entire communist world since 1956, on the historical role of Stalin, indicates the significance of political leadership in Soviet society, even if its decisiveness has never been officially recognized in Soviet ideology. Lenin, the revolutionary activist, by his personal actions and driving will, as well as by his theoretical innovations concerning the role of the professional revolutionary party, the primacy of "consciousness" over "spontaneity", and the telescoping of the bourgeois and socialist revolutions in Russia, cut deeply into Marxism's determinist pretensions and elevated the role of political leadership far beyond that envisaged by Marx. Although proclaiming his devotion to the Marxist theory of historical development, Lenin, in effect, as early as the turn of the last century asserted that the Russian revolution would hinge on the organization of a professional revolutionary party composed of a small, politically skilled group of leaders who, through their insight into the dialectics of history, would themselves transmit the proper revolutionary consciousness to the masses.

Following the October Revolution, the Bolsheviks, after a brief period of indecision, resolutely declined to share power with other parties or groups. The intransigence of opposition parties, the rigors of war, the disintegration of civil society, the lack of a deep-rooted democratic tradition in Russia, and other circumstantial factors contributed to this outcome. But of at least equal significance in the Bolsheviks' determination to monopolize power were their dogmatic belief in the validity of Marxism–Leninism and their singular ability to interpret it, a naked power drive, the centralist tendencies in Leninism, and contempt for "bourgeois democratic" procedures.

Lenin — and his successors — of course, never publicly suggested that ultimate responsibility be delegated to a single individual; they always maintained that decisions should be, and were, made collectively by the leadership. However, the very factors leading to the monopolization of power in Russia by the Communist Party, as a collective entity, in the absence of any firmly held belief of the right or need of opposition views and any institutionalized process whereby dissenting opinions could be voiced, in fact led to the consolidation of power in the hands of a single man. That one-man dictatorship would be the likely result of Lenin's organizational principles was suggested as early as 1904 by Trotsky, who was then in opposition to Lenin:

> According to Lenin's plan, the working class is replaced by the Party; the Party is replaced by the Party organization; the Party organization is replaced by the Central Committee; and finally the Central Committee is replaced by the dictator.

Concurrent with the consolidation of the position of the Communist Party over Soviet society, power was increasingly concentrated within the Party. Lenin's dominant position in the Party rested largely on his personal authority as father of the revolution; and he was willing to consult with his colleagues and rely heavily on his powers of persuasion to achieve his ends. Nevertheless, he could, on occasion, act in a highly authoritarian manner. Although during his reign force was not unleashed against Party members, he did employ it against other elements of the society. Moreover, at the crucial 10th Party Congress in March 1921, he deplored what he termed the "excessive luxury" of widespread debate over policies which had taken place within the Party in the preceding year, and sponsored a resolution that outlawed the existence of organized factions within the Party.

During the 1920's Stalin, building on the Bolshevik organizational principles bequeathed by Lenin, proceeded to fulfill Trotsky's 1904 prophecy by adeptly and ruthlessly consolidating the Party's control over Soviet society and, at the same time, his own personal control over the Party and the international Communist movement. As General Secretary of the Party, he rapidly expanded the functions and powers of the Party cadre — the full-time, paid Party workers at every echelon of society — at the expense of the Party as a whole and the state administration. By controlling the Party apparatus, he was gradually able to gain control of the lower Party organizations and eventually pack the Party Central Committee with his supporters. While the organizational support of other members of the Politburo was thus being choked off, Stalin, by forming one coalition and then another, successfully played his Politburo opponents off against each other, picking them off one at a time. By 1927 he had defeated the so-called Left Opposition of Trotsky, Zinoviev, and Kamenev. Then, adopting significant portions of the program of the Left Opposition, he turned on the so-called Right Opposition of Bukharin, Tomsky, and Rykov.

By 1928 the twin processes whereby the Party machine extended its control over the Party and the society as a whole, and Stalin consolidated his hold over the Party, had proceeded to the point where Stalin could launch the "second revolution" of forced-draft industrialization and collectivization of agriculture. Such a drastic and swift program of social engineering, which ran counter to the habits and interests of large portions of the population, required the prior existence of a reliable political machine firmly directed by an uncontested leader who was prepared to use not only all means of persuasion but also widespread force. During this "revolution from above" the authoritarian political regime was transformed into the personalistic Stalinist totalitarian system.

Although the Marxist concept of the role of the leader was never officially repudiated, in effect leadership became the watchword of the times. Rather than merely reflecting the economic and social forces of a society, stern leadership now became the means to transform the society. Stalin became the great *Vozhd* who fixed the battle order by which the Soviet people were to storm the economic barricades. The population was mobilized by the use of force and by a strategy of leadership which relied heavily on propagating a "cult" of an omniscient and omnipotent leader. Blended into the cult of this one-time student for the priesthood was a large potion of witchcraft and inscrutability. Stalin was in unique communion with the Soviet deity, the scientific laws of social development, and was the supreme practitioner of the occult art of directing communist construction. He was given personal credit for every major (and minor) achievement of the Soviet Union. The goal to create a direct psychological bond between Stalin and the individual citizen was at least in part successful and for many citizens Stalin became a personification of the Soviet Union itself.

The Party apparatus had been decisive in Stalin's defeat of his Politburo opponents in the 1920's; but, once victorious, he was no longer dependent on the Party for his power base. In the 1930's he created a personal dictatorship which did not rest on a single lever of support to which he might be indebted. His dictatorial formula ensured that he retained final authority on all major issues by deliberately creating institutional instability and overlapping authority below. The political–administrative–punitive administration of the state was divided into various centralized bureaucratic structures which overlapped, penetrated, and supervised each other. The major power structures were the Party apparatus, the governmental administration united in the Council of Ministers, the secret police, and the military command; but these entities were further splintered. For example, Stalin's personal Party secretariat, supervised by Poskrebyshev, was distinct from the formal Party chain of command. Similar divisions could be detected in the government, police, and military hierarchies.

Even in the most powerful organ of the nation, the Party Politburo, Stalin jealously divided power. His lieutenants, who composed the Politburo, were charged with supervising particular areas of national life and/or specific bureaucratic hierarchies. He deliberately played them off against each other and, in addition, placed subordinates in their bailiwicks who reported on their superiors directly to Stalin. The Politburo in Stalin's later years rarely met as a body, even though it was small (having usually less than a dozen full members), but was divided into various committees over which Stalin presided. In short, Stalin's power was enthroned on the basis of institutional insecurity and instability below.

An important ingredient in this governing recipe was the use of capricious and widespread terror against both individuals and particular segments of the population. The imminent threat of ubiquitous terror, which pervaded the entire society, effectively prevented the development of centers of resistance to Stalin's commands — to say nothing of any effective political opposition to his rule — and reinforced the instability and insecurity institutionalized in the system of overlapping chains of command.

The Succession Problem and Elite Politics

The officially promoted image of Soviet politics (or lack thereof) notwithstanding, political struggles and policy disagreements do occur, sometimes bitterly. Even when a dictator like Stalin had consolidated his position and ruled by the sword unchallenged, political intrigue continued among those who contended for his favor to promote their own political fortunes and to obtain favorable consideration for their policies and the bureaucratic organizations they headed. Upon the death of Stalin, these political struggles were given new significance and an additional fillip.

For the outsider, the best glimpse into this normally obscure world is afforded during a transition of political leadership. In the jockeying for position after the deaths of both Lenin and Stalin, the outside world was treated to rare views of the underside of the Soviet political iceberg. As contenders for power lost out, they were indicted for actions which throw light on the policy-making process and political intrigue. Moreover, as the contestants maneuver for political support during a succession crisis their actions are more clearly visible.

Warning should be given that since Soviet elite politics receives greater exposure during a succession struggle, our knowledge of the character and operations of Soviet leadership is greater for these periods than when a single leader has consolidated his position and the transition is consummated. Clearly the leadership operates differently when one leader is dominant than when several individuals and groups are maneuvering for supreme power. To construct a general picture of Soviet elite politics by extrapolating from our knowledge of succession periods requires judgment and caution.

As the following chapters will demonstrate, a succession crisis may also provide information about the previous period which permits insights into the operations of leadership when there is a single dictator, i.e., under Stalin. Even the information about the Stalin regime revealed after 1953, however, must be viewed with caution since it was made public not to set the historical record straight, but to serve some current political purpose. Moreover, since conditions change and the nature of political leadership in the Soviet Union depends heavily on the character of the personalities involved, one should not assume that the Stalin and the post-1958 Khrushchev regimes necessarily operated similarly. In fact, Khrushchev's leadership probably varies markedly from Stalin's. Not only are conditions altered, but the styles of the two men are different. However, our knowledge of post-1958 elite politics is much less extensive than that for 1953–1958; consequently there is considerable disagreement among Western observers about the nature and extent of Khrushchev's power.*

Why is there a particularly serious problem with the succession of political leadership in the Soviet system, and what are the dimensions of this problem? Why, at least thus far, has the question of leadership succession been resolved only when one leader has been able to assert his dominance? By seeking some general answers to these closely intertwined questions, we may be able to develop some general hypotheses about the Gestalt of Soviet politics which will assist in coping with the detailed source material in later chapters.

At the outset, a caveat is in order to the effect that another succession "crisis" and the emergence of a pre-eminent leader after Khrushchev leaves the scene are not *inevitable*. If historical evidence and our conception of the political dynamics of the Soviet system are relevant, however, these eventualities are *likely*.

Since power in the Soviet Union is so highly concentrated and wielded so extensively and intensively, the death of the supreme leader, as in the case of Lenin and Stalin, poses a particularly difficult problem for the system to handle. For one thing, after over twenty years of a single-minded propaganda barrage on the person of Stalin, his death left a psychological void in the mass consciousness that complicated the job of his successors, who had been largely eclipsed by his manufactured radiance. Moreover, the stakes in the outcome of the struggle to find a replacement for the dead dictator are so high as to make difficult a resolution of the succession through a process of give-and-take and political compromise governed by ground rules upon which all participants agree. After Stalin's death, with the methods of his rule vividly impressed on the minds of his heirs, the succession struggle was especially

* For a debate among several Western specialists on the nature and extent of Khrushchev's power after 1958, see: Carl Linden, Thomas A. Rigby, and Robert Conquest, "Conflict and Authority," *Problems of Communism*, No. 5 (September–October 1963); and Carl Linden, Robert C. Tucker, Wolfgang Leonhard, and Michel Gordey, "How Strong Is Khrushchev?" *Problems of Communism*, No. 6 (November–December 1963).

intensified because of the fear that the losers might suffer the same fate Stalin meted out to his defeated opponents. As Khrushchev told the 22nd Party Congress in October 1961:

> When the anti-Party group was smashed, its participants expected that they would be treated in the same way they had dealt with people at the time of the cult of the individual and in the way they hoped to deal with those who favored the restoration of Leninist norms of Party life. . . .
>
> Kaganovich called me on the telephone and said:
>
> "Comrade Khrushchev, I have known you for many years. I ask you not to let them treat me in the vindictive way people were treated under Stalin."

While Khrushchev obviously recited this episode to demonstrate his benevolence and adherence to "Leninist norms," it does indicate the miasma pervading elite politics after Stalin's death.

Not only are the stakes of the game high, but institutionalized procedures for the transfer of political power, legitimized and deeply ingrained in the national consciousness through long usage and theoretical justification, simply do not exist. Neither the Party statutes nor the Constitution recognize the problem of leadership transference because they maintain the myth of the monolithic Party, organically a part of the entire population, which is governed by collective organs. No office or title bears any particular authority, for their occupants are supposedly only the agents of the Supreme Soviet or the Party Central Committee.

In fact, the Party Statutes and the Constitution are formalistic documents which bear little relation to the actual organization of the political regime. Constitutionally the government, or the Council of Ministers, is responsible to the Supreme Soviet, which is popularly elected. In reality, elections to the Supreme Soviet are uncontested and that body itself is cumbersome and meets only a few days each year to approve — unanimously — decisions that have been made elsewhere in the Council of Ministers and the Party Presidium. The highest Party organ is theoretically the unwieldy Congress, composed of delegates from lower Party organizations, which is supposed to meet every four years. The Congress "elects" a Central Committee, which in turn chooses a Presidium (formerly Politburo) and a Secretariat to handle daily administrative matters. De facto authority resides in the Presidium and Secretariat, whose members are co-opted, and only rarely has even the Central Committee had an opportunity to exercise important decision-making powers. In sum, political struggles and decision-making proceed beyond, and are unregulated by, the formal legal structure of the society.

Not only are there no legal or traditional procedures for transferring political leadership; it is a fundamental ideological tenet that the collective leadership is unified in the pursuit of communism to be achieved by the application of policies scientifically derived from a correct Marxist–Leninist reading of the laws of social development. The possibility and legitimacy of organized political opposition in the tradition of Western constitutionalism is flatly denied. According to the official ideology, multi-party political systems, political conflict, and the "political process" as a whole are the products of a strife-torn capitalist society, hopelessly rent by class struggle. In contrast, it is alleged that Soviet society is basically harmonious and hence by definition the leadership is unified. Where the idea of the right of a "loyal opposition" and the spirit of moderation and compromise accompanying it have not taken root, the ability of a group of political leaders to share power and agree on pragmatically grounded compromises is reduced. Opposition to policies is tantamount to an "anti-Party" attitude and therefore minor disagreements can easily become intensified. Moreover, it should be remembered that those leaders at the apex of power have demonstrated their capacity to operate successfully in this ruthless political system where miscalculations can have swift and disastrous personal consequences, and where the ability to compromise and articulate the diverse interests of a number of groups in society is less rewarded than the brute projection of one's own or his superior's will. The Soviet political elite is the product of a system wherein the contest for political power is played for keeps.

The rivalry for Stalin's mantle involved a great deal more then mere court intrigue even though Soviet elite politics are more personalistic than in most Western political systems. The Soviet leadership, whether engaged in open factional struggle or dominated by one man, must deal with reality. Even the dictator cannot simply project his will. He may intend to do something and indicate this in a public communication, and then discover that the situation has changed and that the original reason for his intended action no longer exists. He may then act otherwise. This need not necessarily mean that someone or some group compelled him to give up his original plan of action; it may mean that it no longer would serve his purposes. Moreover, while what is called the "power struggle" is an inherent feature of Soviet politics, being a substitute for political actions of various kinds that go on in open societies, it is not pursued in a vacuum without regard to consequences. It takes place in a certain milieu in which the actors care about the effects of their actions upon the society they rule, and which can be disregarded by them only at the risk of almost certain defeat in the power struggle itself. The reality with which the Soviet leaders have to deal and which they cannot wholly control includes not only international relations, but also limitations of human and natural resources, economic realities, the built-in dynamics of various institutions, and the difficulties of having their policies translated into action with a minimum of distortion by subordinate officials — to name only a few.

The scientific analysis of Marxism–Leninism does not, after all, provide concrete answers to the myriad foreign and domestic problems facing the leadership. The various leaders may differ on the appropriate policy to be applied in a given situation, depending on their background and experience and the impact on their personal fortunes. Even if we were to assume that policy preferences are determined by personal political considerations alone, it is obvious that a leadership struggle inevitably tends to focus on policy issues as the contestants attempt to enlist support from various segments of the lower elite and differentiate themselves from one another.

It is the nature of political dialogue in the Soviet Union, however, that policy differences tend to harden into ideological disputes, thus reinforcing the intensity of the disagreement. Ideological considerations are drawn into policy disagreements because each side attempts to justify its own position and discredit that of its protagonists by reference to the Marxist–Leninist scriptures. It is not easy to compromise and agree to disagree if an issue becomes encrusted with a doctrinal veneer.

On the other hand, victorious contestants may sometimes dramatically reverse their positions (while always maintaining publicly that the new line is merely a logical extension of the earlier position); both Stalin and Khrushchev later adopted some of the policies of the rivals they had defeated. Stalin's scheme for industrialization in 1928 was in large measure borrowed from Trotsky's program of the mid-1920's. Khrushchev's consumer-mongering after 1956 was not unlike that of Malenkov's in 1953–54. Moreover, even though one or several of a leader's policies are failures, he may not be shaken politically, especially after he has consolidated his position. It is even possible to blame these failures on defeated rivals, a procedure employed by both Stalin and Khrushchev. It should be noted parenthetically at this point that several of the most important of Khrushchev's programs, which figured prominently in the leadership struggle, did not prove viable in the long run —

and largely for the very factors that were criticized by his Presidium opponents. The highly touted Virgin Lands scheme ran afoul of drought, weeds, and heavy costs by the late 1950's and in 1963–64 it was largely laid to rest. Likewise, the 1957 reorganization of industrial management, a policy which appeared to catalyze the opposition to Khrushchev, did not prove to be an enduring solution for Soviet managerial problems and by late 1962 it had been largely undone.

The policies that a leader espouses will often be designed to appeal to a political–administrative clientele which he judges to have the most potential muscle for any political showdown. Khrushchev, for instance, after 1953 made an obvious pitch for the support of the military command by opposing Malenkov's advocacy of a greater output of consumer goods. Moreover, at least some leaders over the years appear to build up personal political followings from the ranks of the lower power elite. Such support may be based on a mixture of friendship through long association in some working relationship, mutual advantage, and cool power calculations on both sides. Since political position in the Soviet Union is based not on popular mandate or influence because of wealth or leadership of some independent interest group, the future of a member of the lower political–administrative elite depends significantly on, in addition to competence, his relations with his superiors. If he can identify a political leader on the rise and gain his confidence through loyalty and good performance, his mentor may reward him with rapid advancement through the ranks. On the other hand, if he puts his money on the wrong leader, the consequences for his career can be severe.

By the same token, if a leader appears to falter, he may find his political following rapidly dissipated as his supporters — those who can — scramble to the winning side. An important aspect of the factional struggle among the leaders is the maneuvering of the contestants to have their supporters placed in key positions and either to woo over the supporters of their opponents or to replace them. Obviously, therefore, it is particularly important for a leader to convey the appearance of having the initiative at all times. More than once after 1953, important secondary figures apparently switched sides to seek personal advantage. For example, D. T. Shepilov, whose elevation into the Party's inner circles appeared to be closely tied to Khrushchev's patronage, threw in his lot with the opposition to Khrushchev in June 1957. It is noteworthy that Khrushchev subsequently characterized him as a "double-dealer." The Shepilov affair further serves to point up the fact that even those close to the power struggle cannot always accurately predict the winner.

A leader's personal political following may be based primarily within a particular bureaucratic structure or it may cut across a number of institutions. Beria, for instance, had supporters not only in the secret police, which he headed for fourteen years, but also in the governmental and Party organizations of the Transcaucasian republics. A striking number of high officials, promoted after 1954 mostly in the Party but also in the military, police, and government, had worked in the Ukraine when Khrushchev had been Party boss there. Some of the more important of these men, whose names will be encountered later, include: A. I. Kirichenko, L. R. Korniets, R. A. Rudenko, A. I. Kirilenko, V. P. Mzhavanadze, V. V. Matskevich, V. E. Semichastnyi, L. I. Brezhnev, and I. A. Serov. Several men who served under Khrushchev when he was Party First Secretary of Moscow Oblast also rose to prominence at the same time. During World War II, Khrushchev worked with a number of military commanders on the Ukrainian front, including Moskalenko, Konev, and Chuikov, who later became Marshals and appeared to play some role in the leadership struggles.

In addition to the personalities, capabilities, and personal followings of the top leaders, and various policy considerations, the leadership succession struggle also involves various institutions. As indicated earlier, no office formally carries with it the prerogative of supreme power. Moreover, because Stalin had set one institution against another and had ensured that none had inherent authority aside from its relationship to him, no office in 1953 could have been regarded as a certain avenue to power. By fragmenting authority, Stalin had guaranteed his own position; he had also created a situation where no office could be regarded as the primary lever for catapulting a leader into the position of dictator.

The most important single body in the Soviet Union, since shortly after the Revolution, has been the Politburo (later Presidium) of the Party Central Committee. However, the Presidium is not the head of a single administrative chain of command. It is composed of the heads of the most important power centers in the Soviet Union and may be regarded as the interlocking directorate of the entire political–administrative system. (Likewise, the Party Central Committee, on a broader scale, embraces representatives of all the important bureaucratic chains of command.) For most of the period under review here, there were more representatives on the Presidium from the central government than from the Party apparatus. The Presidium is supposed to set the policies and co-ordinate the work of both the Council of Ministers and the Party bureaucracy, headed by the Central Committee Secretariat. On occasion after 1953, the majority of the Presidium and the Secretariat were at loggerheads.

On the other hand, since the members of the Party Presidium also occupy positions of leadership in institutions and organizations, during a factional struggle these bureaucratic hierarchies tend to get drawn into the fray. Indeed, a succession crisis involves a greater risk than merely unstable leadership: as the leaders mobilize support within the institutions they head, the leadership struggle might spill out of the Party Presidium and convulse the entire system.

Each major institution at the time of Stalin's death offered certain advantages and disadvantages for those who attempted to use them for support. Because of Stalin's reliance on terror, the secret-police apparatus was strongly entrenched and possessed broad, arbitrary powers. Through informer networks and other intelligence-gathering techniques, the police could keep close watch on all political developments, including those at the highest level. The police had, in effect, a large standing army which, in addition to normal militia duties, guarded border areas, key military installations, and the Kremlin. The Ministry of Internal Affairs (MVD) also had a huge economic empire based on the millions of persons imprisoned in the labor camps. On the other hand, the police were intensely disliked by the population and were regarded with justified suspicion by all elements of the power elite.

The military, as the wielder of the largest concentration of force, appeared on the surface to be a formidable contender for power. However, its forces were somewhat counterbalanced by those of the MVD, its ranks were penetrated and supervised by the Party and the police, and its representatives at the highest levels were not professional military men but political marshals like Voroshilov and Bulganin. After World War II, Stalin, by exiling Marshal Zhukov to a remote and minor military command and by other measures, had ensured that the military high command could not capitalize politically on the strength and popularity it had built up during the war.

The importance of the governmental administration (excluding the police and the military) was indicated by the fact that in 1952–1956 the majority of the Party Presidium came from the Council of Ministers. Under Stalin, the state had attempted to expand its control directly over all societal activities, largely through the ramification of a huge governmental bureaucracy. Moreover, with the single-minded concentration on economic growth under rigid central direction, the industrial administration, organized around centralized, industrial-branch ministerial empires which extended throughout the nation, quite naturally became extremely powerful. The governmental administration embraced economic managers and technical specialists who could perhaps be considered those groups best educated and most concerned about rationalizing the economy and society by reducing terror and ideological taboos which interfered with scientific and technical progress.

But the Council of Ministers was not an organic body necessarily speaking with one voice. Its many, diverse ministries — both industrial and non-industrial — competed with each other for favors and resources. Moreover, the governmental administration was increasingly fettered by a highly centralized and top-heavy bureaucracy.

The Party apparatus had the advantage of forming the core of the Party. Its position was legitimized, indeed sanctified, by being the pristine kernel of the Party founded by Lenin. Moreover, the position of senior or First Secretary of the Party Central Committee — and hence boss of the Party apparatus — carried particular weight because it was the post most closely associated with Stalin's name.

The Party apparatus at the time of Stalin's death numbered somewhere between 300,000 and 600,000 full-time Party cadre, from a Party membership totalling nearly seven million. The Party apparatus was organized into departments and sections at each territorial–administrative level which mirrored the governmental administration. In each territorial unit — raion (district), oblast (province), city, and republic — the First Secretary of the territorial Party committee served as a general manager who co-ordinated, and was responsible for, the many diverse activities in his bailiwick. Normally the Party secretary was the most influential member of the territorial Party committee which united the governmental, military, and police elite at that level. Hence, the Party First Secretaries were in a strategic position to make their influence felt. The republic, city, and provincial Party secretaries composed a large bloc of the membership of the All-Union Party Central Committee.

The prerogatives of the Party to appoint, or at least ratify, the most important officials throughout the nation could be used to advantage by an aggressive First Secretary. Malenkov for years had overseen the personnel work of the Party Central Committee for Stalin and, in this position, had undoubtedly had the opportunity to place his supporters in key roles. Not long after Khrushchev became First Secretary, his handiwork was evident in the replacement of a number of provincial

First Secretaries. It should be emphasized, however, that patronage is a crucial lever of power in the Soviet Union as elsewhere and Khrushchev, even as First Secretary, certainly did not have an undisputed right of appointment.

While the office of First Secretary thus gave its occupant certain advantages in the contest for power, these were not automatic and had to be realized. The Party Presidium was loaded against the Secretariat, and the Party apparatus did not have any military force of its own to mobilize. The governmental administration and the military, chafing under Party supervision, were pressuring for a restriction on the role of the Party apparatus. The hierarchy of Party secretaries, many of whom had patterned their style of operation on that of Stalin, were under attack for the use of dictatorial methods. In this connection, an attack on Stalin by his successors could possibly lead as well to downgrading the role of the First Secretary as the position from which he had been able to seize total power. Manifestly, de-Stalinization also carried dangers for the current occupant of the position of First Secretary.

Since the leadership struggle extended to institutional conflicts, the reader should give particular attention to these conflicts to notice whether any lasting institutional changes resulted and, further, whether any organization began to develop authority in its own right apart from its connection with a particular leader. Did the Party Central Committee, for example, at any time become a truly significant decision-making body? If so, was this situation lasting?

Communications and Elite Politics

Since the story of the Stalin succession crisis is related in this volume exclusively through the use of published Soviet sources (with the exception of Khrushchev's Secret Speech to the 20th Party Congress), and since the Soviet press does not provide commentary on elite politics, a few words need to be said about the nature and use of Soviet materials. The Soviet press is highly propagandistic and Soviet documents are not intended to provide evidence for those outside the Soviet Union who wish to understand the nature and meaning of events that occur within the system.

There is a public world and a private world of Soviet politics. The private world is that of ambition, pushing and pulling for place (and for the avoidance of demotion and even punishment); it is the world in which production managers try to keep their assigned targets low so that they can exceed them and collect a bonus; it is the world of personal connections and influence; it is the world of bitter political conflicts. These are all part of the normal operation of the system; but, if discussed at all in public documents, they must be treated as aberrations that are to be dealt with severely. A great part of the private world of Soviet politics is unrevealed, smothered under the official standard of monolithic unity and universal devotion to the tasks of building communism; and only disclosed as necessary to punish excesses, or to weaken factional opponents, or in an effort to institute reforms in the system.

In particular, the relations among the members of the political elite are normally shrouded in secrecy. It is difficult, sometimes impossible, for a Western observer to chart with any accuracy the various considerations and pressures playing upon the policy-making process and the configuration of political forces and personalities in the Soviet Union. This pervasive penchant for secrecy is, in part, a legacy of the Leninist tradition of conspiratorial leadership; it is also promoted by the official denial of the legitimacy of organized political conflict in the tradition of Western constitutionalism. There is no press coverage of the decision-making processes, no speculation on motives for particular leadership actions, no well-informed columnists providing the "inside dope." As a propaganda weapon for both domestic and foreign consumption, the picture of reality presented in published Soviet sources is regularly subject to distortion.

At the same time, the Soviet press is also regarded as an important organizer of the populace and it must convey information to the people about policies and activities to which they are to contribute. The press is also a vehicle of criticism of the bureaucracy to keep it honest and efficient; and, on occasion, it may stimulate discussions about how best to implement certain policies. Finally, as we shall see, the press in sometimes indirect and obscure ways may become involved in the jockeying for power.

To use Soviet sources for the study of elite politics, the reader must know something about the situation in which they occur. He must also know, or try to guess, the purpose they are meant to serve. He cannot simply accept what is said at face value, nor can he reject it, but he must ask what is plausible and what is not — what is supported by other information. Frequently a statement that a particular decision has been taken (e.g., changes in the prices of goods) can be accepted as true if its effects are immediately apparent. Also, an expression of intent can frequently be accepted as true: e.g., a plan to produce a certain quantity of goods. But here, already, the need to interpret arises: How strong is the intention? How high a priority will be given to the achievement of a particular target? Have provisions been made to provide the resources necessary to fulfill the plan, or is the target more a slogan than a real economic plan?

Moreover, the reader must ask himself, does the author of a document have any reason to mislead the audience? For example, if Khrushchev makes certain charges against the "anti-Party group" after they have been purged from the leadership, it is necessary to scrutinize such charges very carefully. Were they made previously? Are they consistent with what Khrushchev said earlier? Are the charges supported by contemporary evidence? Were the members of the "anti-Party group" really in a position to commit such actions at the time? Might they have been compelled to do them, or would they have been able to refuse to do them if ordered?

One must study closely important texts to determine precisely what they assert explicitly, what they logically imply, and what they simply insinuate to the unwary reader. Often Soviet documents insinuate what they would not assert, or imply what they would not say explicitly.

What is the intended audience for a communication — or are there several? Is the audience likely to be well- or ill-informed about Soviet leadership politics? It must be remembered that there is an extensive system of internal communications among the more politically oriented segment of the Soviet population, so that public documents must be interpreted by the outsider without the benefit of information that may be available to the intended readers. Of course, the reader of this book has the advantage of hindsight which was not available to the authors or intended readers of many of these documents. He knows how things turned out; and this may assist him, if he is careful, in understanding a document. But, of course, he must avoid the assumption that the author of a document knew just how things would turn out; he knew for certain only what he was about to do, although he expected certain consequences to flow from his actions. Those consequences may or may not have transpired, and in many instances quite unexpected results may have occurred.

There is a whole ritual of communication in the Soviet system in which important items of information are often swamped in an avalanche of stereotyped boasting which may throw the unwary off the trail. Minor changes in the ritual may have considerable importance, because this is one way of getting a message across unobtrusively.* These clues may be found in slight alterations in official slogans traditionally published for certain public occasions, in small differences in emphasis or omissions in the statements of various leaders, in the listing of leaders in attendance at functions, or in the nature and number of laudatory public references to a leader. To handle this kind of evidence, one must develop a feel for Soviet sources, read through great quantities of materials in order to establish what the ritual is, have a knowledge of Soviet history and the nature of elite politics, and read Soviet materials *carefully* and *thoughtfully*. It is possible that some departure from the established ritual may be due to inadvertence, and this must be considered in interpreting such a departure, but there are many built-in checks against mistakes in the Soviet system of communications. The disgrace of Molotov in September 1955 for a minor divergence from the standard formulation about stages of historical development of Soviet society (pp. 134-37) and Ilyichev's revelation about the political significance of an editor's correction in the publication of a Khrushchev statement in 1951 (pp. 287-88) should indicate that what at first glance might appear to be an unimportant and unintentional slip by an author may have great political significance.

How important minor alterations in phrases and other similar clues are regarded in the Soviet Union was suggested by Khrushchev himself in his Secret Speech of 1956. After condemning the Stalinist cult, he proceeded to recommend that the naming of localities and institutions after leaders be discontinued:

> Many of us participated in the act of assigning our names to various cities, districts, factories and collective farms. We must correct this.
>
> But this should be done calmly and slowly. . . . I can remember how the Ukraine learned about Kossior's arrest. The Kiev radio used

---

* Dr. Myron Rush has labelled this type of information "esoteric communications" and has suggested that it plays an important role in the dissemination of information by top leaders to lower officials, who are accustomed to reading these communications, about the power relationships at the center and the policies under contention. If, as was suggested earlier, a leader's success in a factional struggle rests in part on building a following among the lower power elite, he will attempt to convey an image of strength to sub-elites by manipulation of symbols. For a discussion of "esoteric communications," see: Myron Rush, *The Rise of Khrushchev* (Washington: Public Affairs Press, 1958), Appendix Two.

to start its programs thus: "This is Radio Kossior." When one day the programs began without naming Kossior, everyone was quite certain that something had happened to Kossior, that he had probably been arrested.

Thus, if today we begin to remove the signs everywhere and to change names, people will think that the comrades in whose honor the given enterprises, collective farms or cities are named also met some bad fate and that they also have been arrested.

How is the prestige and importance of this or that leader judged? By the number of cities, industrial enterprises, factories, collective and state farms that bear his name. Is it not time we ended this "private property" . . . ?

The following chapters are replete with examples of indirect and obscured indications of leadership conflict and policy disagreement. Perhaps the most outstanding is the article "On Lenin" by Molotov printed in *Pravda* on April 22, 1957 (pp. 225-26). On the surface this piece appears to be a standard discussion of Lenin's early writings and activities, but in reality it is a sweeping indictment of the policies of the Khrushchev faction.

These esoteric clues scattered throughout the Soviet press must be judiciously balanced against other kinds of evidence. They are often open to varying interpretations, especially since the outsider is not privy to inside knowledge about political conflicts which may provide a key for deciphering them. If used alone without restraint, they can lead to far-fetched, speculative hypotheses about the leadership struggle.

In addition, the unlikelihood of carelessness in Soviet communications should not confuse the question of whether all that happens in the Soviet Union is intentional. Particularly at times when there is no single leader determining policy, the interaction of rival leaders and factions may produce developments intended by none of the parties. It is at least possible, for example, that the 20th Party Congress developed in this manner, ending with Khrushchev's Secret Speech which, as some have argued, was not the planned culmination of the Congress, not even in Khrushchev's own mind. Certainly the twists and turns in Soviet administrative policy in late 1956 and early 1957 were not intended by any single group but were the outcome of the struggle among various groups. Particularly in conditions of open factional conflict, such as those that existed after 1953, it is important to assess the power of a group that is responsible for a particular policy or communication. There can be dramatic turns in events if a policy orginates in a group that is too weak to maintain itself in power.

The Stalinist Legacy

What was the broad social and economic heritage bequeathed by Stalin to his successors which provided the context for the post-1953 leadership struggle? Inevitably, this struggle had to revolve around questions about how best to cope with the problems left by Stalin and whether or not Stalinist solutions were still applicable.

By 1953 the Soviet economy had made a remarkable recovery, one that probably surprised even the leadership, from the low point at the end of the war when destruction had crippled much of the economy. Restoration of the economy to the pre-war level was largely accomplished by 1949. As in the 1930's, priority was given to developing heavy industry, the output of which by 1952 considerably exceeded that of 1941. Living standards were also improved, though at a far slower rate and from a base-line in 1945 that was hardly bearable for a modern country in peacetime. Housing, in particular, was extremely bad. Thus, while the population certainly had a sense of improving well-being, the absolute level of living standards when Stalin died was probably lower than when the war began in 1941; and the people held strong aspirations for greater rewards as a result of their labor.

Agricultural production was stagnant. As Khrushchev was to reveal in 1953, in some sectors agricultural production was below even that of 1913. The peasants' morale was bad because they received little reward for their labor on collective farm lands, and the agricultural bureaucracy was unwieldy and overly centralized. Supplies of mechanized equipment, chemical fertilizers, and other tools of modern agriculture were woefully short. The collective farm system, by putting the peasant in an administrative strait jacket, had enabled the regime to squeeze the countryside in order to industrialize; but, thus far, it had manifestly failed to raise production. Moreover, improvement in agriculture was a prerequisite for any substantial enlargement of the consumer-goods industry as a whole.

The economy was run by a highly centralized bureaucracy, using forced-draft methods, at breakneck speed. During the first five-year plans in the 1930's and again in the restoration of the economy after World War II, the regime, by operating the economy essentially by administrative fiat from the top with the assistance of severe measures of punishment for those who failed, was able to direct resources toward high priority projects and achieve impressive results. The growth of a top-heavy bureaucracy and the extreme centralization of decision-making authority in Moscow, however, gave rise to production bottle-necks, dampened managerial initiative, impeded timely resolution of problems and, in general, threatened to fetter economic growth. Considerations of cost and efficiency indicated the need to revamp the industrial administration to permit some devolution of administrative authority. The critical question was (and is) how the administration of the economy could be reformed without diluting political control from Moscow.

In literature and the other creative arts, the picture was gloomy. The Stalinist regime hewed to very rigid limits in its interpretation of the dogmatic standard of "socialist realism." During 1947–48, Stalin's lieutenant, A. A. Zhdanov, waged an intense and occasionally bloody campaign on "cosmopolitanism" and any deviations in the arts, which effectively snuffed out even the timid efforts that had been made by some writers, artists, and composers to experiment in new directions in the mid-1940's. The creative intelligentsia was supervised by bureau-cratic guardians of the official orthodoxy and cowed into the production of largely prefabricated and hackneyed works. Nevertheless, although outwardly conforming to the canons of socialist realism, a number of writers yearned for greater freedom of expression and even experi-mented in private. After Stalin's death, they were the first to test the tolerance of the new leadership and throughout the post-Stalin period have been a potent source for change.

In foreign policy the Soviet Union seemed to be cautiously experi-menting with new directions which were to be extended after 1953. The blatant Soviet subversion of Eastern Europe in the wake of World War II, culminating in the communist take-over of Czechoslavakia in 1948, and the initiation of the Korean War in 1950 had brought about a Western determination to resist further communist expansion, ex-pressed in the Truman Doctrine for Greece and Turkey, the creation of NATO, the Marshall Plan, and U.S.-led U.N. resistance in Korea. The unification of the Western Alliance — with the inclusion of West Germany — and the growing stability and economic prosperity of West-ern Europe indicated the desirability of new, less directly belligerent and more flexible policies to undercut Western unity.

At the same time, the growing economic and military power of the

Soviet Union probably gave her leaders a greater sense of security and provided them with more options in the conduct of foreign policy. No doubt they also anticipated that this economic and military power could be translated into political gains abroad.

Still another factor was making itself increasingly felt in the conduct of foreign policy by 1953: the development of nuclear weapons. The Soviet Union exploded an atomic bomb in 1949 and a thermonuclear weapon in 1953. By 1954 it would acquire an intercontinental jet bomber, to be followed in 1957 by an intercontinental ballistic missile. While these achievements added impressively to Soviet military might, they also brought increased Soviet awareness of the destructiveness of these weapons. The stalemate of force in Europe was reinforced by the knowledge that any showdown in that critical area would in all likelihood result in a thermonuclear war. As in the United States, so somewhat later in the Soviet Union, policy-makers and military men would ponder and debate the effect of these new holocaustic weapons on the military doctrines developed in World War II and on the over-all conduct of foreign policy. Also involved in this debate was the high cost of the new military technology, which precluded the pursuit of other desired economic goals.

By the early 1950's the Soviet leadership also began to pay more attention to Asia, Africa, and Latin America. The Chinese Communists had demonstrated the vulnerabilities of these transitional societies to communist encroachment; and, in addition to subversive tactics, the Soviet Union was in a position to extend her influence through the use of aid and trade and by playing on strongly held residual feelings of anti-colonialism. That an increasing number of colonies were achieving independence (and the fact that the Soviet leaders had finally become convinced that they were really independent) provided the Soviet Union with more opportunity to influence their regimes.

Stalin had ruthlessly asserted Soviet domination over the world communist movement — enforced, if necessary, by the secret police and the threat of military intervention. When Tito, a good communist but also a self-established nationalist leader of Yugoslavia, failed to knuckle under to Stalin's dictates, he was expelled from the Soviet bloc in the unrealized expectation that he would fall. To ensure conformity to Moscow's rule, those Eastern European leaders suspected of being susceptible to a "Titoist deviation" (i.e., some independence of thought and action) were purged in 1949–50 and the economies and political structures of Eastern Europe were rigidly patterned after those of the Soviet Union.

However, the seeds of ferment existed in the world communist movement. Although anathematized, Tito's Yugoslavia nevertheless provided an appealing example of a viable national communist regime which acted independently of Moscow's orders. The communist regimes in Eastern Europe had difficulty in arousing the loyalty of their populations because they were so obviously Russian puppets and were following policies designed more to benefit the Soviet Union than their own countries. Economic conditions were bad, in large measure because for some time after the war the Russians had bled their economies and because the Soviet economic model was imposed blindly in Eastern Europe even though it did not fit conditions there. Collectivization of agriculture was especially resented and led to reduced farm production. Finally, long-standing national resentments against Russian domination continued to exist.

The victory of the Chinese Communists in 1948–49 added to the might and prestige of the communist world, but it also complicated the Stalinist command system because the Chinese Communists could not be dictated to in the familiar manner. They had come to power largely under their own steam; they were rulers of a country with thrice the population of the Soviet Union; and they were deeply conscious of their ancient cultural heritage.

The new challenges in both domestic and foreign affairs in Stalin's last years apparently stimulated discussion behind the scenes about how best to meet the changing environment. Some modifications in foreign policy could be detected well before Stalin's death but, by and large, Stalin's tendency was to stand firm and ruthlessly enforce the economic and political formulas that he had developed during his long reign. In October 1952, on the eve of the 19th Party Congress, Stalin published what was to be his last treatise, "The Economic Problems of Socialism." He intended it to serve as the basic text to elucidate the principles on which the Soviet system was to operate and the manner in which communism was to be achieved. In vitriolic language he condemned those economists who had put forth suggestions for more rational methods to run the economy. In so doing they had cast doubts on the wisdom of some of Stalin's pet formulas such as the blind pursuit of ever greater production in heavy industry and the value of the Machine Tractor Stations, a key lever of control in Stalin's collectivized agriculture. Stalin asserted *ex cathedra* that the economic policies he had followed since 1928 were in accord with the economic laws immanent in a socialist society and that any attempt to alter these laws would court disaster. Although promising improved living conditions, Stalin in essence reaffirmed the validity of his economic model which sacrificed everything to production of those items which increased national power and placed emphasis on centralized administrative control. Particularly in agriculture, he demanded that the collective farm system be tightened up even further and gradually transformed into state farms rather than, as some had suggested, that the collective farms be provided with more autonomy and the peasants given greater economic incentives. He foresaw the interchange of goods between town and country on a natural basis, in which money would play no role, under the control of a central administrative agency.

In the political realm, Stalin continued and accentuated the style he had developed in the 1930's. Although the great purge of the 1930's was not repeated, neither did Stalin simply rely on the memory of this bloodbath to keep his subordinates and the population in line. With several notable exceptions in the aftermath of A. A. Zhdanov's death in August 1948, terror was not directed explicitly at the top leadership. Rather, it was turned chiefly at certain lower officials and particular cultural and social groups; e.g., "bourgeois nationalists" in the non-Russian republics; the "cosmopolitan" Jews; intellectuals who were indulging in "subjectivism" and imbibing dangerous ideas from abroad; lower Party and economic officials who were charged with damaging national property, ideological deviations or sabotage and still other crimes. In the late 1940's and early 1950's there were also purges which centered around geographical areas such as Leningrad, Georgia, Byelorussia, and the Ukraine.

Despite these widespread purges of the middle and lower officialdom after the war, the composition of the top leadership remained fairly stable. Top leaders were reshuffled frequently and their power suffered ups and downs, but basically the leadership in the late 1940's was much like that of the late 1930's. By 1950 the purge began to move into the leadership itself, although in a selective and, at least for the time being, bloodless way. Politburo member A. A. Andreyev was deprived of his responsibilities for agriculture. Beria's control of the secret police was loosened and his geographical base in Transcaucasia was weakened by the purge of the so-called Mingrelian bourgeois nationalists in Georgia. Voroshilov, according to Khrushchev's Secret Speech in 1956, was also largely isolated from Presidium proceedings.

During the last six months of Stalin's life, there were several indications that a massive reshuffling of the top leadership was imminent. In mid-October 1952, after the conclusion of the 19th Party Congress, it was announced that the newly selected Party Central Committee had replaced the old Politburo with a Presidium whose membership was increased from eleven to 25 full members and from one to eleven candidate members. Likewise, the Central Committee Secretariat was enlarged from four to ten secretaries. This dramatic appearance of a large number of new and younger faces in the top Party organs reasonably suggests that Stalin was setting the stage for the removal of a number of the old leaders like Voroshilov, Beria, Molotov, Mikoyan, and others.

Soon after the end of the Party Congress, the press began to adopt noticeably more militant attitudes toward offenders against economic directives and toward the dangers of domestic penetration by foreign enemies. The mounting campaign for vigilance against enemies took an ominous turn on January 13 when *Pravda* announced the arrest of nine medical doctors in the Kremlin who were charged with having murdered several Soviet leaders — including Zhdanov — and with plotting to kill a number of others on the orders of American and British intelligence services and a Jewish organization (a majority of the doctors were Jews). Since a number of those allegedly threatened by this plot were high military officers, it seems reasonable to suppose that if a purge were in the wind, this was a device to reassure the military that it was not a target. On the other hand, the fact that the doctors had supposedly been able to penetrate the Kremlin for some years boded ill for at least some of the secret police officials, who were charged with the security of the leadership, and perhaps for some members of the Presidium.

The witch hunt for spies and "secret enemies" continued to expand during January and February, 1953; and from afar it appeared as though the large-scale purges of the 1930's were to be repeated. If the net for supposed "enemies of the people" was to be cast wide, almost certainly some big fish were potential victims.

Although Stalin aspired to immortality and certainly did not like to think of his approaching death, it does appear that he made some tentative arrangements to pick a successor. For a suspicious tyrant, Stalin had concentrated in Malenkov's hands a considerable amount of power. Malenkov's position was particularly strengthened with the death in 1948 of Zhdanov, Malenkov's major rival for Stalin's favor. Malenkov had worked in leading positions of the Central Committee staff since 1934. In 1939 he was made a Secretary of the Central Committee; in 1941 he was elevated to candidate membership in the Politburo and became a full member in 1946. Thus, he had worked closely with Stalin at the center of power for a decade and a half. In 1953, he was 51 years old.

Stalin was loathe to concentrate too much power in the hands of any subordinate, however, for fear that the latter might speed up the succession process. Partly as a counterbalance to Malenkov in the Party apparatus, Khrushchev was brought to Moscow from the Ukraine in 1949 after Zhdanov's death and made a Secretary of the Central Committee. At the 19th Party Congress, Malenkov gave the major report of the Central Committee and Khrushchev reported on changes in the Party statutes. It should be noted that if Stalin had tabbed Malenkov to be his successor, but had been unwilling to give him sufficient power to consolidate his position as supreme ruler immediately upon the death of the old dictator, then Malenkov's position was particularly perilous since the other leaders would concentrate their efforts to whittle down his power.

After the war, the cult of Stalin reached even greater proportions, but in his last years he rarely appeared in public and even gave up delivering long speeches on special occasions. He seemed to be conserving his energies. His chief form of public activity was the writing of long "theoretical" tracts by which he apparently hoped to assure his place in the Communist pantheon for all times.* He was growing increasingly peculiar but there is little hard evidence to show that he was mad or, if mad, was growing madder. Khrushchev said later that the leaders wept real tears at his grave. They were certainly released from a very real fear of him when he died, yet they showed their respect for his ability to rule Russia by their apprehension of what might happen when he was gone.

* One might note here a seeming parallel with the behavior of Mao Tse-tung in recent years.

II · THE IMMEDIATE SUCCESSION PROBLEM AND THE CASE OF BERIA

On March 6, 1953 *Pravda* announced:

Dear comrades and friends: The Central Committee of the Communist Party, the USSR Council of Ministers, and the Presidium of the USSR Supreme Soviet announce to the party and all workers of the Soviet Union that on March 5, at 9:50 P.M., the Chairman of the USSR Council of Ministers and Secretary of the Central Committee of the Communist Party of the Soviet Union, Joseph Vissarionovich Stalin, died after a serious illness.

The heart of Lenin's comrade and brilliant disciple, the wise leader and teacher of the Communist party and the Soviet people — Joseph Vissarionovich STALIN — has stopped beating.

The name of STALIN is eternally dear to our Party, to the Soviet people, to the workers of the world. Together with Lenin, Comrade

STALIN founded the great Party of Communists, nourished and strengthened it; together with Lenin, comrade STALIN was the inspirer and
leader of the Great October socialist revolution, the founder of the
world's first socialist state. Continuing the work of Lenin, Comrade
STALIN led the Soviet people to the world–historic victory of socialism
in our country. Comrade STALIN led our country to victory over fascism
in the second world war, which radically transformed the entire international situation. Comrade STALIN armed the Party and the people with a great and clear program for building Communism in the
USSR. . . .

The Soviet people have boundless faith and deep love for their
Communist Party because they know that the highest law governing all
of the party's activity is to serve the people's interests. . . .

The Central Committee of the Communist Party of the Soviet
Union, the USSR Council of Ministers, and the Presidium of the USSR
Supreme Soviet, appealing in these sorrowful days to the Party and the
people, express firm confidence that the Party and all working people of
our motherland will join even more closely around the Central Committee and the Soviet Government. . . .

Long live the great, all-conquering teachings of Marx–Engels–
Lenin–Stalin!

Long live our mighty socialist motherland!

Long live our heroic Soviet people!

Long live the great Communist Party of the Soviet Union!

At the same time *Pravda* gave notice that:

The USSR Council of Ministers and the Central Committee of the
Communist Party of the Soviet Union announce: The formation of a
Commission to organize the funeral of Chairman of the Council of Min-
isters of the Soviet Union of Socialist Republics and Secretary of the
Central Committee of the Communist Party of the Soviet Union, Gen-
eralissimo Joseph Vissarionovich STALIN, to consist of comrades N. S.
Khrushchev (Chairman), L. M. Kaganovich, N. M. Shvernik, A. M.
Vasilevsky, N. M. Pegov, P. A. Artemyev, and M. A. Yasnov.

The week following Stalin's death witnessed a frenzy of activity by the
top leaders as they acted to preclude the acceleration of any divisive
forces in Soviet society or the outbreak of disturbances, while, at the
same time, under the mantle of professed unity, they jockeyed for position in the uncertain race for political power which inevitably followed

"In the Hall of Columns of the House of Unions, March 8, 1953. In the photograph (from left to right): Comrades V. M. Molotov, K. Ye. Voroshilov, L. P. Beria, G. M. Malenkov, N. A. Bulganin, N. S. Khrushchev, L. M. Kaganovich, A. I. Mikoyan at the coffin of J. V. Stalin." (Pravda, March 9, 1953, page 1)

the demise of the old dictator. Already on March 7, *Pravda* and *Izvestia* announced a wholesale reorganization of the top Party and governmental organs which largely undid the system created by Stalin at the 19th Party Congress in October 1952. This reorganization consolidated power among a handful of the most important leaders, squeezing out a number of lesser figures brought into the upper ranks by Stalin in late 1952. As such, it provides clues to the immediate distribution of power in the wake of Stalin's death.

The preface to the announcement of the new ruling organs indicates the leadership's anxiety over the public's reaction to Stalin's death:

The Central Committee of the Communist Party of the Soviet Union, the USSR Council of Ministers, and the Presidium of the USSR Supreme Soviet in this difficult time of our Party and country consider it the most important task of the Party and the government to maintain uninterrupted and correct leadership of the whole life of the country, which in turn demands the greatest solidarity of leadership and the prevention of any kind of disorder and panic in order to ensure unconditionally the successful implementation of the policy established by our Party and government for the internal affairs of our country as well as for international affairs.

In view of this and in order to prevent any confusion in the direction of the activities of the government and Party organs, the Central

Committee of the Communist Party of the Soviet Union, the USSR Council of Ministers and the Presidium of the USSR Supreme Soviet deem it essential to carry out a number of changes in the organization of the Party and government leadership.

I. ON THE CHAIRMAN AND FIRST DEPUTY CHAIRMEN OF THE USSR COUNCIL OF MINISTERS

1. To appoint as Chairman of the USSR Council of Ministers, Comrade Georgy Maximilianovich Malenkov.

2. To appoint as First Deputy Chairmen of the USSR Council of Ministers, Comrades Lavrenty Pavlovich Beria, Vyacheslav Mikhailovich Molotov, Nikolai Alexandrovich Bulganin, and Lazar Moiseyevich Kaganovich.

II. ON THE PRESIDIUM OF THE USSR COUNCIL OF MINISTERS

1. To recognize the necessity of having in the USSR Council of Ministers, instead of two organs — the Presidium and the Bureau of the

Presidium — a single organ, the Presidium of the USSR Council of Ministers.

2. To establish that the Presidium of the USSR Council of Ministers shall consist of the Chairman of the USSR Council of Ministers and the First Deputy Chairmen of the USSR Council of Ministers.

III. ON THE CHAIRMAN OF THE PRESIDIUM OF THE USSR SUPREME SOVIET

To recommend the appointment of Comrade Kliment Yefremovich Voroshilov as Chairman of the Presidium of the USSR Supreme Soviet, freeing Comrade Nikolai Mikhailovich Shvernik from these duties. . . .

To appoint as Secretary of the Presidium of the USSR Supreme Soviet, Comrade Nikolai Mikhailovich Pegov, freeing him from his duties as Secretary of the Central Committee of the CPSU. . . .

IV. ON THE MINISTRY OF INTERNAL AFFAIRS OF THE USSR

To combine the USSR Ministry of State Security and the USSR Ministry of Internal Affairs into one ministry, the USSR Ministry of Internal Affairs.

To appoint as USSR Minister of Internal Affairs, Comrade Lavrenty Pavlovich Beria.

"Comrade J. V. Stalin in the Presidium of the 19th Congress of the Communist Party of the Soviet Union. At the tribune, comrade G. M. Malenkov presenting the report of the Party Central Committee on October 5, 1952." (*Pravda,* March 8, 1953, page 2)

V. ON THE USSR MINISTER AND DEPUTY MINISTERS OF FOREIGN AFFAIRS

1. To appoint Comrade Vyacheslav Mikhailovich Molotov as USSR Minister of Foreign Affairs. . . .

VI. ON THE USSR MINISTER OF DEFENSE AND FIRST DEPUTY MINISTERS OF DEFENSE

1. To appoint Marshal of the Soviet Union, Comrade Nikolai Alexandrovich Bulganin as USSR Minister of Defense.

2. To appoint as First Deputy Ministers of Defense, Marshal of the Soviet Union Comrade Alexander Mikhailovich Vasilevsky and Marshal of the Soviet Union Comrade Georgy Konstantinovich Zhukov.

VII. ON THE MINISTRY OF DOMESTIC AND FOREIGN TRADE

To combine the Ministry of Foreign Trade and the USSR Ministry of Trade into one Ministry, the USSR Ministry of Domestic and Foreign Trade.

To appoint Comrade Anastas Ivanovich Mikoyan as USSR Minister of Domestic and Foreign Trade. . . .

VIII. ON THE MINISTRY OF MACHINE BUILDING

To combine the Ministry of the Automobile and Tractor Industry, the Ministry of Machine and Instrument Construction Industry, the Ministry of Agricultural Machine Building, and the Ministry of the Machine Tool Industry into one ministry, the Ministery of Machine Building.

To appoint Comrade Maxim Zakharovich Saburov Minister of Machine Building, relieving him of the duties of Chairman of the USSR State Planning Committee.

ON THE MINISTRY OF TRANSPORT MACHINERY AND HEAVY MACHINE BUILDING

To merge the Ministry of Transport Machine Building, the Ministry of the Shipbuilding Industry, the Ministry of the Heavy Machine Building Industry and the Ministry of Construction and Road Building Machinery Industry into one ministry, the Ministry of Transport Machinery and Heavy Machine Building.

To appoint Comrade Vyacheslav Alexandrovich Malyshev Minister of Transport Machinery and Heavy Machine Building.

ON THE MINISTRY OF POWER PLANTS AND THE ELECTRICAL EQUIPMENT INDUSTRY

To merge the Ministry of Power Plants, the Ministry of the Electrical Equipment Industry and the Ministry of the Communications

Equipment Industry into one ministry, the Ministry of Power Plants and Electrical Equipment Industry.

To appoint Comrade Mikhail Georgiyevich Pervukhin Minister of Power Plants and the Electrical Equipment Industry. . . .

X. ON THE CHAIRMAN OF THE ALL-UNION CENTRAL COUNCIL OF TRADE UNIONS

To recommend the appointment of Comrade Nikolai Mikhailovich Shvernik as Chairman of the All-Union Central Council of Trade Unions, relieving Comrade Vasily Vasilyevich Kuznetsov of these duties.

XI. ON THE PRESIDIUM OF THE CENTRAL COMMITTEE OF THE CPSU AND THE SECRETARIES OF THE CENTRAL COMMITTEE OF THE CPSU

1. To recognize the need to have in the Central Committee of the CPSU, instead of two agencies of the Central Committee — the Presidium and the Bureau of the Presidium — one agency, the Presidium of the Central Committee of the CPSU as set forth in the Party Statutes.

2. In order to achieve more effective leadership, the Presidium shall consist of ten members and four candidates.

3. To affirm the following composition of the Presidium of the Central Committee of the CPSU:

Members of the Presidium of the Central Committee: Comrades G. M. Malenkov, L. P. Beria, V. M. Molotov, K. Ye. Voroshilov, N. S. Khrushchev, N. A. Bulganin, L. M. Kaganovich, A. I. Mikoyan, M. Z. Saburov, and M. G. Pervukhin.

Candidate members of the Presidium of the Central Committee of the CPSU: Comrades N. M. Shvernik, P. K. Ponomarenko, L. G. Melnikov, and M. D. Bagirov.

4. To elect as Secretaries of the Central Committee of the CPSU Comrades S. D. Ignatyev, P. H. Pospelov, and N. N. Shatalin.

5. To recognize the necessity for Comrade N. S. Khrushchev to concentrate on work in the Central Committee of the CPSU, and, in this connection, to relieve him of his duties as First Secretary of the Moscow Committee of the CPSU.

6. To confirm Secretary of the Central Committee of the CPSU, Comrade N. A. Mikhailov, as First Secretary of the Moscow Committee of the CPSU.

7. To relieve of their duties as Secretaries of the Central Committee of the CPSU Comrades P. K. Ponomarenko and N. G. Ignatov in connection with their transfer to executive work in the USSR Council

"Comrades J. V. Stalin, Mao Tse-tung, and G. M. Malenkov. Photograph taken February 14, 1950, at the time of the signing of the Soviet-Chinese Treaty of Friendship, Co-operation, and Mutual Assistance." (*Pravda,* March 10, 1953, page 3)

of Ministers, and Comrade L. I. Brezhnev in connection with his transfer to the post of head of the Political Department of the Navy Ministry.

XII. ON THE CONVOCATION OF THE FOURTH SESSION OF THE USSR SUPREME SOVIET

To convene the Fourth Session of the USSR Supreme Soviet on March 14, 1953 in Moscow to review the decisions of the joint meeting of the plenary session of the Central Committee of the CPSU, the USSR Council of Ministers and the Presidium of the USSR Supreme Soviet, which are subject to confirmation by the USSR Supreme Soviet.

Several features of this announcement merit some elaboration. The notification of the convocation of the Supreme Soviet to ratify the organizational decisions already made, most probably by a handful of the top leaders, evidenced the post-Stalin regime's concern to observe, for public benefit, the constitutional forms so often blatantly ignored under Stalin. The reader should pay special attention to the order in

"Signing the Treaty and Agreement between the Soviet Union and the Chinese Peoples Republic. A. Ya. Vyshinsky is signing the Treaty. In the photograph (from left to right): A. A. Gromyko, N. A. Bulganin, N. V. Roshchin, Chou En-lai, A. I. Mikoyan, N. S. Khrushchev, K. Ye. Voroshilov, V. M. Molotov, J. V. Stalin, Mao Tse-tung, B. F. Podtserob, N. T. Fedorenko, Van Tsa-san, G. M. Malenkov, Chen Bo-da, L. P. Beria, S. Azizov, L. M. Kaganovich." (*Pravda*, February 15, 1950)

which the members of the Central Committee Presidium are listed. They are not placed in alphabetical order but appear to be listed in order of de facto authority. The announcement leaves unclear, perhaps deliberately, the precise membership of the Central Committee Secretariat. Immediately before Stalin's death, the Secretariat consisted of: Stalin, Aristov, Brezhnev, Ignatov, Malenkov, Mikhailov, Pegov, Ponomarenko, Suslov, and Khrushchev (in Russian alphabetical order, except for Stalin). Malenkov on March 7, therefore, apparently was both Chairman of the Council of Ministers and senior Secretary of the Central Committee.

At this point it is relevant to introduce some pictorial evidence of the course of leadership maneuvering during the four days after March 6. The enlarged photograph, showing Malenkov with Stalin and Mao Tse-tung, is actually a montage, made from the earlier photograph showing the large group, which originally appeared in *Pravda* on February 15, 1950.

A plenum of the Party Central Committee was convened on March 14; its decisions, which made substantial alterations in the Secretariat, were not reported until a week later. They evidenced continued jockeying among the top leaders as each endeavored to enhance his own position and preclude a grab for total power by one of the contestants. The resolution provided:

1. To grant the request of Chairman of the USSR Council of Ministers, G. M. Malenkov, to be relieved of the duties as Secretary of the Central Committee of the CPSU.

2. To elect the following Secretariat of the Central Committee of the CPSU: Comrades N. S. Khrushchev, M. A. Suslov, P. N. Pospelov, N. N. Shatalin, and S. D. Ignatyev.

3. In conformity with Article 32 of the Statutes of the Communist Party of the Soviet Union, to transfer Comrade N. N. Shatalin from candidate to member of the Central Committee of the CPSU. (*Pravda*, March 21, 1953)

In interpreting the significance of these personnel changes, it should be noted that in the West, Shatalin was generally considered to be closely associated with Malenkov. The removal of Malenkov from the Secretariat left Khrushchev as senior secretary, although at this time his position was not given any formal recognition.

That no single leader had succeeded in appropriating dictatorial power was made clear the following month in an article by L. Slepov, an editor of the Party newspaper *Pravda* and a prominent authority on Party affairs. His emphasis on the need for collective discussion and decisions, which doubtless had been authorized by the top leaders, was an implied downgrading of Stalin's place in Soviet history, a process that began cautiously and indirectly shortly after the announcement of his death; and it may also have been intended to weaken the authority of the "First Secretaries," the little Stalins, at all levels of the Party organization:

. . . The Party committees are organs of political leadership. In their practical work they cannot use methods inherent in administrative–managerial agencies. There were instances of this during the war. Wartime conditions caused certain particular features in leadership methods which were to some extent justified by circumstances. However, this led to serious shortcomings in the practical work of Party organizations. . . .

One of the basic principles of Party leadership is collectivity in the decision of all important problems of Party work. It is impossible to provide genuine leadership if inner Party democracy is violated in the Party organization, if genuine collective leadership and highly developed criticism and self-criticism are absent. Collectivity and the collegium principle represent a tremendous force in Party leadership. . . .

The principle of collectivity in work means, above all, that decisions taken by Party committees on all major questions are the result of collective discussion. Regardless how experienced leaders may be or what their knowledge and ability are, they do not possess and cannot replace the initiative and experience of an entire collective. In any collegium, in any leadership collective, there are people who possess diverse experience without which the leaders cannot make correct decisions and exercise qualified leadership. . . .

We still find leaders who violate the principle of collective decision, who decide important matters individually without consulting bureau members. This incorrect method is used, for example, by Comrade Alamanov, First Secretary of the Dzhalal-Abad Oblast City Committee. In deciding important questions, he often ignores the opinion of bureau members, fails to consult them, fails to create conditions so that criticism can be expressed, and resents critical comment. Comrade Svirin, Secretary of the Valuiki Raion Party Committee in Kursk Oblast, often decides questions of the selection and assignment of personnel on his own initiative without discussion before the raion committee bureau.

It is obvious that in these cases, the officials have functioned not as political leaders but as poor administrators. The political leader may not counterpose himself to the collective; he always seeks to rally the Party *aktiv,* to absorb the experience of the Party masses, to operate not by administrative rule but by his authority . . .

Leaders cannot regard criticism of themselves as a personal affront. They must be able to accept criticism courageously and be ready to bend their will to that of the collective. Without such courage, without the ability to overcome one's vanity and to bend one's will to that of the collective, there can be no collective leadership, no collective. . . .

Actually, the function of collective leadership is to correct and criticize each other. Where there is an intolerable atmosphere of kowtowing, which excludes businesslike, critical discussion of problems, where criticisms of comrades, who are officials, are not expressed, there are, as a rule, serious shortcomings in work. . . . (L. Slepov, "Collectivity Is the Highest Principle of Party Leadership," *Pravda,* April 16, 1953)

Charting a New Course—A Bid by Beria

The new leadership, faced with uncertainties during the transitional period and anxious to establish its authority with the population, announced a number of measures designed to woo popular support by making concessions to widely-held but long-denied cravings for better living standards and more personal security. The policy of greater economic allocations for consumer goods was first hinted at by Malenkov in his funeral oration for Stalin and his speech to the Supreme Soviet on March 15; in the succeeding months he endeavored to associate his name closely with this popular line. As we shall see, however, before long this policy became a bone of contention among the leadership and figured in later political in-fighting.

The first tangible manifestation of the new course came on April 1 with an announcement in the central newspapers of a "New Reduction of State Retail Prices for Foodstuffs and Manufactured Goods":

The USSR Council of Ministers and Central Committee of the CPSU has decreed:

1. As of April 1, 1953, to lower state retail prices for foodstuffs and manufactured goods in the following amounts: *Bread, Flour and Macaroni Products.* — Rye bread, whole-wheat bread, rolls, cracknels and other bakery products of bread type, 10%; rye flour, whole-wheat flour, corn meal and other flour, 10%; and macaroni, vermicelli, noodles and other macaroni products, 10%. . . . [The total list contained 21 different categories of food and manufactured consumer goods, for which price reductions ranged from 5% for such items as wool fabrics and furniture to 50% for many fruits and vegetables.]

Pravda editorialized on the price reduction as follows:

. . . This decree is a vivid expression of the unceasing concern of the Communist Party and the Soviet Government for the peoples' welfare, for the maximum satisfaction of their material and cultural needs. This decree will be greeted with great satisfaction by all working people of our country. . . .

The constant rise of the Soviet people's living standards is striking proof of the superiority of the socialist system over the decaying capitalist system, which has condemned the working people to poverty, unemployment and cruel deprivations because of the militarization of the economy and preparations for a new war. . . . (*Pravda*, April 1, 1953)

The Soviet consumer was given further relief in late June when the Minister of Finance revealed that the 1953 state loan was only half that for 1952. Since public subscription to the state loan was far from voluntary, this move constituted a type of tax reduction.

Of a different order, but equally designed to curry popular favor, was a decree of the USSR Supreme Soviet "On the Amnesty," published on March 29:

As a result of the consolidation of the Soviet social and state system, improvement in the living and cultural standards of the population, and growth in the citizens' civic consciousness and honest attitude toward fulfilling their social duty, compliance with the law and socialist order have been strengthened and the incidence of crime has significantly decreased in the country.

The Presidium of the USSR Supreme Soviet considers that, in these circumstances, it is no longer necessary to detain in places of custody persons who have committed offenses which present no great danger to the state and whose conscientious attitude toward labor has shown that they are fit to return to an honest working life and become useful members of society.

The Presidium of the USSR Supreme Soviet decrees that: (1) Persons sentenced to imprisonment for up to five years are to be released from places of detention and freed from other measures of punishment not related to deprivation of freedom. (2) Persons sentenced, regardless of the length of the sentence, for offenses committed in an official capacity and for economic offenses, and also for military offenses stipulated in Articles 193-4a, 193-7, 193-8, 193-10, 193-10a, 193-14, 193-15, 193-16, and 193-17a of the Russian Republic penal code, and corresponding articles of the criminal codes of all other Union Republics, are to be released from places of detention. (3) Women having children up to ten years of age, pregnant women, minors up to the age of 18, men over 55 and women over 50, and also convicted persons suffering from serious incurable diseases are to be released from places of detention. (4) Convicts whose sentences include deprivation of freedom for more than five years are to have their sentences reduced by half. . . . (6) Citizens who have been previously convicted and have served their sentences, or who have received an early release from their sentence on the basis of this decree, are to have their criminal record expunged and their civil rights restored. (7) The amnesty is not to apply to persons sentenced to terms of more than five years for counter-revolutionary crimes, major thefts of socialist property, banditry and premeditated murder. (8) The criminal laws of the USSR and the Union republics are to be re-examined with a view to substituting administrative and disciplinary measures for criminal responsibility in cases of offenses committed in an official capacity and in cases of economic, social and other less dangerous crimes, and also with a view to reducing the criminal responsibility for some crimes. . . . (*Pravda*, March 29, 1953)

> Less than a week after the Amnesty Decree of March 29, the Soviet press did a *volte-face* on the so-called Doctors' Plot, which had been rapidly coming to a head just before Stalin's death, and the accompanying campaign for public vigilance against foreign and domestic enemies. As suggested in Chapter I, this affair was, in all likelihood, to set the stage for a purge by Stalin of some of the veteran members of the elite. Hence, while repudiation of the Doctors' Plot was intended, like the Amnesty, to reassure the Soviet public on the arbitrary use of force, it was also pushed by those who had been threatened by this episode.

A COMMUNICATION FROM THE USSR MINISTRY OF INTERNAL AFFAIRS

The USSR Ministry of Internal Affairs has conducted a thorough check of all preliminary investigation materials and other data in the case of the group of doctors accused of sabotage, espionage and terrorist activities against the active leaders of the Soviet state.

As a result of the check, it has been established that the accused in this affair, Professors M. S. Vovsi, V. N. Vinogradov, M. B. Dogan, B. B. Kogan, P. I. Yegorov, A. I. Feldman, Ya. G. Etinger, V. K. Vasilenko, A. M. Grinshtein, V. F. Zelenin, B. S. Preobrazhensky, N. A. Popova, V. V. Zakusov, and N. A. Shereshevsky and Dr. G. I. Maiorov, were arrested by the former USSR Ministry of State Security incorrectly, without any legal grounds.

The verification has shown that the charges against the above-named persons are false and the documentary data on which the investigators relied are without basis. . . .

The persons accused of incorrect conduct of the investigation have been arrested and held for criminal responsibility. (*Pravda*, April 4, 1953)

> Two days later, *Pravda* attempted lamely to explain this gross violation of "socialist legality":

. . . How could it happen that in the bosom of the USSR Ministry of State Security, which is charged with standing guard over the interests of the Soviet state, there was fabricated this provocative affair, the victims of which were honest Soviet people, outstanding figures of Soviet science?

This happened, above all, because the leaders of the former Ministry of State Security did not show themselves to be of high quality. They were divorced from the people, from the Party. They forgot that they were servants of the people and obligated to stand guard over Soviet legality. The former Minister of State Security, S. Ignatyev, displayed political blindness and carelessness, and was led around by such criminal adventurists as Ryumin, the former deputy minister and head of the investigation section who directed the investigation and who has now been arrested. Ryumin acted as a concealed enemy of our state and people. Instead of working to expose the real enemies of the Soviet state, the real spies and saboteurs, Ryumin embarked on the path of deceiving the government, on the path of criminal adventurism. Desecrating the high calling of employees of the state administration and their responsibilities before the Party and before the people, Ryumin and several other employees of the Ministry of State Security, to further their criminal aims, grossly violated Soviet legality, even so far as the direct falsification of evidence, and dared to violate the inviolable rights of Soviet citizens which are written into our Constitution. . . .

Contemptuous adventurists like Ryumin, by falsification of the investigation, tried to arouse in Soviet society — which is united by moral and political cohesion and ideas of proletarian internationalism — feelings of national antagonism which are deeply alien to Socialist ideology. . . .

The Soviet government openly and directly talks about these matters to the people. This testifies to the great strength of the Soviet state and the socialist system. The source of this strength is the fact that our government is closely and inseparably united with the people, leans on the people in all its activities, and firmly and consistently follows a policy answering the vital interests of the people. . . .

Long ago in the Soviet Union exploiting classes were liquidated. Therefore, foreign reactionary forces in their attempts to take subversive actions against the Soviet state cannot have any significant base of social support within our country. But the Soviet people know that while the capitalist encirclement exists, there will inevitably be further attempts to send spies and saboteurs to us. . . . (*Pravda*, April 6, 1953)

The above editorial revealed to Western observers for the first time that S. D. Ignatyev had been Minister of State Security in the period preceding Stalin's death. As such, he was operating in Beria's province. After Stalin's death, when Beria recovered control of the political police, Ignatyev was made a Secretary of the Party Central Committee. However, on April 7, it was announced that:

By decision of the Plenum of the Central Committee of the CPSU, Comrade S. D. Ignatyev has been released from the duties of a Secretary of the Central Committee.

Beria, who was charged with general supervisory responsibilities over the police for the Party Presidium in the period when the Plot was supposed to have originated, was not mentioned in any of the accusations against the former Ministry of State Security or in any other way connected in the press with the Plot. Indeed, the Doctors' Plot may well have been intended, in part, to undercut Beria's position. If so, its repudiation could hardly have damaged his authority and might, on the contrary, be considered a sign of his strength.

In the spring and early summer, there was a widespread reshuffling of Party and governmental officials in many republics. Judging by press reports, the dismissal of a number of leading republic officials was in part an effort to woo public support for the regime by eliminating unpopular tyrannical local leaders who had patterned themselves on the Stalinist model. There can be little doubt, however, that these purges were managed from Moscow and that they were influenced by the efforts of the top leaders to place their followers in key positions and to settle a number of old political scores. It is doubtful that any single leader dominated these power plays in the republics. Our knowledge of these second-echelon political bosses and their ties with the top leaders is too limited to permit any precise calculation of which Presidium members fared best in these republic housecleanings. Nevertheless, some clues are available.

This overhaul of the second-echelon cadre began when a plenum of the Georgian Republic Party Central Committee on April 14 replaced its first, second, and third secretaries. The following day, the Georgian Republic Supreme Soviet approved a new Council of Ministers containing a number of new faces. The new Council Chairman, V. M. Bakradze, in his speech before the Georgian Supreme Soviet, shed some light on the political intrigue which had gone on in the republic:

. . . Comrades! I do not think I need to describe individually the proposed heads of ministries I have named. . . . I only wish to emphasize that the proposed heads of ministries presented here are members of our great Communist Party; they have been trained and tested by the Georgian Party organization of Lenin and Stalin, the organization which for many years has been led by the best son of Georgia, the talented disciple of Lenin, comrade-in-arms of Stalin and outstanding figure of the Communist Party and the great Soviet state, Comrade Lavrenty Pavlovich Beria. . . .

I want to give you a short explanation in regard to the candidates for membership in the Government of Georgia, Comrades Baramia, Zodelava and Rapava. . . .

As has now been completely revealed and verified by the appropriate agencies, the enemy of the people and the Party, the former Georgian Republic Minister of State Security, Rukhadze, fabricated against Comrades Baramia, Zodelava and Rapava and certain other officials devoted to the Party and the Soviet people, a provocative "affair" which was falsified from beginning to end, concerning a nonexistent nationalism to which certain prominent officials of our republic had fallen victim. . . .

Former Secretaries of the Georgian Communist Party Central Committee, Charkviani and Mgeladze, not only failed to show a rudimentary capacity to assess critically the provocative "materials" fabricated by Rukhadze but, on the contrary, furthered his malicious activities.

The adventurist Rukhadze and his colleagues have been arrested and will be severely punished. . . . In accord with appropriate directives by USSR agencies, all those who were arrested on the grounds of the materials fabricated by the enemy of the people, Rukhadze, have been released, completely exonerated and have had their rights restored. It has been proved that Comrades Baramia, Zodelava and Rapava have always been devoted to the Communist Party and the Soviet regime. (*Zarya Vostoka*, daily newspaper of the Georgian Republic Party and government organizations, April 16, 1963)

> That the overhaul of republic officialdom began in Georgia is of special interest because there is strong evidence that in 1951–52 a number of Beria's followers had been purged from office in this republic which had long been considered his stronghold.
>
> The charge that Rukhadze had fabricated a plot about "nonexistent nationalism," the reader will remember, is similar to the accusations against Ryumin in the Doctors' Plot for his alleged efforts to foment "national antagonism." Leonid Melnikov, the First Secretary of the powerful Ukrainian Republic Party organization, was also dis-

graced on grounds which similarly included a charge of excessive Russification:

> Recently a plenum of the Ukrainian Party Central Committee was held. The plenum discussed shortcomings in political work and in the leadership of economic and cultural work. . . .
>
> The plenum noted that the Central Committee bureau and the Central Committee Secretary, Comrade Melnikov, had distorted the Leninist–Stalinist nationality policy of our Party, manifested in the harmful practice of promoting to leading Party and Soviet work in the western provinces of the Ukraine officials mainly from other provinces of the Ukraine Republic and also in converting the teaching in Western Ukrainian higher educational institutions to the Russian language. . . .
>
> The plenum removed Comrade L. G. Melnikov from the post of First Secretary and from the bureau of the Ukraine Communist Party Central Committee for failing to provide leadership and for committing grave errors in the selection of personnel and in carrying out the Party's nationality policy.
>
> The plenum elected Comrade A. I. Kirichenko to the post of First Secretary of the Ukraine Communist Party Central Committee, releasing him from the duties of Second Secretary of the Ukraine Communist Party Central Committee. . . . (*Pravda,* June 13, 1953)

Kirichenko also replaced Melnikov as a candidate member of the Central Committee Presidium.

Similar criticisms were heard from the Baltic area. A plenum of the Latvian Republic Party Central Committee, for example, noted in late June "grave shortcomings in the work of leading republic Party, Soviet and economic agencies, which have committed gross distortions in carrying out Soviet nationality policy. The Leninist–Stalinist policy of selecting, training and promoting Latvian national cadres to leading work in Party, Soviet and economic organizations has been violated in the republic." Within a month, accusations about manipulating nationalist sentiment of quite a different order were to be heard.

One final aspect of these republic purges needs mentioning: the republic ministries of Internal Affairs were particularly hard hit. Between April and June, the Ministers of Internal Affairs were changed in Georgia, the Ukraine, Estonia, Latvia, and Lithuania.

The second performance of the opera "The Decembrists" was performed in Moscow's Bolshoi Theater on June 27. On June 28, the central newspapers carried a list of dignitaries in attendance which omitted one important name:

. . . The performance was attended by Party and government leaders, Comrades G. M. Malenkov, V. M. Molotov, K. Ye Voroshilov, N. S. Khrushchev, N. A. Bulganin, L. M. Kaganovich, A. I. Mikoyan, M. Z. Saburov, M. G. Pervukhin, N. M. Shvernik, P. K. Ponomarenko, and V. A. Malyshev.

Thirteen days later, on July 10, *Pravda* carried an "Information Bulletin on the Plenum of the Central Committee of the Communist Party of the Soviet Union":

Recently a plenum of the Central Committee of the Communist Party of the Soviet Union was held.

Having heard and discussed a report of the Presidium of the Central Committee by Comrade G. M. Malenkov on the criminal anti-Party and anti-state activities of L. P. Beria, which were directed toward undermining the Soviet state in the interests of foreign capital and which became manifest in the treacherous attempts to place the USSR Ministry of Internal Affairs above the government and the Communist Party of the Soviet Union, the plenum of the Central Committee of the CPSU adopted a decision to remove L. P. Beria from membership in the Central Committee of the CPSU and to expel him from the ranks of the Communist Party of the Soviet Union as an enemy of the Communist Party and the Soviet people.

This communique was followed by an announcement from the Presidium of the USSR Supreme Soviet:

In view of the criminal anti-state activities of L. P. Beria directed toward undermining the Soviet state in the interests of foreign capital, which have recently been uncovered, the Presidium of the USSR Supreme Soviet, having examined a report of the USSR Council of Ministers on this matter, has decreed:

1. That L. P. Beria be relieved of the post of First Deputy Chairman of the USSR Council of Ministers and of the post of USSR Minister of Internal Affairs.

2. That the case of L. P. Beria's criminal activities be referred to the USSR Supreme Court for consideration.

The exact circumstances surrounding Beria's arrest and execution are unknown in the West. According to the official account, he was found guilty by a special session of the USSR Supreme Court, composed of a number of prominent Party, government, and military leaders, during December 18–23, 1953, and shot on December 23. On several occasions, however, Khrushchev himself has privately provided differing versions of how Beria was killed during the very June meeting of the Party Presidium convened to consider his case. Precisely how Beria was caught off guard and his police and military forces neutralized remain unexplained.

The chief reason for the removal of Beria was doubtless his colleague's fear that he might employ the secret police against them. Other reasons for his downfall, beyond those that may be reasonably inferred from Soviet materials, have been provided by Eastern European sources. One of the most widespread of these explanations is that Beria had advocated greater relaxation in Soviet relations with the West and in Soviet controls over the Eastern European satellites, and in addition had urged a course of moderation in domestic policy on the Eastern European regimes. Thus, according to this line of reasoning, the uprisings in East Germany on June 16 were largely blamed on Beria. Khrushchev himself gave some weight to this charge in a speech before a conference of Soviet artists and writers on March 8, 1963:

> Immediately after Stalin's death, Beria began to take steps to disorganize the Party's work and disrupt the friendly relations of the Soviet Union with the fraternal countries of the socialist camp. For example, along with Malenkov, he put forward the disruptive proposal that the German Democratic Republic be liquidated as a socialist state and that it be recommended to the Socialist Unity Party of Germany that it renounce the slogan of building socialism.

However, our primary purpose here is to relate the story through Soviet media of the time. In the scope and depth of the charges and the vituperativeness of the language, the indictments of Beria closely resemble those of the great Stalin purge trials of the late 1930's. Because the leadership obviously attempted to discredit Beria completely, by throwing the entire book of heinous crimes against him, and to use him as a scapegoat for failures, to reconstruct from Soviet sources a reasonable estimation of the issues in dispute between Beria and his Presidium colleagues requires discernment and caution.

The first official account of Beria's "crimes" was given on July 10:

On June 26, 1953, the Presidium of the USSR Supreme Soviet. having examined the report of the USSR Council of Ministers on the criminal activities of L. P. Beria as an agent of foreign capital directed toward undermining the Soviet State, decreed: to remove L. P. Beria from the post of First Deputy Chairman of the USSR Council of Ministers and from the post of USSR Minister of Internal Affairs, and to bring Beria to trial. The USSR Supreme Soviet on August 8, 1953 approved the Decree of the Presidium of the USSR Supreme Soviet of June 26.

At the present time the USSR Procurator General's Office has finished its investigation of the case of the traitor to the Motherland, L. P. Beria.

This investigation has established that Beria, using his position, formed a treacherous group of conspirators hostile to the Soviet State, whose criminal goal was to use the organs of the Ministry of Internal Affairs, centrally and locally, against the Communist Party and the Government of the USSR in the interests of foreign capital. In their treacherous schemes they also strove to place the Ministry of Internal Affairs above the Party and the Government in order to seize power and liquidate the Soviet worker–peasant system for the purpose of restoring capitalism and the domination of the bourgeoisie.

The following accused, linked with Beria for many years through their joint criminal activity in the organs of the NKVD–MVD, were active members of the treacherous group of conspirators: V. N. Merkulov, former Minister of State Security of the USSR, and more recently the USSR Minister of State Control; V. G. Dekanozov, former head of one of the administrations of the NKVD of the USSR and more recently the Minister of Internal Affairs of the Georgian Republic; B. Z. Kobulov, former Deputy People's Commissar of Internal Affairs of the Georgian Republic, later Deputy Minister of State Security of the USSR, and recently Deputy Minister of Internal Affairs of the USSR; S. A. Goglidze, former People's Commissar of Internal Affairs of the Georgian Republic and recently head of one of the administrations of the USSR Ministry of Internal Affairs; P. Ya. Meshik, former head of one of the administrations of the USSR NKVD and recently Minister of Internal Affairs of the Ukrainian Republic; and L. E. Vlodzimirsky, former Head of the Section for the Investigation of Special Cases of the USSR Ministry of Internal Affairs. . . .

Having become USSR Minister of Internal Affairs in March 1953. Beria began increasingly to promote members of the conspiratorial group to a number of leading posts in the Ministry of Internal Affairs.

The conspirators victimized and persecuted honest officials of the Ministry of Internal Affairs who refused to carry out Beria's criminal orders.

With the goal of undermining the collective-farm system and creating food difficulties in our country, Beria sabotaged by various means and hindered the implementation of very important measures of the Party and the Government directed toward raising the economy of the collective and state farms and a steady rise in the well-being of the Soviet people.

It has also been established that Beria and his accomplices undertook criminal measures to stir up the remaining bourgeois–nationalist elements in the Union Republics, to sow enmity and discord among the peoples of the USSR and, in the first place, to undermine the friendship of the peoples of the USSR with the great Russian people. . . .

As has now been established by the investigation, Beria made contact with foreign agents as early as the period of the Civil War. In 1919, Beria, while in Baku, committed treachery by accepting a post as a Secret Agent in the Intelligence Service of the counter-revolutionary Mussavat Government in Azerbaidzhan, which worked under the control of British Intelligence organs. In 1920, while in Georgia, Beria again committed a treacherous act by establishing secret contact with the Menshevik Secret Service in Georgia, which was a branch of the British Intelligence Service.

It has been established by the investigation that in later years, also, Beria continued and widened his secret, criminal contacts with foreign agents through spies sent by them. He was sometimes successful in protecting these spies from exposure and deserved punishment. . . .

Through these criminal methods, he made his way into responsible posts in the Transcaucasus and Georgia, and later into the USSR Ministry of Internal Affairs. Nurturing plans for the seizure of power to accomplish his treacherous goals, Beria and his accomplices committed outrages against people who disagreed with them. They committed arbitrary and lawless acts and deceived the Party and State in a base manner. . . .

The investigation has established the existence of cases when the conspirators committed terroristic murders of persons from whom exposure was feared. Thus, Beria and his accomplices killed M. S. Kedrov — a member of the Communist Party since 1902 and a former member of the Presidium of the All-Russian Extraordinary Commission for Combating Counter-Revolution and Sabotage and the collegium of the

OGPU under F. E. Dzerzhinsky. The conspirators had grounds to suspect that Kedrov possessed evidence on the criminal past of Beria. Other evidence of terroristic murders committed by the conspirators to exterminate honest cadres, loyal to the cause of the Communist Party and the Soviet regime, has also been uncovered. . . .

Facts of other crimes committed by Beria have also been established by the investigation which reveal his profound moral degeneration and, in addition, facts have also been established by the investigation, of criminal mercenary acts committed by Beria and of his abuse of power.

Exposed at the investigation by the testimony of various witnesses and by authentic documentary evidence, the accused admitted their guilt in committing a number of very grave crimes against the State. . . . (*Pravda*, December 17, 1953)

Not unexpectedly, on December 24, *Pravda* reported that the special session of the USSR Supreme Soviet, which had held its proceedings *in camera,* had ordered Beria, Merkulov, Dekanozov, Kobulov, Goglidze, Meshik, and Vlodzimirsky to be shot, and that the sentence had been executed immediately.

A number of organizational and personnel alterations followed in the wake of Beria's fall. In addition to those MVD officials sentenced along with Beria, the MVD was thoroughly purged of his entourage. It is quite likely, for example, that the dismissal of the head of the Byelorussian MVD in late June was directly connected with Beria's arrest. The Supreme Soviet on August 8 affirmed a decree of its Presidium on June 26 which named S. N. Kruglov as Minister of Internal Affairs. At the Supreme Soviet session of April 27, 1954, it was officially announced that a Committee for State Security (KGB) had been created independent from the MVD and that its head was I. A. Serov, a man who had worked for some years in the Ukraine when Khrushchev was First Secretary of the Ukrainian Party Central Committee. This move to ensure control by the Party leadership over the secret police by dividing up the old Beria empire, was, in all likelihood, implemented well before April 1954. Some functions of the MVD — e.g. guarding borders and important military installations — were transferred to regular military units. Yet another important reduction of MVD responsibilities was indicated by *Pravda* of August 9: reporting on the actions of the Supreme Soviet, it revealed that a Min-

istry of Medium Machine Building had been set up with V. A. Malyshev at its head. This Ministry is generally regarded in the West to
have charge of the Soviet nuclear program.

During the summer of 1953, the posts of Commandant of the
Kremlin, Commandant of the City of Moscow, and Commander of
the Moscow Military District all changed hands. On July 19, *Pravda*
reported the removal of M. D. Bagirov as Chairman of the Azerbaidzhan Republic Council of Ministers, although he was not publicly accused of "anti-state" activities and association with Beria until the
spring of 1956. G. A. Arutiunov was removed as First Secretary of the
Armenian Republic Party Central Committee in early December.
There were a number of other personnel changes in the republics during the late summer, but many of them were probably the results of an
extensive revamping of the governmental machinery going on at the
time and were not related to the Beria affair.

All settlements, boroughs, parks, squares, and streets named after
Beria soon received new appellations and all published works that
referred favorably to him were appropriately revised. Subscribers to
the second edition of the *Large Soviet Encyclopedia* were sent re-
placements for pages 21–23 of volume 5, which had been published in
1951. Thus, the portrait and accomplishments of L. P. Beria were
quite literally replaced in Soviet history with pictures of the Bering
Sea and articles on the Bering Sea and the life of Wilhelm Bergoltz.

III · THE MALENKOV ERA

Following the purge of Beria, the remaining leaders appeared to close ranks, and presented a united front to the people. *Pravda* editorialized on July 13:

. . . The highest principle of leadership in our Party is collective leadership. Decisions made by one person are always or almost always one-sided. The Party teaches us that only the collective political experience, the collective wisdom of the Central Committee of the Communist Party, which is based on the scientific foundation of Marxist–Leninist theory, ensures the correct leadership of the Party and the state. . . .

Under the façade of monolithic unity, however, currents of rivalry and disagreement continued to flow unabated. Disagreements over substantive domestic and foreign policies stimulated and exacerbated dissen-

July 1953 to February 1955

sion among the leadership, and these personal rivalries spilled over into organizational rivalry among branches of the Soviet administrative–political structure.

The Issues: Agriculture

It will be recalled that Malenkov gave the report of the *Presidium* of the Central Committee on the Beria case. At the second session of the Supreme Soviet to meet after Stalin's death in early August, Malenkov continued as the primary spokesman for the leadership by delivering the major address on the state of the nation:

Comrade Deputies! The draft of the state budget submitted by the government to the present session of the USSR Supreme Soviet completely guarantees financing the tasks connected with the development of the national economy in 1953, the third year of the Fifth Five-Year Plan. Achieving these tasks will be an important step forward on the path of building a communist society in our nation. . . .

In connection with the discussion of the budget, I should like to speak of certain pressing tasks in the sphere of industry and agriculture, the solution of which would enable us to achieve more successfully our main job — ensuring further improvement in the material well-being of the workers, collective farmers, intelligentsia, and all the Soviet people.

The economic results attained in the first six months of 1953, like the results in 1951 and 1952, show that our industry is successfully meeting the goals of the Fifth Five-Year Plan. The volume of industrial production in 1953 will be approximately two and a half times greater than in the prewar year of 1940. . . .

It is known that the Party began the industrialization of the country by developing heavy industry — metallurgy, the fuel and power industry, and expansion of our machine building. It would have been impossible to assure the independence of our motherland without this policy. The Party firmly and unswervingly maintained its policy in the struggle against the Trotskyite and right-wing capitulators and traitors who opposed building up heavy industry and demanded the transfer of funds from heavy industry to light industry. To have adopted these proposals would have meant the destruction of our revolution and our country, for we would have been disarmed in the face of the capitalist encirclement. . . .

Solving the problem of developing heavy industry as the primary task changed fundamentally the relationship between heavy and light industry in the total volume of industrial output.

Heavy industry now employs approximately 70 per cent of all industrial workers. The means of production constituted 34 per cent of the total goods produced by USSR industry in 1924/25, 58 per cent by the end of the Second Five-Year Plan — in 1937 — and approximately 70 per cent in 1953. . . .

We shall continue in every way to develop heavy industry — metallurgy; the fuel, power, chemical and lumber industries; machine building; and the building industry — and to develop and improve our transport. We must always remember that heavy industry is the basic foundation of our socialist economy, for without its development, it is impossible to ensure further growth of light industry and agricultural production and to strengthen our country's defense capabilities.

Today, on the basis of the progress we have made in the development of heavy industry, we have all the necessary conditions for bringing about a sharp increase in the production of consumers' goods.

We have every possibility to do this and we must do it. During the last 28 years, production of the means of production as a whole in our country increased approximately 55 times while production of consumers' goods increased only about twelve times. Comparison of the 1953 production level with that of the prewar year 1940 shows as well that during this interval the output of the means of production more than tripled while production of consumers' goods increased 72 per cent.

The volume of production of consumers' goods which has been attained cannot satisfy us.

Heretofore we have not had the opportunity to develop light industry and food industry at the same rate as heavy industry. Now we can and, consequently, we must speed up the development of light industry in every way in order to secure a faster rise in the living standards and cultural level of the people. . . .

The government and the Party Central Committee consider it necessary to increase considerably the investment of funds for development of light industry and food industry — particularly fishing and agriculture — to make adjustments in order to increase substantially the plans for production of consumers' goods, and to give machine-building and other heavy industrial plants a greater part in producing consumers' goods. . . .

As you know, the Fifth Five-Year Plan provides that production of consumers' goods in 1955 will be approximately 65 per cent greater than in 1950. We have the possibility of developing the production of consumers' goods in such quantity as to reach this goal of the Five-Year Plan considerably before 1955.

We cannot be satisfied, however, merely with increased output of consumers' goods. The quality of all manufactured consumers' goods is a question of no less importance.

We must admit that we have been lagging behind in the quality of items of mass consumption, and we must resolutely correct this matter. Many enterprises still produce articles of unsatisfactory quality which do not meet the demands or satisfy the tastes of the Soviet consumer. . . .

But, in order to create a sharp expansion in the production of consumers' goods, we must first of all be concerned with the further development and growth of agriculture, which supplies the public with foodstuffs and light industry with raw materials.

Our socialist agriculture has made great progress in its development. The communal economy of the collective farms is growing and becoming stronger each year and the output of agriculture is increasing.

Our country is fully supplied with grain. Deliveries to the state of cotton, sugar beets and meat and dairy products have increased considerably when compared with the prewar period. In 1952, 3,770,000 tons of raw cotton were delivered, 1.7 times more than in 1940, and 22,000,-000 tons of sugar beets were delivered, almost 30 per cent more than in 1940. Deliveries of meat to the state last year amounted to 3,000,000 tons, one and a half times more than in 1940; and deliveries of milk amounted to 10,000,000 tons, almost 1.6 times more than 1940. In addition to deliveries to the state, our agriculture provides large quantities of meat, milk and other foodstuffs through co-operative and collective farm trade.

It would be a serious mistake, however, to ignore the lag in a number of important branches of agriculture and the fact that the present level of agricultural production does not correspond to the increased technical equipment of agriculture and the potentialities inherent in the collective farm system.

We still have quite a number of collective farms, and even entire raions, where agriculture is in a neglected condition; in many raions, the collective and state farms obtain low yields of grain and other crops and have big losses in harvesting; as a result of poor development of the communal economy, some collective farms still have insufficient incomes in cash and in kind, and pay little in cash, grain and other products for the workdays of the collective farmers.

It must be admitted that matters are still unsatisfactory in regard to the development of animal husbandry, and we are still far from satisfying the growing requirements of the public for meat, milk, eggs and other livestock products. . . .

It is our duty to ensure an additional, more rapid increase in the production of grain, keeping in mind that this is necessary for the country, not only to satisfy the population's growing requirements for bread, but also for the rapid development of animal husbandry and the supply of grain to districts which produce technical crops. . . .

It is our immediate task to ensure in the next two to three years the establishment in the country of an abundance of foodstuffs for the public and of raw materials for light industry on the basis of a general development of agriculture as a whole and further organizational and economic strengthening of the collective farms.

In order to achieve this task, the government and the Party Central Committee have judged it necessary to implement a number of important measures to ensure the further rapid development of agriculture: first and foremost, measures to raise the economic interest of collective farms and collective farmers in developing the backward branches of agriculture. One cannot consider as normal the present situation in which necessary economic incentives have been established for collective farms and farmers to develop some branches of agriculture and some crops, such as cotton, sugar beets, tea, and citrus fruits, while the state does not provide sufficient economic incentives for developing production in a number of other branches — potato and vegetable cultivation and especially animal husbandry. . . .

Without increasing the retail trade prices and while unswervingly maintaining the policy for further lowering them, the government and the Party Central Committee have decided to raise the prices paid this very year for meat, milk, potatoes, and vegetables supplied to the state by the collective farms and collective farmers as obligatory deliveries; to organize extensive state purchases of surpluses of grain, vegetables, potatoes, meat, milk, eggs and other farm products at higher prices from collective farms and collective farmers who have completed their obligatory deliveries; to develop collective farm trade extensively, aiding the collective farms in organization of the sale of surpluses of farm products at collective farm markets and through consumers' co-operatives.

Together with raising the material interest of the collective farmers in developing the communal economy of the collective farms, the government and the Party Central Committee have decided also to amend and alter substantially the incorrect attitude which has arisen among us toward the private supplementary holding [private plot] of the collective farmer. . . .

In consequence of the defects existing among us in tax policy toward the collective farmers' private supplementary plots, there has been a decrease in recent years in income to the collective farmers from their private plots and a reduction in the number of cattle, particularly cows, privately owned by the collective farm households. This contradicts our Party's policy in the sphere of collective farm development.

In this connection, the government and the Party Central Committee have judged it necessary to reduce considerably the quotas of obligatory deliveries from the collective farmers' private supplementary plots and have decided, as Finance Minister Comrade Zverev has already announced, to alter the system of assessing the collective farmers' agricultural tax, reducing the cash tax on each collective farm household by an average of approximately one half and cancelling entirely the existing arrears of the agricultural tax of past years. . . .

In order to satisfy the growing purchasing power of the population, the government has taken additional measures in recent months to develop trade by increasing the production of mass consumers' goods and deliveries of goods to the market from other sources; a large number of machine-building factories have been converted to production of mass consumers' goods. As a result of these measures, goods valued at 32,-000,000,000 rubles will be sold in the current year beyond the 312,-000,000,000 rubles' worth originally allocated for sale to the public between April and December, 1953. . . .

These measures are beginning to bear results. As you well know, the volume of retail trade in 1952 rose 10 per cent in comparison with the previous year. In the first quarter of the current year it increased 7 per cent and in the second quarter 23 per cent compared with the corresponding periods of last year.

But this is not enough. The present volume of trade cannot satisfy us. There are serious shortcomings in the very organization of trade itself; in a number of raions not all articles needed by the population are sold. There are frequently occasions when a buyer has to go to another city or raion to buy some article or another.

Trade and planning organizations must carefully study the public demand for goods. The need for thorough consideration of the public's demand and all its various needs stem from the very nature of Soviet trade. Only thus is it possible to organize better distribution of stocks of goods throughout the country.

The task is to have sufficient stocks of food and manufactured goods in the next two to three years so that all necessary goods may be bought in every city and every raion. . . .

Comrades! Further improvement of housing conditions and health services, and the enlargement of the network of schools and children's institutions are of great importance in improving the public welfare.

Despite the fact that we engaged in extensive housing construction prior to the war and even more so in the years since the war, the need for housing is still far from met and an acute shortage of housing is felt everywhere. This is especially true for the cities, because the urban population of our country has greatly increased. While the urban population was 26,000,000 in the 1926 census and 61,000,000 in 1940, today it is approximately 80,000,000. . . .

State capital investments in housing construction for this year have been considerably increased, and the total volume is almost four times the expenditures for this purpose in prewar 1940. But housing construction is still proceeding badly, plans for housing construction are still not fully met, and funds allocated by the state for this purpose are still not fully utilized. . . .

We also need more schools, medical establishments and children's institutions. The national economic plan for 1953 provides a 30 per cent increase over last year in the construction of schools, a 40 per cent increase in the construction of kindergartens and nurseries, and a 54 per cent increase in the construction of hospitals. . . .

It would be wrong to gloss over the substantial defects in the work of state and economic agencies, defects which cause considerable damage to the national economy. The decisions of the 19th Congress of our Party noted this. It must be admitted that the ministries and local Party and Soviet agencies are still not fulfilling the directives of the Congress satisfactorily and are not taking the necessary steps to improve the work of directing enterprises. The task is to eliminate energetically the existing shortcomings. . . .

The task is to put an end to the negligent attitude toward questions of the unit cost of products, to see to a systematic lowering of unit costs, and to make every enterprise profitable.

In order to solve more successfully the task facing us, it is necessary to raise substantially the responsibility and quality of the work of all parts of the state administration and economic management.

Amalgamation of the Ministries was implemented and the powers of Ministers considerably expanded in recent months. The measures are yielding good results in the management of the economy and have made it possible to save almost 6,500,000,000 rubles this year. It must be admitted, however, that the maintenance of administrative staffs is still costly. The government will continue to improve the work of the state apparatus and cut its maintenance costs more determinedly. At the same time, it must be said that we shall have to make certain corrections in the reorganization of the Ministries in connection with the new tasks of further growth of various branches of the national economy. . . ." [Editor's note: A lengthy section on foreign policy has been omitted here.] (*Pravda*, August 9, 1953)

> Malenkov's report to the Supreme Soviet was important not only as a vehicle for him to increase his national visibility but also because it enunciated — albeit cautiously and with suitable qualifications — a series of policies, several of which were to be challenged in the following two years.
> That Malenkov had not reaped all the benefits of Beria's fall was indicated by *Pravda's* information bulletin of September 13:

A plenum of the Central Committee of the Communist Party of the Soviet Union was held a few days ago.

1. The plenum heard and discussed the report by Comrade N. S. Khrushchev on measures for the further development of agriculture in the USSR and adopted a resolution on the subject.

2. The plenum elected N. S. Khrushchev First Secretary of the Party Central Committee.

> Thus, Khrushchev's de facto position of senior secretary was given formal status.
> Two days later, *Pravda* and *Izvestia* carried the full text of Khrushchev's nearly 25,000-word speech which rambled through six newspaper pages. The excerpts from this speech of September 3 printed below were chosen to illustrate several points. If carefully compared with Malenkov's speech of August 8, it will be seen that Khrushchev painted the existing situation in agriculture in somewhat different hues than did Malenkov, and that he hedges on some of Malenkov's economic projections — even to the point of qualifying several of Malenkov's phrases. The great length and scope of the speech and the abundance of detailed information it contained, indicated that Khrushchev was staking out a claim to be the major spokesman on agriculture for the regime. The free-wheeling nature of the address, the use of aphorisms

and numerous specific and often personalized references to local situations and individual collective farmers give a flavor of what might be termed Khrushchev's public style — a style which he was to use with considerable political acumen in following years. The very holding of this plenum on agriculture, and the publicity devoted to it, gave notice that the Party, as well as the Council of Ministers, had the right to proclaim policy in the economic sphere and that meetings of the Central Committee would be used as forums for propounding these policies. Khrushchev called for additional measures, beyond those advocated by Malenkov, to raise agricultural production — measures which were to be carried out by the Party as well as the government. In one poignant paragraph, Khrushchev stated that according to his Party rulebook one could not make distinctions between political and economic work, and that lower Party cadres in the countryside were to get their hands dirty in the battle for production. Although at this point of time Khrushchev presented his proposals on agriculture in the name of the Presidium of the Central Committee, he quite explicitly called for an increased role by the Party *apparatus* in agricultural administration.

. . . Under the leadership of the Communist Party, the Soviet people have developed an integrated heavy industry — the mighty foundation of the socialist economy. With the existence of such a foundation, there is now the practical possibility for decided advances in all branches of light industry and food industry. A considerable expansion in the output of consumers' goods for the maximum satisfaction of the steadily growing material and cultural needs of the entire society is the basic goal and major task of socialist production.

To organize this decided advance in consumers' goods, however, our agriculture must advance rapidly.

A very urgent and important national economic task at the present time is to achieve a sharp rise in all branches of agriculture, while continuing to develop further heavy industry, and in two to three years to increase greatly the food supply for our country's entire population in addition to guaranteeing the collective farm peasantry a higher level of living standards.

In this connection the Presidium of the Party Central Committee has considered it necessary to introduce for consideration by the plenum proposals for realizing a number of urgent measures to ensure the rapid growth and all-round development of agriculture. . . .

We must say frankly that we are making poor use of the tremendous resources hidden within large-scale socialist agricultural production. We have many backward and even neglected collective farms and entire raions. The crop yield continues to be low on many collective farms and raions. Agricultural productivity has grown very slowly, especially in animal husbandry, forage and feed crops, potatoes, and vegetables. An obvious disparity exists between the growth rate of our large-scale socialist industry, urban population and the living standard of the working masses on the one hand and the present level of agricultural production on the other. . . .

The rate of socialist agricultural development has obviously lagged behind the rate of industrial development and the growth in the population's need for consumers' goods. It is sufficient to note that although industrial output increased 2.3 times from 1940 through 1952, gross agricultural output increased only 10 per cent (in comparable prices).*

In general we are satisfying the country's requirement for grain crops, in that our country is well supplied with bread. We have the necessary state reserves and are exporting wheat on a limited scale. With the growth in the living standard of the working people, the population's demand is moving increasingly from bread to meat and dairy products, vegetables, fruits, and so forth. An obvious disparity between the population's growing needs and the level of production has taken place during the past few years particularly in these branches of agriculture.* The lag in a number of important branches of agriculture has impeded further development of light and food industry and is a hindrance to increasing the profitability of the collective farms and farmers. . . .

If we exert all our ability and efforts in solving this task and do not restrict ourselves in leadership to general directives but are occupied with strengthening each collective and state farm and each MTS [machine and tractor station], then we shall attain this level of consumption in a very short time, and for certain kinds of production in two to three years. . . .

Raising the material self-interest of collective farms and farmers to increase crop yields and develop communal animal husbandry is of great importance. For this purpose the USSR Council of Ministers and the Presidium of the Party Central Committee have deemed it necessary to increase the present procurement and purchase prices for animal husbandry products, potatoes, and vegetables. Thus, the procurement prices

* Compare these statements with those of Malenkov on page 62.

for produce turned over to the state as obligatory deliveries are more than 5.5 times larger for livestock and poultry, double for milk and butter, 2.5 times larger for potatoes, and 25 to 40 per cent more on the average for vegetables. As for purchase prices, they have risen an average of 30 per cent for meat and 50 per cent for milk. It is important to note here that retail prices for animal husbandry products, potatoes and vegetables have not risen, but, on the contrary, are dropping every year. The policy of lowering retail prices will be steadily followed.

Given these circumstances, it has also been regarded expedient to lower the norms for the collective farms' obligatory deliveries to the state of animal husbandry products and the norms for the collective farms' deliveries of potatoes and vegetables. The norms for obligatory deliveries of animal husbandry products from the holdings [private plots] of workers and employees have been substantially reduced.

With the reduction in the obligatory delivery norms, the collective farms and farmers will have more surplus produce for sale at the higher purchase prices and for sale on the collective farm markets. . . .

In addition, the Soviet government will spend more than 15,000,-000,000 rubles in 1953 and more than 35,000,000,000 rubles in 1954 to implement the urgent measures for furthering agricultural development. A large part of these expenditures is allocated for further additional capital investment in agriculture and for increasing the interest of collective farms and farmers in developing animal husbandry and raising yields of potatoes and vegetables in order to advance decidedly these branches of agriculture in the next few years. As a result of carrying out the above-cited measures, the collective farms and farmers will receive more than 13,000,000,000 rubles extra income in 1953 and more than 20,000,000,000 rubles extra income in 1954. . . .

Our most pressing tasks are in the field of animal husbandry, since lagging there has become chronic and we shall not be able to improve the situation rapidly without decisive measures.

Our animal husbandry was lagging even before the war. Much has been achieved since the war to restore and further develop animal husbandry. During the period from July 1945 to July 1953, cattle in the USSR increased 11,300,000 head, sheep and goats 53,900,000, and pigs 25,100,000.

At first glance these growth figures, which are really considerable, seem to present no cause for alarm. In fact this is not so.

I cite data on the number of livestock in the USSR (in millions, over comparable areas, for the beginning of each year):

	Cattle	Cows	Pigs	Sheep and Goats	Horses
1916	58.4	28.8	23.0	96.3	38.2
1928	66.8	33.2	27.7	114.6	36.1
1941	54.5	27.8	27.5	91.6	21.0
1953	56.6	24.3	28.5	109.9	15.3

These figures show that the number of cows at the beginning of 1953 was 3,500,000 less than at the beginning of 1941 and 8,900,000 less than at the beginning of 1928. . . .*

More attention must be given to raising wheat, sunflowers, kale and certain other silage crops.

Separate attention must be given to such a valuable feed crop as corn. It is no accident that corn growing has become widespread in a number of countries with developed animal husbandry. In the USSR corn occupies an extremely small area, even in those regions where it grows best.

Conditions are favorable for corn growing in many oblasts of the USSR. One can cite many examples where increased corn yields have been obtained by Ukrainian collective and state farms. Back in 1948, Comrade Taran, an agronomist on the Comintern State Farm in Poltava Oblast, obtained an average harvest of 70 centners of corn per hectare over a large area by using the square-cluster method of sowing. On the Chkalov Collective Farm in Dnepropetrovsk Oblast (Comrade Shchervina, Chairman) the average corn harvest for five years was 50 centners per hectare. Not to mention the remarkable successes in corn raising of Mark Yevstafyevich Ozerny — the famous master of this method from the Red Partisan Collective Farm, Likhovka Raion, Dnepropetrovsk Oblast — who has obtained high yields year after year and in 1949 had a record harvest of 224 centners of corn per hectare.

In Moscow Oblast experience has shown that corn provides high yields of silage in the central raions. The square-cluster method of sowing completely ensures harvests of up to 500 and more centners of silage per hectare. Thus, the Path of the New Life Collective Farm and the Gorki II State Farm in Moscow Oblast have raised no less than 700 to 800 centners of corn for silage on every hectare. . . .

Certain local officials complain of feed shortage and yet raise the question of reducing corn crops. Our Ukrainian comrades in particular are at fault here. One may ask, what more abundant feed crop can they cite? . . .

* Compare these statements with those of Malenkov on page 62.

Nevertheless, many Party and Soviet officials regard feed output and procurements as a matter of secondary importance. Some comrades have replaced concrete and comprehensive guidance of this work on every collective and state farm with last-minute campaigns and flowery declarations.

For example, here is how Comrade Semin, Secretary of the Vologda Oblast Party Committee, envisages the solution of problems linked with feed procurement. In a report to a plenum of the oblast Party committee . . . he stated: "One must be convinced of the fact that the feed base is not primary or fundamental in animal husbandry. First comes leadership, then the feed base." In addition, he proposed handling the haying in ten to fifteen days by the tactics of a last-minute campaign. "Only by a general frontal attack," he said, "can we win this battle." Comrade Semin demands that intercollective farm or raion headquarters be set up to organize and direct all operations.

Let us ask, where are the raion Party committees or the raion Soviets and what is their role if some sort of farfetched intercollective farm headquarters directs the haying? . . .

It is necessary to state that officials of the USSR Ministry of Agriculture and Procurements have taken an incorrect stand on this matter. They have planned potato planting by the square-cluster method in terms of existing equipment. Because we still have few machines, the ministry proposes that we plant only half the area. One cannot agree. We must remember that the square-cluster method grew up on collective farms when we did not have a special machine. Nevertheless, it was applied on advanced collective farms with excellent results. . . .

A word must be said about seeds. The people have a sage saying: "Don't expect a good breed from a poor seed." Unfortunately there is among us a negligent and sometimes criminal attitude toward potato seed. Many collective and state farms sow poor seed and also fail to meet the full sowing norm. Yet, the sowing norm for potatoes has a special and even decisive importance in achieving high yields. For example, progressive collective farms in Moscow Oblast sow two to three tons of seed per hectare. With good care they achieve a harvest of 20 to 25 tons per hectare. . . .

Particular attention must be given to wheat. Great possibilities exist for increasing the output of winter and spring wheat; in addition to the old areas for growing this crop, there are many raions in the central Black-Earth oblasts, the Volga area, the forest steppes of the Ukraine and a number of the non-Black-Earth zone areas. When basic agrotechnical measures are observed, these regions obtain high yields of winter and spring wheat. . . .

It should be noted that even the apparatus of the USSR Ministry of Agriculture and Procurement and its local agencies do not meet the demands for an efficient solution of the problems posed by the collective farms and the MTS. The apparatus is very cumbersome; it includes numerous administrations and departments which duplicate each other and are often idle. It is no surprise that the Ministry does not manifest efficiency and accuracy in guiding local agencies, that it permits bureaucracy and red tape in solving pressing problems. The USSR Ministry of Agriculture and Procurement is only weakly linked with practice and is isolated from the collective farms and the MTS. Without knowledge of the true conditions locally, the Ministry, nevertheless, attempts to regulate from the center all phases of the work of local agricultural agencies, collective farms and the MTS, giving instructions which are often undesirable locally.

Ask the comrades from the North Caucasus if they have ever asked the Ministry how to raise wheat. I am certain the answer will be no. Workers in the Ukraine do not ask the Ministry how to raise sugar beets, nor do those in Uzbekistan ask how to grow cotton. This is understandable, for experienced workers have grown up in the localities. But the Ministry officials continue to guide in the old manner, proceeding on the false assumption that only they know everything and can do everything. . . .

The defects in the Ministry's work are graphically revealed in the work of agricultural planning. Many unnecessary items, which inhibit the initiative of local agencies, the MTS, and collective farms, are included in the plans. It is sufficient to say that the planned tasks for the collective farms in agriculture and animal husbandry alone list from 200 to 250 goals. . . .

In the course of the year, each collective farm presents to raion agricultural agencies reports covering approximately 10,000 items. Collective farm reports have almost tripled since the war by number of items.

While we criticize the USSR Ministry of Agriculture and Procurement, this does not imply that its role has been downgraded. On the contrary, the Ministry must play an increasingly greater role. The Ministry apparatus must be overhauled to meet changed conditions and its staffs considerably decreased. . . .

In this connection Union and autonomous republic Ministries of

Agriculture and Procurement and krai and oblast agriculture and procurement administrations must assume greater importance. This means that local agricultural agencies must be strengthened with qualified personnel, their structure reviewed, their staffs decreased and the agencies brought closer to production. . . .

The Russian Republic, unlike the other Union republics, until recently has not had a full-fledged Ministry of Agriculture with the necessary rights and powers. Even the republic's MTS were not within the Ministry's jurisdiction.

This Ministry formerly had the job of concentrating on the output of potatoes and vegetables, but in fact it did not have the required material and technical base even for this. As a result, the ministry had to limit its activity to problems of rabbit breeding, bee keeping and wild life. This sounds fantastic, but, unfortunately, it is not fantasy but fact. . . .

The draft decree [for Central Committee approval] provides for the dispatch by the spring of 1954 of not less than 100,000 agricultural specialists to work in the MTS so that each collective farm will be served by an agricultural specialist and each large farm by an agricultural specialist and an animal husbandry specialist. . . .

Comrades! Successful solution of the tasks confronting us in agriculture demands great organizational and political work by Party organizations. It would be wrong to assume that the further development of agriculture will come about quietly, smoothly and spontaneously. . . .

Our rural Party forces are not small. There are collective farm Party organizations on 76,000 farms. At present there are more than 1,000,000 Communists in the countryside. The army of the rural YCL [Komsomol] members numbers more than 2,000,000. If we station and use these forces correctly, we shall successfully cope with all our tasks and overcome every difficulty on the way to the goal. . . .

Nevertheless, we must admit that there are grave shortcomings in the work of Party organizations in the countryside. In many organizations, Party political work is conducted in isolation from economic tasks. There are still officials among us who frequently say that politics is inseparable from economics, that politics must be combined with solving economic tasks and then in practice they separate political activity from the daily work of economic construction. This can be seen primarily in the state of work with agricultural officials, especially with collective farm chairmen.

To achieve success, attention must be concentrated on what is most important, that is, on strengthening the MTS and collective and state farms with qualified, capable personnel, with our best cadres. . . .

Now that a Soviet intelligentsia has grown up among us, why should we not issue a call from the Party and summon the best people from the cities — say, for example, 50,000 Communists — to strengthen rural work? I think that we can do this. It would be well to discuss this matter along with other questions here at the plenum. . . .

An urgent task in improving the leadership of agriculture is to raise the role of the raion Party committees, and [Soviet] executive committees in developing collective farms, MTS and state farms. Unless we strengthen the raion sector, unless we assign Party forces correctly and organize all Party work skillfully, we shall not be able to raise the leadership of the collective and state farms and MTS to the level required by the new tasks.

Many raions are not well staffed with trained Party and Soviet personnel. Officials in many raion Party committees and executive committees do not have the practical qualifications necessary to cope with the increased demands now made of executives. . . .

Work in the countryside is very important and esteemed work. Party organizations should overcome the overbearing and bureaucratic attitude toward the village which has arisen among certain Communists, including those occupying responsible positions. . . .

The lack of personal responsibility in the leadership of MTS and collective farms must be eliminated. There is a large apparatus in the raions of Party, Soviet and agricultural administration officials which amounts to approximately five or six officials for each collective farm. Despite this, no one is actually responsible for conditions on the collective farms and MTS or for political work among the masses.

One may say that the raion Party committee secretary, the raion executive committee chairman, the head of the agricultural department of the raion executive committee, the MTS director and many others are responsible for the collective farms and MTS. But who is really responsible for a particular collective farm in the raion? You will not get a concrete answer to this question from anyone, because there is no one responsible for a particular collective farm. Herein lies the fundamental shortcoming in the guidance of collective farms. . . .

The following considerations for an exchange of opinions on this question might be given. It seems to us that for every MTS, the raion committees should have a group of workers, headed by a raion Party committee secretary. For example, there are three MTS in a raion. In such a raion it would be possible to create three groups of instructors — one group for each MTS — so that one instructor serves one or a maximum of two collective farms and is responsible to the raion Party committee for his work. The role of instructor in the Party apparatus in general and in the raion Party committees in particular must be increased. Attention must be paid therefore to selecting and training instructors.

A raion committee secretary who heads a group should supervise the instructors under him, serve the collective farms throughout the entire MTS zone, organize Party work among the MTS workers and also on the collective farms and be responsible to the raion Party committee for conditions on these collective farms. In order that guidance of collective farms and primary Party units be concrete, the raion committee secretary will have to spend all his working time at the MTS. And this is good; there will be less paper work and red tape and more active leadership. In this connection there is no longer any need for an assistant director for political affairs in the MTS. The bureau of the raion Party committee, headed by the first secretary, must guide the work of the groups serving the MTS and collective farms and also manage the entire economic and cultural life of the raion. . . . (*Pravda*, September 15, 1953)

Khrushchev's allusions to the possibilities of utilizing idle lands and increasing the production of corn for fodder indicate that even at this time he was mulling over ideas that were to blossom forth soon in his "Virgin Lands" and corn–hog campaigns. Similarly, his criticisms of the Ministry of Agriculture were to be repeated and intensified during 1954. In fact, Khrushchev's September speech, as a whole, proved to be the kickoff of a mounting national campaign on agricultural problems.

To focus attention on the regime's agricultural program and to stir up agricultural cadres, three conferences on agriculture were held in early 1954: the All-Soviet Conference of MTS Personnel (January 25–28), the All-Soviet Conference of State Farm Personnel (February 3–5), and the All-Russian Conference of Agricultural Leaders (February 11–15). Each conference was attended by some 2000 regional and local officials, specialists and leading farmers. The format of these three conferences warrants mention. In each case the opening address was delivered by the relevant minister, followed by numerous shorter speeches by members of local cadres and by specialists. Khrushchev then wound up each session with a major speech. Although his speeches were not published at the time, newspaper reports noted that they were received with "thunderous applause." Most of the Presidium members attended, but Khrushchev was the only top leader to address the conferences.

On March 6, 1954, precisely one year after Stalin's death, *Pravda's* major item was entitled: "On Further Increasing the Country's Grain Production and Developing Virgin and Unused Lands. Decree of the Plenum of the Central Committee of the CPSU, adopted on March 2, 1954 on the basis of N. S. Khrushchev's Report." The most radical proposal of this broad-gauged decree was to increase drastically land under cultivation and thus attempt a dramatic breakthrough in grain production. Eventually, some 90 million acres of previously uncultivated land, primarily in Siberia and northern Kazakhstan, were put to the plow.

It was over two weeks after this decree before Khrushchev's marathon speech to the Central Committee plenum on February 23 was published. Two sections of this speech are especially noteworthy:

. . . The problem is to increase considerably the gross grain yield in 1954 and 1955 and to increase state procurements and purchases of grain by at least 35 to 40 per cent compared with 1953. . . .

There are large amounts of undeveloped land in eastern areas. For example, there are up to 40,000,000 hectares of overgrown, idle and virgin lands, unirrigated fields and pastures in 14 oblasts of the Russian Republic and eight of the Kazakh Republic. . . .

Conservative estimates show that in the northeastern oblasts and certain other areas of the Kazakh Republic, in Western Siberia and the Urals, as well as the Volga area and to some extent the North Caucasus, grain cultivation can be expanded by 13,000,000 hectares in the next two years, 8,700,000 hectares on the collective farms and 4,300,000 on the state farms. The area under grain can be expanded by more than 2,300,000 hectares in 1954 alone.

We have every opportunity for increasing the area planted above the 13,000,000 hectares planned.

.   .   .   .   .

Comrades! Serious shortcomings in the leadership of MTS and collective and state farms were revealed at the previous plenum of the Central Committee. Since then we have made a detailed study of affairs and have uncovered new facts indicating neglect in a series of branches of agriculture; I have reported these at the present plenum. One asks who is to blame? First of all the officials who were working in this very important sector.

Comrade Skvortsov headed the administration of state farms for a long time. Now you see the results of his management. On a number of state farms the land is managed uneconomically and as a result the country has failed to obtain a large amount of agricultural products. Comrade Skvortsov enjoyed our confidence, but in fact he turned out to be a poor organizer and a shortsighted official. . . . Great doubt has arisen whether he will be able to improve the situation as First Deputy Minister of State Farms. . . .

A large share of the blame for mistakes in planning rests on Comrade Demidov, who was in charge of agricultural questions, and on Comrade Dmitriyev, the former chief of the Agricultural Planning Administration of the USSR Gosplan. Demidov and Dmitriyev saw that grain sowing was being sharply curtailed on collective farms and especially on state farms, but they not only failed to oppose this, on the contrary, they supported and pursued actively this incorrect and anti-state policy. . . .

The incorrect behavior of Comrade Benediktov, Minister of Agriculture, must be noted. Comrade Benediktov is an agronomist and has proven himself to be an effective administrator and a man of principle. How then did he not notice these mistakes in time and oppose them? Evidently bureaucracy entangled him.

Comrade Kozlov, USSR Minister of State Farms, is even more to blame for these errors. One may say that he is a young minister who has worked at this post for only a few months; but even in his former work he had direct contact with agriculture and exercised direct influence on the decision of agricultural questions — influence on Gosplan, the Ministry of Agriculture, the Ministry of State Farms and agricultural research institutions. . . .

A reorganization of the Ministries of Agriculture, State Farms and Procurements has recently been conducted, but this was only a small part of the matter. Although the staffs of these ministries have been substantially reduced, their apparatus is still cumbersome and the style of their work has changed little.

The officials of the ministries are still remote from the MTS and collective and state farms; they seldom appear in the field. . . .

It is necessary to continue the work of cutting staffs of the ministries and sending part of the staff out to practical work. . . .

It is necessary to wage a ruthless struggle with bureaucracy and red tape, which, incidentally, are found not only in the agricultural agencies. . . . It must be kept in mind that we will meet strong resistance from the bureaucrats who have become accustomed to dealing with papers alone and cannot live without them. . . .

Kazakhstan's agriculture is now confronted with a great new job — bringing under cultivation more than 6,000,000 hectares of virgin and idle land. Without improved Party leadership in the republic, it will be impossible to meet successfully this complex task. In this connection the members of the Kazakhstan Party Central Committee bureau were invited before the Central Committee. We discussed with them the problem of how to carry out the tasks confronting agriculture in the republic. The discussion led to the unanimous conclusion that Party leadership in the republic must be strengthened. This matter was brought up for discussion at a plenum of the Kazakhstan Party Central Committee [some time before February 12]. The plenum decided to strengthen the republic's leadership and to release Secretaries Shayakhmetov and Afonov from their responsibilities. Comrade Ponomarenko was elected First Secretary of the Kazakhstan Party Central Committee and Comrade Brezhnev Second Secretary. . . . (*Pravda,* March 21, 1954)

The boldness with which Khrushchev criticized by name important governmental officials and the near-personal credit publicly given to him for the Virgin Lands project indicate the distance he had come in leadership power and authority in the year since Stalin's death. Just how much the Virgin Lands was in fact his personal project is revealed in a collection of Khrushchev's statements on agriculture published in 1962–63, entitled *The Construction of Communism in the USSR and the Development of Agriculture*. This collection contains a "note" from Khrushchev to the Party Presidium dated January 22, 1954 in which he strongly urges the Virgin Lands scheme.

The audacity of the new lands program is indicative of Khrushchev's political ability. As a showy project promising a rapid cure for grain and fodder shortages, it provided considerable publicity mileage, especially for its author. However, as Khrushchev himself acknowledged, it involved a risk because of the scanty rainfall in the areas involved. Moreover, the Virgin Lands program required heavy inputs of agricultural equipment, some of which had to be transferred from traditional agricultural areas where machinery was already in short supply. The competition for agricultural equipment and for rail facilities required to ship it led to a sharp intervention in agricultural administration by the Central Commitee Secretariat, which demanded that priority be given to the Virgin Lands.

In June and July, 1954 Khrushchev stumped the agricultural areas of Siberia and Kazakhstan, inspecting farms, talking with local officials, addressing conferences and sending back "notes" to the Party Presidium. On June 27, the newspapers reported the meeting of a Central Committee plenum:

The plenum examined the results of spring sowing, crop care, harvest preparations and fulfillment of the plan for procuring farm products in 1954.

The session heard and discussed the reports of Comrade I. A. Benediktov, USSR Minister of Agriculture; Comrade P. I. Lobanov, RSFSR Minister of Agriculture; Comrade A. I. Kozlov, USSR Minister of State Farms; Comrade T. A. Yurkin, RSFSR Minister of State Farms; and Comrade L. R. Korniyets, USSR Minister of Procurement. It also adopted an appropriate decree.

Significantly, no mention is made of Khrushchev's participation in the June plenum. However, the previously cited collection of his statements on agriculture (published in 1962–63) contain a speech to this plenum. Some of his remarks were highly critical of agricultural operations, the lack of machinery and the poor work of USSR and RSFSR Ministries. He raked T. A. Yurkin, RSFSR Minister of State Farms, over the coals and had the following to say about the USSR Minister of Agriculture, Benediktov: "Am I really speaking about things that are unknown to the minister, Comrade Benediktov? No, he knows about them, but does not take measures to correct the situation." The published resolution of the plenum did reprimand the USSR Ministries of Agriculture, State Farms, and Automobile, Tractor and Farm Machine Building, the RSFSR Council of Ministers and the Kazakh Republic Council of Ministers for failures in equipment deliveries, inadequate supervision of MTS and mistakes in allotting Virgin Lands; but the criticisms were generalized. On August 12, however, these criticisms were repeated and sharpened:

The Party Central Committee has examined the question of transferring combines and trucks to Siberia and Kazakhstan and has concluded that the transfer of combines and trucks to Siberia and Kazakhstan from other regions is conducted in an unsatisfactory manner. The

Party Central Committee pointed out that some leaders of local agricultural agencies take an incorrect attitude toward the task of shipping combines and trucks and hold up their dispatch. . . .

The Central Committee declared that the RSFSR Council of Ministers (Comrade Puzanov) and the USSR Ministry of Agriculture (Comrade Benediktov) do not exercise the necessary control over the shipping of combines and trucks and do not employ the necessary measures in order to ensure the timely completion of this work.

The Ministry of Transport (Comrade Beshchev) behaves irresponsibly toward the transport of combines and trucks, does not ensure the prompt delivery of freight cars for the shipping of machinery and does not exercise daily control over their progress on the railway route.

The Party Central Committee has ordered the RSFSR Council of Ministers, the Ukrainian Party Central Committee, the Ukrainian Council of Ministers, oblast and raion party committees, oblast and raion executive committees of oblasts and raions that are assigned to ship combines and trucks to Siberia and Kazakhstan to take immediate measures for the timely completion of the work of shipping combines and trucks, as well as combine operators, combine mechanics, drivers, mechanics, and other workers of motor brigades. . . .

Personal responsibility was placed on Comrade Beshchev, Minister of Transport, for the prompt delivery of freight cars, the shipping of combines and trucks and their rapid transportation.

The Central Committee, placing great emphasis on the prompt delivery of combines and trucks to Kazakhstan and Siberia, have obligated the political leadership of the Ministry of Transport and Party organizations of the Department of Railway Junctions and Stations to explain in detail to the railway transport workers the importance of the speedy shipment of combines and trucks to the virgin lands and to organize the railroad workers so that they will carry out this important assignment of the Party and Government in a positive manner. . . . (*Pravda*, August 12, 1954)

> Despite the difficulties with the Virgin Lands project indicated by this statement, plans to expand the program were announced five days later:

In the Party Central Committee and the USSR Council of Ministers: ON THE FURTHER CULTIVATION OF VIRGIN AND IDLE LANDS FOR INCREASED GRAIN PRODUCTION.

The Party Central Committee and the USSR Council of Ministers note with satisfaction that the Party and government appeal for increasing the country's grain production by developing many millions of hectares of virgin and idle lands has evoked a warm response and nationwide approval. . . .

In the spring of 1954 an area of 3,600,000 hectares was planted to wheat and other crops on the newly developed lands, as against the planned figure of 2,300,000 hectares. The plan for planting grain crops on virgin and idle lands was fulfilled 156 per cent on collective farms and 176 per cent on state farms.

As a result of the measures taken, the total grain harvest in areas of West Siberia and Kazakhstan will be considerably increased in the current year. By August 10, 1954 there had been plowed 13,400,000 hectares of virgin and idle land, or 103.2 per cent of the established plan. . . .

Taking into consideration the experience in developing new land in 1954 and the existence of real possibilities for further increasing grain production in the country by cultivating additional virgin and idle lands, the Party Central Committee and the USSR Council of Ministers call upon collective farmers, MTS and state farm workers and local Party, Soviet, and agricultural agencies to overfulfill substantially in 1954 the goal set for cultivating virgin and idle lands, in order to ensure in 1955 the sowing of grain and other agricultural crops in these areas on at least 15,000,000 hectares of fallow land instead of the 13,000,000 hectares planned. . . . (*Pravda*, August 17, 1954)

It should be noted that this was the first decree after Stalin's death in which the Party Central Committee took precedent over the Council of Ministers in the announcement.

The Issues: Light versus Heavy Industry

Closely intertwined with agricultural policy was the question of consumers' goods production, or what may be loosely termed the issue of light versus heavy industry. After Malenkov's speech to the Supreme Soviet in August, public attention was focused on the consumers' goods campaign during the remainder of 1953, as illustrated by the following sampling from the Soviet press:

A conference of *aktiv* from Moscow and Moscow Oblast light industry was convened in Moscow recently by the Moscow Oblast Party Committee.

More than 1,500 innovator–workers, engineers and officials from textile, footwear, garment, knitwear, and other light industry enterprises and officials from ministries and research institutions attended the conference. Comrade N. A. Mikhailov, Moscow Oblast Party Committee Secretary, also participated.

Comrade A. N. Kosygin, USSR Minister of Light and Food Industry, reported on the efforts of workers in light industrial enterprises to improve production, increase the variety, raise the quality and lower the unit cost of consumers' goods. . . . (*Izvestia*, August 27, 1953)

*   *   *

Reconstruction has begun on the State Department Store building on Red Square. A department store will soon open here — the largest in the country. It will occupy the entire State Department Store building and the adjacent building at 17 Vetoshny Lane. The new department store will have more than 47,000 square meters of floor space and 2½ kilometers of counters. A thousand sales people will serve customers. . . . (*Izvestia*, August 28, 1953)

*   *   *

The Communist Party and the Soviet government view as their major job guaranteeing the further improvement of the living standard of the workers, the collective farmers, the intelligentsia, and all the country's working people. The program enunciated at the Fifth Session of the USSR Supreme Soviet for a decided increase in consumers' goods output is being constantly and thoroughly implemented. The Soviet people are showing tremendous enthusiasm in the struggle to carry out the decree of the September plenum of the Party Central Committee on measures for further developing agriculture. . . .

The vital need for a decided increase in consumers' goods output requires workers in all branches of heavy industry and transportation to show concern for, and give all possible aid to, the demands and needs of light and food industry. In the first place, this means filling accurately the orders of the Ministries of Consumers' Goods and the Food Products Industry and those of local industry and the producers' cooperatives, supplying the needs of these enterprises on time with the required equipment and various types of raw materials and other items.

It must be recognized that not all heavy industrial enterprises have paid proper attention to orders from light and food industry. *Pravda* has reported previously that certain machine-building plants were far behind in supplying modern equipment to textile, clothing, footwear, and other enterprises. The USSR Ministry of Machine Building discussed this question recently and adopted measures to eliminate existing short-comings. . . .

The incorrect attitude which considers the manufacture of consumers' goods a petty, second-rate matter must be vigorously uprooted. The time has come to understand that the production of goods for the population is a job of great importance to the state, one which calls for a persistent struggle to increase the output and expand the variety of these goods and improve their quality and appearance. . . . (*Pravda*, October 9, 1953)

*   *   *

In the USSR Council of Ministers and the Communist Party Central Committee: CONCERNING AN INCREASE IN CONSUMERS' GOODS OUTPUT AND IMPROVEMENT IN THEIR QUALITY.

. . . The relative proportion of heavy industry is more than two-thirds the total volume of industrial production. On the basis of the success achieved in developing heavy industry, we now have everything necessary to organize a sharp increase in consumers' goods production, and we have the opportunity to increase significantly capital investment in the development of those branches of industry producing consumers' goods.

In addition, it has become possible to make broader use of machine-building, metallurgical, chemical and other heavy industrial enterprises for consumers' goods production.

The USSR Council of Ministers and the Party Central Committee, in connection with the major task of ensuring further improvement in the living standard of workers, collective farmers, intelligentsia and all other Soviet people, deem it necessary in the next two or three years to accelerate in every possible way the development of light industry in order to have a sufficient quantity of manufactured consumers' goods in the country and to increase decidedly the supply of these goods to the population.

To achieve this goal, it is necessary to develop consumers' goods production on a scale that will fulfill as soon as possible the 1955 quota set by the five-year plan for the production of consumers' goods. . . . (*Pravda*, October 28, 1953)

*   *   *

CONCERNING MEASURES FOR EXPANDING PRODUCTION OF MANU-
FACTURED CONSUMERS' GOODS AND IMPROVING THEIR QUALITY: Report
by Comrade A. N. Kosygin, USSR Minister of Consumers' Goods Industry, at the All-Soviet Conference of Light Industry Personnel,
October 29, 1953.

. . . The Soviet people greeted with great satisfaction the statement by Comrade G. M. Malenkov at the fifth session of the USSR
Supreme Soviet that the Party and government have decided to ensure
a sharp increase in consumers' goods output in order to enlarge
markedly within the next two or three years the supply of manufactured
goods and food products for the public.

The September plenum of the Party Central Committee adopted a
decision to carry out a number of important and urgent measures to
ensure the rapid advance and all-round development of agriculture. The
Central Committee plenum, in its resolution based on the report by
Comrade N. S. Khrushchev, "On Measures for Further Development of
USSR Agriculture," outlined means for a sharp advance in all branches
of farming. . . .

It is necessary to study thoroughly and pay close attention to consumers' demands, making timely re-adjustments in industry to create
the required broad variety, good quality and attractiveness of goods and
to make the most widely sold products correspond in quality to the
public's rising tastes and needs. . . .

A necessary condition for sharply increasing production of mass
consumers' goods and markedly improving their quality is the supply
by enterprises of the necessary raw materials, modern equipment, chem-
icals, dyes and materials. Moreover, individual ministries are still failing
to meet government-approved delivery quotas, are slow in developing
and mastering the production of new types of machines, dyes and chem-
icals. . . .

The Ministry of Machine Building has similar shortcomings. This
ministry and its enterprises are very slow to develop and master the
production of new machine models which would make it possible to turn
out higher quality goods. We have thus far failed to organize the production of machinery to produce worsteds, light dress velvets, carpets,
and thread. . . .

Meanwhile, the Ministry of Machine Building is not meeting plans
for supplying equipment to light industrial enterprises, which include
special machines and units in fixed proportions and variety. Of 160
types of machinery to be delivered over a nine-month period, 51 types

of machines were not delivered and the nine-month delivery plan was not fulfilled for 56 types. . . .

By its decree of October 5, 1953, the USSR Council of Ministers required supplier ministries to ensure immediate supplies to enterprises producing goods for mass consumption and to meet unconditionally plans for providing equipment, raw materials and supplies, regardless of fulfillment of the plan for deliveries to other consumers. . . .

We must ensure a great change in capital construction, and over the next two or three years put more capacity into operation. Our ministry is now building about 400 enterprises above standard size at an estimated cost of more than 20,000,000 rubles. A total of 9,000,000,000 rubles' worth of construction has already been done on them. In the next two years, all these enterprises are to go into production, completely or in part. Small-scale work to expand or rebuild more than 800 enterprises is also being done. . . . (*Pravda*, November 15, 1953)

The sale of consumers' goods did increase sharply after Stalin's death, in part because the government dipped deeply into its warehouse reserves. It is doubtful that any top leader was opposed on principle to raising living standards; but in any society there are competing demands, which have their political partisans, for always limited (even though growing) economic resources. To increase dramatically the output of consumers' goods meant to divert resources from other sectors of the economy. Naturally, those leaders responsible for other areas of national life, such as military security or heavy industry, were concerned to obtain what they believed to be their just share of the economic pie. Although the program to strengthen agriculture was an essential part of the effort to increase living standards and hence complemented the consumers' goods campaign, these two programs were also in competition for resources. To increase agricultural production successfully required stepped-up production of heavy agricultural equipment, to say nothing of fertilizers, insecticides, transportation, and the like.

It seems a reasonable hypothesis that initially any leadership debate on economic policy centered on more technical questions of the proportion of resources to be devoted to various sectors of the economy. As the leadership debate over economic priorities continued, however, it appeared to become more embittered. Economic policy became entwined with questions about the authority of various leaders. The debate over economic policy tended to be raised (or, more accurately, lowered) to the level of a doctrinal dispute, as the protagonists cited Marxism–Leninism to buttress their positions. Those advocating greater production of consumers' goods were accused of the heresy of denying the priority of production of the "means of production," a grave right-wing deviation. Since 1928, Soviet economic planning had been based on the principle that heavy industry must expand more rapidly than light industry. In actual fact, no one argued — at least publicly — that the old doctrine of the priority of heavy industry should be abandoned. Nor, on the other side, did they argue that there should not be some increased production of consumers' goods. But the dispute became distorted as each side attempted to discredit the position of the other.

Several Western observers believe that they can detect disagreement over economic policy in the shading and emphases of various leaders' speeches in late spring of 1954. This evidence is elusive, however; and it was only in the fall of 1954 that more reliable material appeared. M. A. Saburov delivered, on November 6, the major address in commemoration of the 37th Anniversary of the Revolution; in this speech he gave considerable attention to the Soviet economy:

. . . In working out the fundamental principles of building a communist society, the great Lenin pointed out that heavy industry is the cornerstone of the socialist economy, that without heavy industry it is impossible to supply all branches of the national economy with new and completely modern equipment and to guarantee the independence of our motherland. Hence, our Party and the Soviet government are taking measures for the rapid expansion of the output of metals, electric power, fuel and machinery. While the country's industrial output in 1954 will be 2.8 times greater than 1940, heavy industry's output will be 3.4 times greater.

Further electrification of the country is a vital requirement for the growth of all branches of the economy. Electric power output in 1954 will be triple that of 1940. . . .

On the basis of the progress in the development of heavy industry and transport, the Party and government have worked out an extensive program for increasing the production of consumers' goods to satisfy abundantly and in the immediate future the working masses' growing demands. This year a start has already been made on the practical achievement of this program. In 1954 there will be produced more than 5,500,000,000 meters of cotton fabrics, 6 per cent more than in 1953 and 43 per cent more than in 1950; 242,000,000 meters of woolen fabrics, 17 per cent more than in 1953 and 56 per cent more than in 1950; 520,000,000 meters of silks, 30 per cent more than in 1953 and four times as much as in 1950. Production of other consumers' goods will also increase substantially this year. . . . (*Pravda*, November 7, 1954)

During November and the first three weeks of December, some difference in emphasis could be detected between *Pravda*, the central Party newspaper, and *Izvestia*, the central government newspaper, in items concerning economic policy. On December 21, the seventy-fifth anniversary of Stalin's birth, *Pravda* and *Izvestia* printed commemorative articles which exemplify these differing foci:

Izvestia: . . . The Soviet people are proud that at the cradle of our mighty Soviet state stood its founder, Lenin; that J. V. Stalin worked untiringly to strengthen its power; that our ship of state is being led onward with honor by the glorious Communist Party and its Central Committee, headed by disciples of Lenin and comrades-in-arms of Stalin. . . .

The enemies of the Party and the people — Trotskyites, Bukharinites, bourgeois–nationalists and other traitors, capitulators and men of little faith — tried to undermine the unity within the ranks of the Party, to divert the Party from the Leninist way, to liquidate the revolution's achievements and to restore the ways of capitalism. Under the leadership of J. V. Stalin, the great continuator of Lenin's cause, the Communist Party defended the Leninist unity of the Party, defeated the traitors and capitulators and steered a course toward the building of socialism. . . .

The program being implemented by the Party Central Committee and the Soviet government, which is one of a great advance in agriculture, of increasing the material interest of the collective farmers in the results of their labor, and forcing production of consumers' goods, will further the development and the strengthening of Soviet society's moral–political unity.

The Communist Party's chief concern in the area of domestic policy is for the further advance in the nation's productive capacity, for the steady rise in the prosperity and cultural level of the masses, so that each year the life of millions of working people may improve.

The policy, delineated by the Party and being successfully implemented, of increasing rapidly the production of consumers' goods and of promoting a sharp new upturn in agriculture — along with constant care for the unslackening development of heavy industry — is an integral part of the program of communist construction. . . . (F. Konstantinov, "The Great Continuator of Lenin's Immortal Cause," *Izvestia*, December 21, 1954)

Pravda: . . . After the Party's heavy loss in January, 1924 — the death of V. I. Lenin — the Trotskyites and right opportunists, the enemies of Marxism, the Party and the Soviet people, intensified their struggle against the Party's general line. At that time, Stalin, along with other disciples and comrades-in-arms of Lenin, headed the Party's struggle to maintain the purity of Lenin's teaching regarding the possibility of the triumph of socialism in a country encircled by capitalists, and the struggle to apply Lenin's theory. . . .

The program of socialist construction, which Lenin scientifically delineated, foresaw the complete and thorough industrialization of the country, the comprehensive development of heavy industry, and the electrification of the entire national economy.

Lenin called for a powerful machine building industry as the only material base for socialism and saw it as the key to the socialist transformation of agriculture. Heavy industry is the solid base for developing the country's productive capabilities, for raising the productivity of social labor, for increasing the prosperity of the working masses and raising their cultural level.

V. I. Lenin taught that only socialist industrialization of the country would make the Soviet state technically and economically independent of capitalist countries. He warned that "unless we save and restore heavy industry, we shall not be able to build any industry, and without it we shall perish altogether as an independent country."

J. V. Stalin's historic achievement was to give further creative development and practical meaning to Lenin's programmatic instructions on the economic transformation of our country and to work out major theoretical problems of building communism. In its practical work, the Party, guided by Lenin's theory of building socialism, steered a firm course toward industrializing the country and developing heavy industry and achieved outstanding successes.

J. V. Stalin saw in modern heavy industry the real and dependable basis of the Soviet regime. He rightly considered forced growth of machine building, the production of the means of production, to be the main link, the core of development of heavy industry; he also attached equally great importance to developing ferrous and nonferrous metallurgy and the chemical industry, to increasing the output of electric power, the mining of coal and the extraction of oil. Experience has shown that it was the growth of these branches of industry that subsequently played the decisive role in the fundamental technical reconstruction of the entire national economy.

The works of J. V. Stalin outlined the special Soviet method of industrializing the country. Unlike the capitalist method, the Soviet method proceeds from the fact that it is necessary to begin industrialization of the country with heavy, not light, industry. . . .

High rates of development of heavy industry constituted the Party's sacred duty to the USSR's working class and peasantry and to the entire world's proletariat, and this meant fulfilling a patriotic duty and an international obligation. . . .

The transformation of our motherland into a mighty industrialized, collective farm socialist power was decisive in ensuring the victory of the Soviet people in the great patriotic war. In organizing defeat of the enemy, the socialist state made good use of the powerful productive potential created during the prewar five-year plans. Major credit for the victory of the Soviet people in the patriotic war belongs to the Communist Party and to J. V. Stalin, who headed the State Defense Committee and the Soviet armed forces during the war. . . .

Today, when we are solving the tasks of completing the building of socialism and making the gradual transition to communism, the Party summons the Soviet people to direct their main attention to fulfilling plans for the further growth of heavy industry. The Party sees in heavy industry the very foundation of the socialist economy, the firm basis for further development of the entire national economy.

A new and mighty advance in the development of heavy industry will further strengthen the country's defense capability and will provide a reliable guarantee for the inviolability of our motherland's frontiers.

The growing prosperity of the Soviet Union's working people and the possibility to satisfy better their increasing demands for foods and consumers' goods depend on the steady development of heavy industry.

At the same time, the Party and government have outlined urgent measures for ensuring rapid growth in agriculture; they are aimed at considerable increases in the yields of all crops, the rational use of land and machinery, the further development of large, new areas of virgin and idle lands, substantial upgrading of the role of the MTS in the organizational–administrative strengthening of all collective farms, and strengthening and enlarging the state farm network. A great deal of organizational–administrative work has been done to eliminate the lag in livestock raising, to increase the cattle herd and to raise meat and dairy yields. The measures being carried out will considerably improve the raw materials base for light industry. . . .

Generalizing the experience of socialist construction, Stalin creatively developed Lenin's theses on the socialist state. He explained the significance of the Soviet state as a mighty tool in the struggle for communism and showed the need for further strengthening the state, the need for heightening the vigilance of the Soviet people, and for constantly improving the armed forces in the face of the mobilization of the aggressive forces of reactionary imperialism. . . .

In the conditions of the general crisis of capitalism, the aggressiveness of the monopoly circles is rising, and international tension and the threat of new wars are increasing. Through war and arms races the imperialists attempt to find a way out of the crisis, a way out of the rising internal contradictions between labor and capital.

The intensification of aggressive tendencies among imperialist circles, especially in the USA and Britain, is due to both the sharpening in the contradictions within the imperialist system and their hatred of socialism, the desire by any means, including violence and war, to prevent the growth of socialism in the USSR and the people's democracies. This explains the efforts of the imperialists to rearm Western Germany and to turn it into a center for a new world war, into a springboard for attack on the USSR and the countries of the democratic camp. . . . (V. Kruzhkov, "J. V. Stalin — The Great Continuator of the Cause of V. I. Lenin," *Pravda*, December 21, 1954)

> On September 25, 1954 Khrushchev had given an interview to Professor John Bernal, which was subsequently published in the *London Times*. Not until three months later did *Pravda* and *Izvestia* carry this interview which is of interest for Khrushchev's interpretation of the consumers' goods program:
>
> . . . The Communist Party, based on successes in industrializing the country, has established the task of achieving a marked advance in consumers' goods output within two or three years. It is understandable that in order to increase the output of consumers' goods it is necessary to develop agriculture at faster rates and especially to increase sharply the output of grain. . . .
>
> Our Party is consistently and persistently pursuing a policy of overall expansion of consumers' goods output and maximum satisfaction of

the growing needs of the working people. However, to increase the output of goods, it is necessary to raise the level of grain production because in the final analysis grain is the basis of all other food products — even more, it is the basis of the production of many consumers' goods. . . .

I know that people abroad are saying that the new measures in the sphere of agriculture supposedly represent a radical change in over-all Soviet economic policy. These allegations do not match reality. We are not relaxing attention to industrial development, we are not sacrificing industry to agriculture. The development of all branches of industry will continue in the future in accord with the plan outlined; in the future, too, main attention will be devoted to the development of heavy industry. The caterpillar tractors, plows, seed drills and other farm machinery, which will be produced by factories this year and next, will be sent mainly to the new lands. . . . (*Pravda*, December 24, 1954)

> Khrushchev was again featured in the central press on December 28 when his long speech of December 7 to a conference of construction officials and architects was printed:

. . . Only on the basis of further development of heavy industry will we be able successfully to promote all branches of the national economy, and to raise steadily the material well-being of the people and ensure the inviolability of the frontiers of the Soviet Union.

This is the main thing. The further development of heavy industry — an increase in the output of metal, coal, oil, electric power, chemical products, the development of heavy machine building, machine tool construction, and the production of forge-press equipment — is the powerful basis for successful development of all branches of industry and agriculture.

Relying on the progress in the development of heavy industry, the Party and government are devoting great attention to expanding the production of consumers' goods.

Much work has been done this year in implementing the decisions of the Party Central Committee plenums on further development of agriculture. . . . (*Pravda*, December 28, 1954)

> The most polemical attack on the supporters of the consumers' goods policy was made by D. Shepilov in *Pravda* on January 24:

. . . Views entirely foreign to Marxist–Leninist political economy and to the general line of the Communist Party on several fundamental questions of the development of the socialist economy have begun to be formulated of late among some economists and teachers in our higher educational institutions.

We have in front of us the theses of a report by Ye. Kasimovsky, Candidate of Economic Science, at the Moscow Financial Institute on the subject, "The Correlation of the Growth Tempos of the Two Subdivisions of Social Production"; articles submitted to the journals *Problems of Economics* and *Problems of Philosophy* entitled, "The Correlation of the Growth Tempos of Subdivisions I and II in the Course of Expanded Socialist Reproduction," by D. Kuznetsov, Candidate of Economic Science, "The Correlation of the Two Subdivisions of Social Production," by Ye. Kasimovsky, and "Certain Questions of the Theory of Socialist Reproduction," by P. Mstislavsky; speeches by A. Paltsev, Candidate of Economic Science, at two discussions of problems of expanded socialist reproduction and other materials.

The basic concepts presented in these articles and speeches may be summarized as follows:

Under capitalism the goal of production is profit. Expansion of production is the means of increasing profits. Production for production is a characteristic of capitalism. Under capitalism, production is divorced from consumption and in profound contradiction to it. Production of consumers' goods lags systematically behind production of the means of production because of the fall in the public's purchasing power. The rule of the capitalist system of production is preponderant development of production of the means of production which advances faster than production of consumers' goods.

An entirely different pattern is inherent in the socialist system of production. Here the purpose of production is for man and his needs. Therefore, these economists say, preponderant development of production of the means of production, of heavy industry, cannot be the law of the socialist system of production, for, if this were the case, it is alleged, a contradiction between production and consumption would inevitably arise and constantly increase. Preponderant development of production of the means of production, of heavy industry, was an economic necessity only, if you please, in the early stages of development of Soviet society when our country was backward. Now that we have built a great industry, however, the situation has changed radically. Production under socialism is production for consumption. Faster production of the means of production, of heavy industry, they say, contradicts the basic economic law of socialism. Thus, they reach a conclusion of broad ramifications: The policy pursued by the Party of forced development of branches of heavy industry has supposedly entered into conflict with the basic economic law of socialism since forced development of heavy industry retards public consumption.

Grossly distorting the meaning of Party and government decisions to increase production of consumers' goods, the authors of this conception assert that since 1953 the Soviet nation has entered a new stage of economic development, the essence of which is allegedly a radical change in the Party's economic policy. While the Party used to put emphasis on developing *heavy* industry, now, if you please, the focus has shifted to developing *light* industry, to production of consumers' goods. Attempting to present their imaginary formulae as requirements of the basic economic law of socialism, these economists propose setting an identical rate of development for heavy and light industry or even providing for the preponderant development of light industry as compared with heavy industry throughout the whole period of the final construction of socialism and the gradual transition from socialism to communism.

If views of this nature were to become widespread, it would create great damage to the entire cause of communist construction. It would lead to complete disorientation of our cadres on the basic question of the Party's economic policy. It would mean in practice that development of our heavy industry, which is the backbone of the socialist economy, would take a descending path leading to decline in all branches of the national economy, to a drop instead of a rise in the working people's living standards, to an undercutting of the economic power of the Soviet nation and its defense capability.

As we know, in their day the rightist restorationists pressed the Party to take this path. But the Party rebuffed these formulae of surrender. Guided by the economic theory of Marxism–Leninism, the Party spurred on at a forced pace the production of the means of production, of heavy industry; and, on this basis, ensured a tremendous development of the national economy, for heavy industry was, is and will be the granite foundation of the might of the Soviet country and of the well-being of its people. . . .

The heart of the matter is that the above-cited economists pervert the Marxist theory of reproduction and, in so doing, attempt to cover the revisionist essence of their conception with hypocritical references to Marx and Lenin. . . .

Concern for the public welfare is a first principle of Party policy.

The Party has been guided by this principle at all stages of the development of Soviet society. The *maximum* satisfaction of the ever-growing material and cultural needs of the working people has characterized the design of the socialist system's advance and is a task of the Party's program which derives from the requirements of the basic economic law of socialism. The Party is solving this task in the Marxist manner — on the basis of forced development of productive forces, forced development of production of the means of production, modern industrial technology and a steady rise in the productivity of social labor. . . .

The preponderant rate of growth of production of the means of production, as a *law* of socialist economics, does not at all exclude the fact that in some years it may be practically expedient and necessary to eliminate a lag in the production of consumers' goods and to pull up light and food industry and agriculture. The Party constantly adopts measures of this nature when it discovers disproportions arising in the national economy.

The above-quoted statements by economists, however, do not refer to such specific, practical corrections in this or that proportion between light and heavy industry. Nothing of the kind. They advance before the Party the point of view that a more rapid growth of the production of consumers' goods in comparison to the production of the means of production is a *law* of the socialist system of production. . . .

The Party and government have recently adopted a whole series of important decisions on further advancing socialist agriculture and increasing the output of consumers' goods. These decisions are of tremendous importance to the national economy. At the same time, major Party documents have invariably emphasized that only on the basis of a further mighty development of *heavy* industry is it possible to achieve a sharp advance in all branches of agriculture and to increase considerably the supply of food products for our country's whole population. . . .

The Soviet people's entire great creative activity is taking place in an international situation which obligates the Soviet people to display great vigilance. The forces of imperialist reaction, armed to the teeth and arming even more, are harboring plans for another world war. In this situation, a consistent and resolute struggle for world peace and the strengthening of the might of the Soviet nation and its defense capability in every way possible is the primary, sacred, patriotic and international duty of the Soviet people. . . . (*Pravda*, January 24, 1955)

The reader may have noted that the connection between heavy industry and national defense, so pointedly stressed by Shepilov, was first
noted only in passing by Saburov on November 6 and was repeated
more emphatically by Kruzhkov on December 21 and by Khrushchev
on December 28. On January 27, an editorial in *Red Star*, the daily
newspaper of the Ministry of Defense, left little doubt where the
military stood on economic policy:

. . . Certain individual "theoreticians" among our economists and
teachers at higher educational institutions, under the cover of a "creative
approach" to the study of the economic theory of Marxism–Leninism,
however, have begun to propagate views which distort radically the
meaning of the Communist Party's policy on economic construction.
These views are nothing less than an attempt to revise the Party's general line. These would-be theoreticians maintain that preponderant
development of the production of the means of production, of heavy
industry, was economically necessary only during the initial stages of
the development of Soviet society, when our country was technically
backward and still agrarian. . . .

From this anti-scientific and anti-Marxist point of view, these so-
called "theoreticians" proceed to just as anti-scientific and anti-Marxist
a conclusion. . . . It would lead to a decline in all branches of the
national economy, to a decline in the living standards of the working
people. It would undermine the economic might of the USSR and
weaken its defense capacity at a time when the imperialist states are
openly preparing for a new war. . . .

Socialist heavy industry has been, and remains, the fundamental
basis of the indestructible defense capability of the Soviet state, of the
inviolability of its frontiers. . . . (*Red Star*, January 27, 1955)

The Issues: Foreign Policy

Foreign policy was a third important issue in dispute during this period. In addition to the relationship of economic policy and defense
capacity, there occasionally appeared vague glimpses of differing evaluations of the "capitalist threat" and of Western unity, and of the impact of nuclear weapons on military doctrine and ultimately on foreign
policy. However, Soviet sources provide few clues to the course of this
debate and the positions taken by the various leaders. The leadership

attempted especially to preserve the façade of monolithic agreement on policy in the sensitive area of national security.

Nevertheless, in their published election speeches during March 1954, the various leaders did appear to put slightly differing emphases on the foreign threat and the need for increased military outlays. The most pronounced departure from the standard line was made by Malenkov in the following statement:

It is universally recognized that 1953 marked a certain reduction of international tension. Peace-loving men brought about the end of the Korean war.

Every thinking person cannot but ponder the question of how to take another step forward, how to find a real basis for the firm foundation of peace and security among peoples. It is not true that mankind faces only two choices: either a new world holocaust or the so-called cold war. The peoples are vitally interested in strengthening peace. The Soviet government stands for a further relaxation of international tension, for a firm and lasting peace, and resolutely opposes the policy of the cold war for this is a policy of preparation for a new world holocaust which, with modern means of warfare, means the destruction of world civilization. . . . (*Pravda*, March 13, 1954)

A month and a half later, in a speech before the Supreme Soviet, Malenkov backtracked to a more orthodox position on the impact of nuclear weapons:

The Soviet government has maintained and continues to maintain that capitalist and socialist systems can peacefully co-exist and compete economically with each other. Proceeding from this position, we have consistently pursued the policy of peace and the strengthening of international co-operation. If, however, aggressive circles, placing their hopes on atomic weapons, should decide foolishly to test the power and strength of the Soviet Union, they can rest assured that the aggressor will be crushed by the same weapon and that such an adventure would inevitably bring the downfall of the capitalist social system. . . . (*Pravda*, April 27, 1954)

Although the evidence is not clear-cut, resting on subtle nuances of emphasis, other members of the Presidium, such as Khrushchev, Molotov, Bulganin and Voroshilov, in their March 1954 election speeches appeared to lay greater stress on the danger of military attack and the resulting need to improve the Soviet military capability. At the same time, Pervukhin, Pospelov, and Saburov — like Malenkov — tended to set a more optimistic tone about the intentions of the Western powers and the strength of the current Soviet military deterrent. At any rate, as we have seen, by the winter of 1954–55 national security had become a major bone of contention among the leadership, exacerbated perhaps by the issue of German rearmament. Although, in fact, international tensions were not acute at the time, those persons advocating renewed emphasis on heavy industry to gird up national defense in late 1954 seemed to be whipping up a minor war scare.

One other event in foreign affairs during this period merits attention for the light it may shed on leadership infighting. On September 29, 1954, *Pravda* announced the departure of an important, high-level delegation for China. The composition of the group shou'd be carefully noted:

In connection with the celebration of the fifth anniversary of the Chinese Peoples Republic, a Governmental delegation of the Soviet Union has departed by plane from Moscow for Peking consisting of the First Secretary of the CPSU Central Committee and member of the Presidium of the USSR Supreme Soviet, N. S. Khrushchev (the leader of the delegation); First Deputy Chairman of the USSR Council of Ministers, N. A. Bulganin; Deputy Chairman of the USSR Council of Ministers, A. I. Mikoyan; Chairman of the All-Union Central Council of Trade Unions, N. M. Shvernik; USSR Minister of Culture, G. F. Alexandrov; chief editor of the newspaper *Pravda,* D. T. Shepilov; Secretary of the Moscow City Party committee, Ye. A. Furtseva; Minister of Industrial Construction Materials of the Uzbek Republic, Ya. S. Nasriddinova; Ambassador to the Chinese Peoples Republic, P. F. Yudin (located in Peking); head of a department of the Central Committee of the CPSU, V. P. Stepanov. (*Pravda*, September 29, 1954)

The Organizational Context

As discussed in Chapter I, a major reason for the leadership struggle after Stalin's death was the absence of firmly established institutionalized procedures for transferring political power and authority in the Soviet political system. In contrast to most constitutional democracies, the formal position which an individual holds in the Soviet political structure does not necessarily confer on him certain powers. The Chairman of the Presidium of the Supreme Soviet, the titular head of state, has long been a secondary post. The Chairman of the Council of Ministers and the First Secretary of the Party Central Committee have traditionally been of primary importance; but, following Stalin's death, it was anyone's guess — apparently even among Stalin's heirs — which, if either, of these posts would ultimately become more decisive. Beria, we may recall, made his bid as Minister of Internal Affairs and member of the Party Presidium. In short, although true to some degree in all political systems, in the Soviet Union particularly, the authority of an office depends largely on the political capacity of its occupant.

Although Soviet political dynamics are highly personalized, this does not mean that institutions and offices play no role. A leader will attempt to enhance his power by building up a following among Soviet officialdom at all levels. This endeavor is facilitated if he operates from an institutional base. Although Molotov apparently ranked number two in the leadership for some months after March 1953 because of his long tenure at the seat of power and his vast knowledge of Soviet politics, policies and administration, his lack of an important organizational base, in time, proved to be a crucial political liability.

A leader's following may not necessarily be confined to one particular bureaucratic hierarchy. Again, in the case of Beria, he was firmly rooted in the Ministry of Interior, but he also attempted to expand his following among Party and Government officials in several Union Republics. Beria failed, however, and at least initially a leader normally attempts to build up his political machine within the organization with which he is most closely associated. Quite naturally a leader will also attempt to enhance the influence and responsibilities of "his" institution; and, thus, the contention for power among the leadership may extend to institutional rivalry. The policies espoused by a particular leader will tend to be those which will appeal to his organization and will further its role in society, although, of course, these are not the only considerations. By the same token, the leadership will attempt to prevent one of its members from consolidating his institutional base and extending its authority.

With the inability of any single leader to seize Stalin's powers immediately after his death and the resulting period of "collective leadership," there arose a natural predilection to de-emphasize the importance of Stalin and the role of any great leader in history and to underline the benefits of collective deliberations and policy-making. The Party, guided by its Presidium, replaced Stalin as the director of Russia's destiny in the Soviet press. While this substitution was in part merely the reflection of the existing leadership situation, it may well also have been a strategy to inhibit any particular leader from seizing ultimate power under the guise of Stalin's heir. Although the downgrading of Stalin had begun as early as April 1953, as exemplified by the Slepov piece, the process was carried further and given a theoretical foundation in a *Pravda* article by a well-known Soviet authority on the Party and Marxism–Leninism, published on June 28, immediately after Beria's arrest:

. . . The Marxist science of society arose and developed in irreconcilable struggle with reactionary, idealistic sociology which denies the objective nature of the laws of social development. Bourgeois sociology, incapable of comprehending the laws of the development of society, inevitably comes to deny the decisive role of the masses of the people in history. It reduces the history of society to the acts of outstanding personalities — kings, captains, rulers, etc. This reactionary, subjectivist view stems from the conception of history as a chaos of accidents, into which outstanding personalities introduce order. . . .

In contrast to subjective thinkers, Marxism regards the development of society as a natural, historical process which strictly follows laws of development and is independent of the will and desires of this or that historical personality.

A social system in each historical epoch is determined not by the arbitrary acts or will of individual persons or by this or that principle or idea, but by the means of production of material wealth. Society, itself, its ideas and institutions, conform to the nature of the means of production. The means of production of material wealth condition the process of social, political, spiritual and intellectual life of society. And the nature of the means of production is determined in the long run by the level of development of society's material productive forces. Change in the productive forces brings about change in production relations. . . . But since the main force of production is the working people — the producers of material wealth — the history of society is above all the history of the laboring masses themselves, the history of peoples. . . .

A great role in the work of organizing and rallying the forces of the working class is played by the Marxist party which bases itself on the knowledge of objective economic laws and points out the immediate tasks and final goal of the struggle.

The Party is the great mobilizing, organizing and transforming force of society. Without the Communist Party and its Marxist theory, the workers' movement would be doomed to drift, to groping in the dark, and to suffer inestimable losses. . . .

The great transforming role of the masses of people revealed itself both in the course of the struggle for power for the Soviets and in the construction of the new socialist life, in the mighty development of the forces of production, in the creation of socialist culture. Only by the creative labor of tens of millions of persons, led by the Communist Party, was it possible to transform a tremendous, economically-backward country into a first-class socialist industrial power in the course of thirteen years. It was possible to transform many millions of individual peasant holdings into large socialist farms based on advanced technology only because the initiative of the Communist Party and of the state regime from above was supported from below by the vast masses of the peasantry. Without the creative activity and initiative of the masses of people, without their self-sacrifice and heroism, it would have been impossible to build a socialist society. . . . (F. Konstantinov, "The People Are the Makers of History," *Pravda*, June 28, 1953)

> Not only was it felt necessary by the collective leadership (or at least a part thereof) to downgrade the role of Stalin, as an individual, it was also desirable to pare down the stature of the office through which he had risen to become dictator and with which his name was most closely associated, in order to make it more difficult for some other leader to make political capital out of this office. The post, of course, was that of General Secretary, later designated First Secretary, of the Central Committee. If the Party's stock rose in 1953, it was made clear that references to the "Party" meant a collective body and not the professional cadre (or apparatus) of the Party. Articles devoted to Party operations now emphasized the need for lodging authority at all levels in Party committees and their bureaus, rather than in their professional staffs headed by the secretaries. Criticisms of the violation of collective leadership in the Party were directed at its lower levels. And, no doubt, there was considerable sentiment throughout the Soviet Union to cut down the powers of the Party secretaries who frequently acted as petty autocrats within their geographical bailiwicks. However, since the structure of the Party at lower levels mirrors its central organization, criticisms of local procedures, by ready inference, could also be extended to upper echelons. For example, assertions that local authority rested in a city Party committee and its bureau by analogy meant that at the top, authority resided in the Central Committee and

its Presidium. An article by F. Yakovlev entitled "Collective Leadership — The Highest Principle of Party Leadership," in the issue of the Party's monthly theoretical journal, *Kommunist,* which went to press on July 28, provided the most trenchant criticism of the violations of collective leadership by the Party secretaries:

. . . The principle of the collectivity of Party leadership finds itself in complete correspondence with the known positions of Marxism–Leninism about the harmfulness and intolerability of the cult of personality. The cult of personality leads to a reduction of the role of the Party and its leading center, to a restriction on the creative activity of the Party masses and the Soviet people, and has nothing in common with a Marxist–Leninist understanding of the high significance of the directing activity of leading organs and leading figures. Only the collective experience, the collective wisdom of the Central Committee, relying on the scientific basis of Marxist–Leninist theory and the wide initiative of the leading cadres, ensures correct leadership of the Party and the country, the inseparable unity and solidarity of Party ranks and the successful construction of communism in our country. . . .

Marxism–Leninism teaches that the Communist Party is a militant, self-activating organization of the working class which actively thinks, lives a real life, destroys the old and creates the new. Those views of the Party, according to which the Party is presented not as a self-activating organism, but as some sort of a complex of administrative–executive institutions where there are employees above and employees below, are deeply mistaken, having nothing in common with Marxism. Such harmful and dangerous views on the Party lead in practice to bureaucratism in Party activity, when separate leading workers, considering themselves "higher employees," try to build the entire work on issuing instructions alone, when participation of communists in the Party leadership is not valued. . . .

Collective leadership signifies that all members of a Party committee, without exception, invest their knowledge in its general business. In the Party committee are represented the best, most politically prepared members of the Party, working in very many different areas: leaders of industrial enterprises, collective farms, MTS; the best propagandists, agitators, organizers; the leading people of factories and collective farm fields; the representatives of the Soviet Army and Navy; and figures in science, literature and art. Under genuine collective Party leadership, every member of a committee has the full possibility to express freely his disagreement with some other opinion, to correct mistakes of certain people, to interject his experience . . .

One usually observes a contraction of the role of Party committees where the secretaries of the Party committees do not learn the organizational principles of our Party, permit themselves to command, to administer, forgetting about the fact that the vicious method of one man decision-making inevitably leads to grave mistakes, to divorce from the masses and to disregard of the interests of the working people. In such cases a committee plenary session is held only as a formality in order to report to the superior organ that the requirements of the statute have been observed. Preparation for a plenum often is conducted only by the forces of the service apparatus of the Party organ — sectors and departments — and members of the Party committee are not attracted to this business; not infrequently it is determined ahead of time who should speak at the plenum; employees of the apparatus, on instructions of the secretariat of the committee, commission separate workers to prepare the text of a speech on this or that question. At the plenum one hears reports in which achievements and successes are glorified and shortcomings and mistakes are smoothed over . . .

We still, however, encounter cases when members of the bureau forget about their responsibilities before the Party committee, before the Party organization, when at sessions of the bureau, at plenums and in the practical daily conduct of their work, they are worried only about being able to strike the right tone for the First Secretary of the committee. This is a vicious line of conduct: members of the bureau in this case do not risk expressing their own opinion, even if in their heart they consider incorrect the point of view of the committee secretary. And, although decisions in such cases are taken unanimously, such "unanimity" has nothing in common with collectivity . . .

Of course, on the secretaries of the committee, and above all on the First Secretary, is placed a high responsibility and great obligation for the leadership of the current work of the Party organ. But clearly, there is something else: a First Secretary is an authoritative leader of a Party organization only to the degree that he is able, in the interests of the Party, more correctly to take into account and to utilize the experience, knowledge, initiative, and all valuable suggestions of the members of the bureau, members of the committee, the wide Party masses and non-Party working people and only to the degree that he is able to grasp the method of collective leadership. . . .

In a number of cases, the secretariats subordinate the bureau of the committee, take on themselves the decision of such great questions as the consideration of personnel affairs of members and candidates of the Party, the adoption of joint decrees of the oblast Party committee and oblast executive committee, etc. The secretariat of the Bashkir oblast Party committee at one time even affirmed the work plans of the bureau of the oblast Party committee and, moreover, placed itself above the bureau of the oblast committee. Similar facts can be observed where supervision over the work of the secretariat by the bureau has been weakened. . . . (F. Yakovlev, *Kommunist*, No. 11 (July), 1953)

> The Party Central Committee and its Presidium and the lower territorial Party committees and their bureaus are composed of the power elite at each level, i.e. the leading officials from Party, government, military, trade union, and still other organizations at that particular territorial–administrative echelon. Hence, by crediting the Central Committee or its Presidium as the source of authority, the question of which bureaucratic hierarchy is more powerful is avoided and the image of collective leadership reinforced. The reader may wish to review the decrees and speeches of the previous section to see which body is credited in each instance for a policy decision. On many occasions, the Party Central Committee and the Council of Ministers may be cited as joint authors of a policy. In this case, the order in which these bodies are mentioned may have significance.
>
> If Yakovlev, in July 1953, asserted the primacy of the Presidium over the Secretariat, in early 1954, a well known authority on Party affairs, D. Bakhshiev, in a book on Party operations, appeared to blur the relationship of these two bodies and thus increase the stature of the Secretariat:

. . . Our Party proceeds from the fact that policy and organization are inseparable. The Party conducted a determined struggle against the Trotskyites who tried to separate the political activity of the Party from its organizational work. Enemies of Leninism attempted to divorce artificially political from organizational questions, to introduce chaos and dissension . . . Lenin said at the 11th Congress that any political question might be organizational, and vice versa. It is impossible to separate mechanically the political from the organizational. This precept is one of the most important bases of the activity of the Communist Party. . . .

The Party [does] not separate organizational work from political but, on the contrary, links them organically . . . The unity of political and organizational work is embodied in the activity of the Central Committee of the Party and the organs created by it . . . The Presidium and the Secretariat of the Central Committee assure unity of political and organizational leadership. . . . (D. Bakhshiev, *Party Construction in Conditions of the Victory of Socialism* [assigned to the press on January 5, 1954], pp. 17-18.)

The relationship between the Presidium and the Secretariat of the Central Committee in this period was intimately connected with the mutual status of the Party and governmental apparatuses. Stalin had united all institutions in his own person, playing one off against the other and determining the allocation of responsibilities among them. With the decompression after his death, questions of critical importance for elite politics arose concerning the relations between the Party and governmental bureaucracies. What were to be their respective spheres of responsibility? What were to be their practical, day-to-day working relationships?

These questions could not be easily or neatly resolved because of the parallel and duplicative nature of these two administrative hierarchies and because theoretical formulas about their respective roles and past precedents were ambiguous. In theory the Party staff at every level is to exercise policy guidance and supervision of the state administration. The latter is to bear the burden of daily administration. In practice this division of responsibilities is more difficult to define; and the degree of involvement of the Party staff in administration has fluctuated from one period to another throughout Soviet history. Since the Party secretary at every echelon is ultimately responsible for all occurrences within his geographical bailiwick, he frequently finds himself inclined toward direct intervention in the most mundane administrative matters. On the other hand, if the lower Party cadre become too deeply involved in daily administration they run the risk of undermining the governmental bureaucracy and of losing their sense of identity as the centralized watchdog of the regime.

During World War II, Party and governmental affairs became hopelessly entangled and the Party took over direct responsibility for many sectors of national life. In the late 1940's and early 1950's, the leadership took some pains to extract the Party staff from its administrative involvements and to redefine the Party–governmental relationship. In his speech before the 19th Party Congress in October 1952, Malenkov advocated a clearer separation between Party and state.

While the allocation of responsibilities between the Party and governmental administrations at any particular time is thus in part the result of practical administrative considerations, it also influences, and is influenced by, elite politics. In April 1953, the authority of the governmental ministers was increased:

Under the leadership of the Communist Party the Soviet people are successfully constructing a communist society. A powerful weapon in the resolution of this historic task is the Soviet state. The Party considers it its sacred obligation to strengthen constantly and fully our socialist state.

The Soviet state performs the functions of economic–organizational and cultural–educational work, the preservation of public property from enemies and plunderers, and defense of the country from outside military attack. To fulfill successfully all these functions, a well-trained, flexible state apparatus is required. . . .

At the same time, along with measures to strengthen the ministries, there has been realized a broadening of the rights of ministers who have received full powers, within the boundaries established by decisions of the Soviet government, to distribute materials and monetary resources within the ministry, and to decide all basic questions of the activities of enterprises and institutions subordinated to them. The rights of ministers have been broadened in order to raise ministers' responsibilities for business entrusted to them and, also, to ensure the timely decision of economic questions connected with the fulfillment of tasks assigned to the ministers. . . . (K. Ivanov, "Concerning the Soviet State Apparatus, *Pravda*, April 26, 1953)

By the fall of 1953, on the other hand, the press began increasingly to devote more attention to the responsibilities of the Party apparatus, especially in supervising the governmental organs.

Our Soviet institutions, from public services to agriculture, as a whole, constitute the governmental apparatus. With its help the Soviet state exercises supervision over economic and cultural construction in the country.

The Party and Soviet government are currently carrying out a number of important measures directed toward simplifying, reducing the cost, and improving the work of the state apparatus. . . .

The high demands of the Party and government made on the work of the Soviet apparatus obliges the Party organizations in Soviet institutions persistently to raise the level of their work. The Party Statutes state that: "Party organizations of ministries, which, because of the special conditions of work in Soviet institutions, may not employ supervisory functions, are obliged to signal defects in the work of an institution, report shortcomings in the work of a ministry and its individual workers, and submit materials and evaluations to the Central Committee and to the heads of the ministries."

This provision in the Party Statutes shows the principal direction in the work of Party organizations in Soviet institutions. They are the real supervisors of Soviet order in our institutions; the most important questions in the work of the apparatus must always be under their observation. Party organizations must fully feel their responsibility for strict observance of state discipline and socialist legality. . . .

Unfortunately, there are a number of Party organizations in institutions which do not fulfill their obligations and overlook irregularities in work. At a recent report and election meeting of the Party organization in the USSR Ministry of Public Health, communists pointed out serious shortcomings in Party political work, noting that the Party organization had not gone deeply enough into the work of the Ministry's staff and had condoned instances of bureaucratic distortions in the work of some of its links. Serious charges, for example, were made against workers in the Ministry's secretariat and offices concerning long delays in formulating the collegium's decisions. Flagrant instances of red tape and a bureaucratic attitude toward the handling of complaints were brought out at the meeting. These and similar cases show that Party organizations in Soviet institutions at times do not effectively influence the work of the apparatus, but often mark time in their work or conduct it in isolation from the problems of the apparatus.

To carry out successfully their official duties — to struggle in every possible way to improve the work of the apparatus, to point out the shortcomings in the work of institutions, to introduce suggestions for improving this work — Party organizations must delve deeply into the life of institutions and uncover mistakes. It is necessary to keep in mind that the work of Party organizations in institutions is judged not by the number of reports and wordy resolutions on the struggle with bureaucracy, but by actual, real, simple, daily tasks which improve the work of the Soviet apparatus. . . .

A serious shortcoming in Party political work in institutions is that it is often performed apart from the concrete problems of the apparatus, apart from the struggle to improve its work. . . .

The further improvement of the work of local Party organizations in Soviet institutions depends on the directives from [territorial] Party committees. It is not correct for a Party organ to exclude a local Party organization when reviewing the work of some institution. However, there are many such cases. For example, the workers of the Central Committee of the Estonian Communist Party, while studying the work of the republic Ministry of Trade last August, neglected to enlist the services of the local Party organization. At the meeting of the bureau of the Estonian Party Central Committee, where the question of the position of the Ministry was discussed, the secretary of the Party bureau was not even invited to attend. He still does not know the decisions of the Central Committee on the work of the Ministry. As a result, even though the Party organization performs some work in the collective, it does so apart from the life of the apparatus and from the daily problems which confront the Ministry.

The responsibility of the regional and city committees of the Party and all local guiding Party organs is to go into the life of Party organizations of institutions, to react against shortcomings in their work, to give them substantial assistance, and by proper guidance to raise the level of Party work to meet the new problems which stand before the Soviet state apparatus. (*Pravda* editorial, November 27, 1953)

> During the fall of 1954, the campaign against bureaucracy in the governmental administration was noticeably stepped up and closely linked with assertions of Party responsibilities for streamlining administrative procedures.

. . . Party supervision cannot be restricted to the exposure of shortcomings. Party supervision, as assigned to primary Party units, assumes that they themselves actively engage in eliminating the shortcomings exposed and, by every means and with all forces, come to the aid of management and, jointly with it, bring about an improvement in economic work.

It follows from this that the Party organization must engage in day-to-day organizational and political work among the masses. . . .

For competent and authoritative Party supervision it is very important to improve the knowledge of Party organization officials. They must study production methods on the spot, keep up with technical achievements at enterprises of the same type and master economics and specific problems in the economics of the enterprise. . . . (V. Vladimirov, "The Right to Supervise Management," *Pravda*, October 20, 1954)

*   *   *

. . . The Soviet state apparatus is a powerful instrument for building communism. Its record of accomplishment in successfully achieving the political, economic, and cultural tasks established by the Party at each stage in the development of our socialist society is beyond question.

At the same time, one cannot fail to see the many shortcomings in the state machinery's organizational structure and the work of economic management.

A harmful, bureaucratic practice has developed in some sectors of the state apparatus: The Soviet and managerial cadres' main attention and energy are concentrated not on the concrete, vital matter of organizing the masses of working people for the struggle to fulfill Party and government decisions but on drawing up all kinds of directives, resolutions, reports, letters, and accounts. . . .

The Communist Party and Soviet government have drafted and are now implementing extensive measures to eliminate management's grave organizational shortcomings and superfluous staffs. Many unnecessary and duplicative organizations, institutions, administrations, departments and minor offices are being eliminated in administrations, sections, ministries and departments. Measures are being carried out to improve the administrative structure in enterprises and to eliminate superfluous personnel. Record-keeping and accounting departments' forms and indexes have been revised, considerably simplifying them, as have indexes for national economic plans and enterprises' technical, industrial and financial plans. . . . (*Pravda*, November 20, 1954)

*   *   *

Lately the authority of ministries and departments has been considerably expanded. They now make independent decisions on a broad range of questions, and this has already had tangible results.

In my opinion, the time has come also to expand considerably the rights of local agencies. Given the situation today, they sometimes cannot make a move without permission from higher organizations. . . .

In Kemerovo we have a trust of the Russian Republic Ministry of State Farms. One might expect that it would exercise supervision of state farms in the oblast, but this is not the case in practice. The ministry sends plans and goals directly to the state farms, bypassing the trust. . . .

The Russian Republic Ministry of Finance exercises petty, annoying and extreme tutelage over local Soviet, financial and administrative agencies. . . . It has worked out so many bookkeeping forms with so many sections, articles and tabulations that local finance officials have no time for actual supervision and hardly enough time for paper work. . . .

Practices long obsolete and a hindrance to work block reorganization. Instead of relying on their oblast organizations, ministries and departments often bypass them. They try to confine active, vigorous life within graphs and sections of plans, estimates and accounts. All this fetters the creative aims of local officials and gets them into the habit of referring to "higher authority" on the most minor occasion. . . . (P. Morozov, Chairman of the Kemerovo Oblast Soviet Executive Committee and Deputy to the USSR Supreme Soviet, *Izvestia*, October 23, 1954)

Criticism of bureaucracy has been a constantly recurring theme in Soviet literature; and there is little doubt but that efforts to pare down and decentralize the ministries was a response to genuine administrative needs. However, insofar as measures to revamp the ministerial system strengthened the hands of the individual ministers, they served to improve the status of the governmental hierarchy. On the other hand, public criticisms of ministerial malpractices and assertions of Party prerogatives to supervise ministerial activities tended to increase the power of the Party staff. Decentralization of the governmental administration, depending on the circumstances, could also increase the authority of the Party apparatus by enabling Party secretaries at lower administrative–territorial levels to extend their influence over the governmental administration operating within their geographical area.

The extension of the authority of the lower Party apparatus, beginning in the autumn of 1953, was indicated by the increase in the number of provincial secretaries. At the 19th Party Congress, it was decided to limit the number of oblast and krai secretaries to three in each case. At the time Khrushchev himself stated:

In order to prevent the secretariats from supplanting the bureaus, the number of secretaries should be reduced to three and the secretariats should be directed to report the decisions adopted by them to the bureau of the oblast committee, krai committee or the Party Central Committee of the Union republic, as the case may be.

Despite this provision and despite the strictures in Yakovlev's *Kommunist* article, of July 1953, against domination by Party secretaries, in the months following Khrushchev's election as First Secretary, this numerical limitation began to be systematically violated. First in the raions and then in the oblasts and republics, the number of secretaries was increased to four or even five, thus strengthening the capacity of lower territorial Party organs to interfere in the work of other institutions. Since Party secretaries were *ex officio* members of the Party bureau, they were in a strong position to dominate it numerically. The number of full-time, paid Party secretaries of primary Party organizations also appeared to increase rapidly after mid-1953.

Particularly in the countryside, in conjunction with the ambitious new agricultural programs, the raion Party apparatus rapidly expanded its controls through the Party secretary and his group of Party instructors located at each Machine and Tractor Station. For most purposes, the raion Party organization was charged with primary responsibility for grass-roots agricultural administration.

In addition to questions about the role and structure of the Party, beginning in mid-1953, a number of important Party secretaryships in oblasts and republics changed hands. Several of these personnel alterations were connected with Beria's disgrace and have already been mentioned. However, the appointment of new first secretaries in the Kazakh and Kirgiz Republics and in Tula, Smolensk, Moscow, and a handful of other oblasts in late 1953 and early 1954 do not appear to have been directly related to the Beria case. A number of those republic and oblast first secretaries removed had been members of the Central Committee elected in 1952.

One of the most significant personnel rearrangements was announced by *Pravda* on November 29, 1953:

Recently a joint Plenum of the Leningrad Oblast Committee and the Leningrad City Committee of the CPSU was held.

The Plenum of the Party Oblast Committee relieved comrade V. M. Andrianov from the office of First Secretary of the Leningrad Regional Committee of the CPSU. . . .

The Plenum elected comrade F. R. Kozlov to the office of First Secretary of the Leningrad Oblast Party Committee. . . .

Secretary of the Central Committee of the CPSU, comrade N. S. Khrushchev, participated in the work of the Plenum.

Andrianov was widely regarded by Western specialists to have been closely associated with Malenkov.

The Party apparatus, however, did not have a monopoly on personnel appointments. The Bulletin of the USSR Supreme Soviet announced on December 29, 1953 the following changes in the Council of Ministers which, on the surface at least, appeared to strengthen that body:

DECREES OF THE PRESIDIUM OF THE USSR SUPREME SOVIET

I. The following have been appointed as Deputy Chairmen of the USSR Council of Ministers: USSR State Planning Committee Chairman, Maxim Zakharovich Saburov; USSR Minister of Power Plants and Electrical Industry, Mikhail Georgiyevich Pervukhin; USSR Minister of Metallurgical Industry, Ivan Fyodorovich Tevosyan; USSR Minister of Medium Machine Building, Vyacheslav Alexandrovich Malyshev, and USSR Minister of Consumers' Goods Industry, Alexei Nikolayevich Kosygin.

The End of the Malenkov Premiership

Before presenting materials on the last weeks of Malenkov's Premiership, let us review several other important pieces of evidence bearing on the course of the power struggle during 1954. On November 11, 1954 *Pravda* published a "Resolution of the Central Committee of the CPSU" entitled "Concerning Mistakes in the Conduct of Scientific-Atheistic Propaganda Among the Population" which was signed at the bottom simply "Secretary of the Central Committee of the CPSU, N. Khrushchev." Evidence of a different order was provided by the following *Izvestia* announcement of December 31, 1954:

Comrade K. Ye. Voroshilov, Chairman of the Presidium of the USSR Supreme Soviet, on December 29 in the Kremlin presented to Comrade N. N. Shatalin, Secretary of the Party Central Committee, the Order of Lenin, which had been awarded to him on his 50th birthday for his services to the Party and the Soviet state.

Shatalin, it will be recalled, is generally considered to have been a Malenkov supporter.

On December 24, 1954 *Pravda* reported the trial of former Minister of State Security, V. S. Abakumov and five other former police officials:

On December 14–19, 1954, at an open court session in the city of Leningrad, the Military Collegium of the USSR Supreme Soviet . . . tried the criminal case which charged the former USSR Minister of State

Security, V. S. Abakumov, the former Head of the Section for Investigation of Specially Important Cases of the USSR MGB, A. G. Leonov, former Deputy Heads of the Section for Investigation of Specially Important Cases, V. I. Komarov and M. T. Likhachev, and former officials of the USSR MGB, I. A. Chernov and Ya. M. Broverman for crimes covered by articles 58-1-b, 58-7, 58-8 and 58-11 of the RSFSR Criminal Code.

The accused Abakumov, promoted by Beria to the post of USSR Minister of State Security, was a direct accomplice of the criminal conspiratorial group and executed Beria's treacherous orders directed against the Communist Party and the Soviet Government.

Committing crimes similar to those of Beria, Abakumov walked the road of adventures and political provocations. Abakumov fabricated cases against certain officials of the Party and Soviet apparatus and representatives of the Soviet intelligentsia, then arrested them, and, using illegal methods of investigation, together with his accomplices Leonov, Komarov and Likhachev, tried to obtain trumped-up evidence and confessions of guilt to serious state crimes from his prisoners.

In this way Abakumov falsified the so-called "Leningrad Case," in which a number of Party and Soviet officials were arrested without cause, having been falsely accused of the most serious state crimes.

The court inquiry established many other cases of the falsification of trials and criminal violation of Socialist legality by Abakumov and his associates. . . .

The Military Collegium of the USSR Supreme Court found the charges against Abakumov and his associates to be fully proved and sentenced the accused I. A. Chernov to imprisonment in a corrective labor camp for 15 years; the accused Ya. M. Broverman to imprisonment in a corrective labor camp for 25 years; the accused V. S. Abakumov, A. G. Leonov, V. I. Komarov and M. T. Likhachev to the highest criminal punishment — to be shot.

The sentence was received by all those present with great satisfaction.

The sentence has been carried out.

Why was this case not attended to earlier? Beria and his other lieutenants had been officially tried a full year before. Moreover, Abakumov was accused of having a hand in the "Leningrad Case," a charge which had not been levelled at Beria when he was indicted the year before. The "Leningrad Case" refers to a purge in 1949 of a number of important officials, both at the center (e.g. N. A. Voznesensky, Chairman of the State Planning Committee; M. I. Rodionov, Chairman of the RSFSR Council of Ministers, and A. A. Kuznetsov, Central Committee Secretary) and in Leningrad, including all the secretaries of the city and oblast Party committees and other important government and Party officials. It is generally assumed by Western specialists that those purged at this time had been closely associated with A. Zhdanov, a top Stalin lieutenant who died on August 31, 1948; and that Malenkov, who had been Zhdanov's chief rival, was the major beneficiary of this purge. Thus the question arises: was the opening of the Leningrad Case and the mention of it in public a move in the leadership struggle?

The closing act of the Malenkov Premiership was signalled by an announcement in *Pravda* on February 2, 1955:

A plenum of the Party Central Committee was held from January 25 to 31. The plenum heard and discussed a report by Comrade N. S. Khrushchev on increasing livestock production and passed an appropriate resolution.

In view of later events, one suspects that more than agriculture occupied the attention of this plenary session. Indeed, the resolution of the plenum "On Increasing the Output of Livestock Products" opened with a paragraph devoted not to agriculture but to a ringing affirmation of the priority of heavy industry. It may be recalled that Shepilov's militant article on economic policy appeared the day before the opening of the plenum. And, on the opening day of the plenum, *Pravda* announced:

The Presidium of the USSR Supreme Soviet has granted the request of Comrade Anastas Ivanovich Mikoyan, Deputy Chairman of the USSR Council of Ministers, to be relieved of his duties as USSR Minister of Trade. . . . (*Pravda*, January 25, 1955)

Khrushchev's report to the plenary session on January 25 was published on February 3. Like the Central Committee resolution it first dwelt on heavy industry:

As always, the Party regards its major job to be the development of heavy industry, because the whole national economy grows only on the basis of heavy industry, including light industry, food industry, other branches of industry, and our agriculture. . . .

Developing Lenin's directives, J. V. Stalin emphasized that to retard the rate of development of heavy industry "would be suicide, would be to undermine our entire industry, including light industry. It would mean a retreat from the policy of industrializing our country, it would mean subordinating our country to the capitalist economic system."

Under Stalin's leadership, the Party unswervingly applied this only correct policy of all-round development of heavy industry. It is firmly pursuing this policy now and will continue to do so!

In connection with the measures taken recently for increasing the output of consumers' goods, some comrades have confused the question of the rate of development of heavy and light industry in our country. Citing their own misinterpretation and vulgarization of the fundamental economic law of socialism, these pseudo-theoreticians try to claim that at a certain stage of socialist construction the development of heavy industry ceases to be the main task and that light industry can and should surpass all other branches of industry. This is deeply wrong thinking, foreign to the spirit of Marxism–Leninism. This is nothing but slander of our party. This is a belching-forth of right-wing deviation, a belching-forth of views hostile to Leninism, which were at one time propagated by Rykov, Bukharin and their ilk. . . .

In its constant concern for the welfare of the workers, the Communist Party has never lost sight of the need to develop those branches of industry which produce consumers' goods. On the basis of the tremendous advance in heavy industry the Party had encouraged and will constantly continue to encourage the development of light industry and agriculture. The measures being implemented by the Party and the government for increasing the production of consumers' goods testify to this. The greater our achievements in developing heavy industry, the more rapid will these measures be realized. . . .

After a lengthy and detailed review of the agricultural situation, Khrushchev then turned to a pet theme:

Nevertheless, the structure of agricultural ministries remains clumsy and there is still much bureaucracy. Office work in agricultural agencies absorbs the energies of many specialists who, instead of performing real work, waste time making out orders and a variety of instructions and compiling data. . . .

The connections between agricultural agencies and the localities continue to be weak; the characteristics and potentialities of different areas of the country are not sufficiently taken into account, and there are delays in providing information about advanced techniques. . . . (*Pravda*, February 3, 1955)

> The Supreme Soviet convened the same day that Khrushchev's Central Committee report was published. For five days it plodded through a seemingly routine session. Then, on February 9, *Pravda*'s front page reported the bombshell that had been dropped the previous day at a joint session of the two chambers of the Supreme Soviet. The center column reported a "declaration" from Malenkov which had been read (in his presence) to the joint session by A. P. Volkov, the Chairman of the Council of the Union.

I ask you to inform the USSR Supreme Soviet of my request to be released from the post of Chairman of the USSR Council of Ministers.

My request is based on professional considerations concerning the necessity of strengthening the leadership of the Council of Ministers and the expediency of having at the post of Chairman of the Council of Ministers another comrade who has had more experience in governmental affairs.

It is clear to me that in executing the complex and responsible tasks of the Chairman of the Council of Ministers, my insufficient experience in work in the localities has had a negative effect, as well as the fact that I have not directed at first hand separate branches of the national economy either in a ministry or in some economic agency.

I must also state that now when the Communist Party and the workers of our country are concentrating their forces in particular on quickly developing agriculture, I see my guilt and responsibility especially clearly for the unsatisfactory state of agricultural affairs because, for a number of years, I was entrusted with the responsibility for the control and leadership of the work of the central agricultural agencies and for the work of local Party and soviet organizations in the field of agriculture. . . .

> Most prominently featured on *Pravda's* front page for February 9 was a speech by Khrushchev:

On the instructions of the Central Committee of the CPSU and the Council of Elders, I propose that Comrade Nikolai Alexandrovich Bulganin be appointed as Chairman of the Council of Ministers.

We all know Nikolai Alexandrovich Bulganin to be a loyal son of the Communist Party who gives all his strength to serve the Soviet people. A worthy pupil of the great Lenin and one of the closest co-workers of J. V. Stalin, who continued Lenin's work, Comrade Bulganin is an outstanding Party and state administrator. . . .

We are convinced that the government of the Soviet Union, with Nikolai Alexandrovich Bulganin at its head, will successfully solve the problems of further strengthening the power of our socialist motherland, ensuring the development of heavy industry and, on its basis, achieving a new improvement in light and food industry and in the development of agriculture, and raising the level of well-being and culture of the Soviet people.

Let me say that I have confidence that the proposal to appoint Comrade Bulganin to the position of Chairman of the USSR Council of Ministers will receive the unanimous support and approval of all the deputies of the USSR Supreme Soviet.

> Khrushchev, it should be noted, attributed the decision to designate Bulganin Premier to the Party Central Committee, indicating this course of action had been decided upon at the January 25–31 plenum. The Supreme Soviet dutifully ratified Bulganin as Premier and then acted upon Malenkov:

The USSR Supreme Soviet decrees: That Comrade Georgii Maximilianovich Malenkov is appointed USSR Minister of Electric Power Stations and Deputy Chairman of the USSR Council of Ministers. . . . (*Pravda*, February 10, 1955)

> Bulganin's acceptance speech before the Supreme Soviet provided a résumé of the issues in dispute during the previous year. He emphasized the importance of heavy industry — while still promising an improvement in living standards — and the need to improve governmental administration; and he highlighted the programs to stimulate agriculture. Finally, he turned to foreign affairs:

The aggressive policy of the U.S. and its preparation for unleashing a new war cannot be underrated. The reactionary circles in the United States and countries dependent on it are striving for a rebirth of German militarism and the admission of a remilitarized Western Germany into the aggressive military groupings of the Western powers. In Asia, also, they are forging military blocs and organizing provocations against the Chinese Peoples Republic and interfering in its domestic affairs.

The American government has chosen the dangerous path of aggravating the situation in the Taiwan area. It is strengthening its forces there. . . .

The policy of the Chinese government in this matter has our complete approval and support. The Chinese Peoples Republic has the sympathy of the whole Soviet people and all progressive mankind because it is struggling for a just cause — for the honor and independence of its homeland. In this noble cause the Chinese people can expect help from their true friends, the great Soviet people. . . .

For a long time an atmosphere of war hysteria has reigned in the United States. Political and military leaders often make military declarations and threats. Some of them have gone so far as to advocate openly the use of atomic weapons in war against peace-loving states.

It is necessary to bring to their senses those madmen who threaten with an atomic bomb. The government of any state cannot overlook the fact that the people demand this.

The policy of the aggressive forces of the capitalist camp will not take our nation by surprise. The aggressors apparently seriously think that the more they threaten the more they scare us. We have had occasion to hear many threats of all kinds, but the Soviet people are not easily frightened and no one will be able to scare them. . . .

To safeguard Soviet weapons' supremacy for the future, the Party Central Committee and the government have recently . . . achieved great success in supplying our Armed Forces with new, completely modern weapons and combat techniques. . . . (*Pravda*, February 10, 1955)

IV · THE ASCENDANCY OF KHRUSHCHEV

The year 1955 was marked by increased activity on the part of Khrushchev who, in addition to his prominent roles as Party organizer and agricultural specialist, took on the duties of diplomat. Bulganin, as Premier, also gained prominence, and frequently shared the spotlight of publicity with Khrushchev, as when he accompanied him on visits to Yugoslavia and Asia. New departures in foreign policy occasioned serious disagreement among the leadership. The public treatment of Stalin's historical role was vacillating, apparently in part because the issue became entwined with elite politics; and it was only at the very end of this period that it was dramatically resolved. The 20th Party Congress, the first post-Stalin Congress, was scheduled for mid-February, 1956; preparations and organizational maneuverings for the upcoming Congress dominated Soviet domestic affairs during late 1955 and early 1956.

March 1955 to February 1956

Personnel and Organizational Alterations

The demotion of Malenkov was followed by a number of significant personnel changes, especially in the government. Malenkov himself remained a full member of the Party Presidium although his rank in the government did not correspond.

The Council of Ministers formed under Bulganin consisted of Kaganovich and Molotov as First Deputy Chairmen; and Kosygin, Malenkov, Malyshev, Mikoyan, Pervukhin, Saburov, and Tevosyan as Deputy Chairmen. In less than a month, there was a realignment:

The Presidium of the USSR Supreme Soviet, on the proposal of Comrade N. A. Bulganin, Chairman of the USSR Council of Ministers, has adopted the following decisions:

(a) To appoint as First Deputy Chairman of the USSR Council of Ministers, in addition to Comrades L. M. Kaganovich and V. M. Molotov, Comrades A. I. Mikoyan, M. G. Pervukhin and M. Z. Saburov.

(b) To appoint as Deputy Chairmen of the USSR Council of Ministers, Comrades A. P. Zavenyagin, V. A. Kucherenko, P. P. Lobanov and M. V. Khrunichev. (*Pravda*, March 1, 1955)

Thus, there were five First Deputy Chairmen and eight Deputy Chairmen. Whatever the motivations, the effect of elevating Mikoyan, Pervukhin, and Saburov to First Deputy Chairmen was to dilute the stature of Molotov and Kaganovich.

Still other personnel alterations at the ministerial level were made during March.

The Presidium of the USSR Supreme Soviet has accepted a proposal of the Chairman of the USSR Council of Ministers, Comrade Bulganin, and has:

(a) Relieved Comrade A. F. Zasyadko of his duties as USSR Minister of the Coal Industry because of unsatisfactory work.

The Presidium has appointed Comrade Alexander Nikolayevich Zademidko USSR Minister of the Coal Industry.

(b) Relieved Comrade A. I. Kozlov of his duties as USSR Minister of State Farms for not successfully handling his work.

The Presidium has appointed Comrade Ivan Alexandrovich Benediktov USSR Minister of State Farms, relieving him of his duties as USSR Minister of Agriculture." (*Pravda,* March 3, 1955)

*   *   *

The Presidium of the USSR Supreme Soviet, on the recommendation of the Chairman of the USSR Council of Ministers, N. A. Bulganin, has decided to release Comrade G. F. Alexandrov from his duties as USSR Minister of Culture because of his failure to provide proper leadership of the Ministry of Culture.

The Presidium has appointed Comrade N. A. Mikhailov as USSR Minister of Culture, having released him from his post of USSR Ambassador to the Polish People's Republic. (*Pravda*, March 22, 1955)

On March 11, a number of high-ranking military promotions were enacted.

A Decree of the Presidium of the USSR Supreme Soviet confers the military rank of Marshal of the Soviet Union on Generals of the Army Ivan Khrustoforovich Bagramyan, Sergei Semyonovich Biryuzov, Andrei Antonovich Grechko, Andrei Ivanovich Yeremenko, Kirill Semyonovich Moskalenko and Vasily Ivanovich Chuikov; the rank of Chief Marshal of Aviation on Marshal of Aviation Pavel Fedorovich Zhigarev; the rank of Marshal of the Artillery on Colonel Generals of the Artillery Sergei Sergeyevich Varentsov and Vasily Ivanovich Kazakov. (*Pravda*, March 12, 1955)

By and large, these military officers promoted to Marshal of the Soviet Union subsequently had very successful careers. Several of them had been associated with Khrushchev at various times during World War II. The military profession as a whole also benefitted in the shuffling of the government after Malenkov's fall by the elevation of Marshal G. K. Zhukov, a professional military man and hero of World War II, to the position of Minister of Defense, which had been vacated by Bulganin when he became Premier. For many years that post had been occupied by "political" marshals.

Indication of another high-level personnel change was suggested by the listing of the leaders who served as honor guards at the bier of Marshal Govorov on March 21:

. . . the honor guard was formed by leaders of the Communist Party and Soviet government N. A. Bulganin, K. Ye. Voroshilov, L. Kaganovich, G. M. Malenkov, V. M. Molotov, A. I. Mikoyan, M. G. Pervukhin, M. Z. Saburov, N. S. Khrushchev, P. N. Pospelov, M. A. Suslov, and USSR Minister of Defense, G. K. Zhukov. (*Pravda*, March 22, 1955)

This list included all the full members of the Party Presidium and the Secretariat except for Shatalin. Shatalin dropped from sight and was later referred to in the press as occupying a Party post in Siberia. The number of Central Committee secretaries was hence reduced to three: Khrushchev, Suslov, and Pospelov.

These personnel shufflings were accompanied by some revamping of the structure and operations of the economic administration. A joint decree of the Party Central Committee and the Council of Ministers of March 9, for example, ordered a reduction in the degree of centralized planning for agriculture, noting:

The planning system employed, under which collective farms were given sowing plans defining strictly the crops and size of sown areas and the kind and number of livestock to be maintained, in many instances led to irrational management. Arbitrary planning of sowing areas led to incorrect distribution of crops, which did not correspond to the economic, soil and climatic conditions of the collective farms. . . . All this hampered the initiative of the collective farms and MTS and weakened their responsibility for, and interest in, developing production. . . .* (*Pravda*, March 11, 1955)

At a national conference of industrial personnel in mid-May, Bulganin urged the introduction of new technology in industrial enterprises and criticized managers for their conservatism and bureaucratic procedures:

. . . There are serious shortcomings in light industry, the lumber industry and other branches of our industry in the use of current, and in the introduction of new and advanced, equipment and methods.

What is the reason for this? The Party Central Committee and the USSR Council of Ministers have correctly pointed out that the delay in introducing advanced equipment results from the complacency and self-satisfaction of many industrial officials, their loss of any sense of responsibility to the state for the jobs entrusted to them, and their loss of perspective and orientation in technological policy. . . .

Shortcomings in the organization of industry are reflected in the system of enterprise management. The Party and government demand the determined abolition of armchair, bureaucratic methods of manage-

---

* However, since procurement planning — as distinct from the sowing plan — remained highly centralized, the initiative permitted to the collective farms and lower agricultural administrators in practice was not as great as foreseen in this decree.

ment, the restriction of administrative staffs, improvement in their work, and better management. These Party instructions are not yet being sufficiently implemented. At medium-sized and small enterprises, generally speaking, the managerial system differs little from the managerial systems of large plants. . . . (*Pravda*, May 17, 1955)

> Hard on the heels of this conference, the regime took steps to expand the rights of industrial executives in handling surplus equipment, and to rearrange the planning agencies.

The Presidium of the USSR Supreme Soviet decrees that:

1. The decree of the Presidium of the USSR Supreme Soviet of February 10, 1941, "On Prohibiting the Sale, Exchange or Unauthorized Disposition of Equipment or Supplies and on Legal Liability for these Illegal Acts" is rescinded.

2. Persons convicted but who have not completed their sentences for the sale, exchange or unauthorized disposition of equipment or supplies are released from serving out their sentences. . . .

3. The USSR Council of Ministers is instructed to establish a system for the redistribution and sale of excess, unused equipment and supplies in order to increase substantially the rights of USSR Ministers, the heads of chief administrations of USSR ministries and the directors of enterprises in the use of such equipment and supplies. (Bulletin of the USSR Supreme Soviet, No. 8, June 8, p. 223)

> *Pravda,* on May 26, announced a reorganization of the State Planning Committee "in order to improve state planning of the USSR's national economy."

. . . To establish, on the basis of the State Planning Committee, a USSR Council of Ministers' committee for long-range planning of the national economy (USSR State Planning Committee) and a USSR Council of Ministers committee for current planning of the national economy (USSR State Economic Committee); to appoint Comrade Nikolai Konstantinovich Baibakov as Chairman of the USSR State Planning Committee, having released him from his duties as USSR Minister of the Oil Industry; to appoint Comrade Maxim Zakharovich Saburov, First Deputy Chairman of the USSR Council of Ministers as Chairman of the USSR State Economic Committee.

> While these reforms were designed to rationalize the bureaucracy and make it more efficient in administering an increasingly complex econ-

omy, the redistribution of power within the administrative apparatus and the personnel reshuffling which they entailed carried substantial political ramifications. For example, the division of Gosplan into two committees inevitably diminished the authority of Saburov, who had headed the former single committee. Insofar as the economic administration was decentralized, especially in agriculture, the role of the Party apparatus was strengthened as the watchdog over the economy.

Finally, Kaganovich, on May 24, was named Chairman of the State Committee of the Council of Ministers on Labor and Wages and, as such, was in a powerful position as a sharpshooter to implement or obstruct further rationalization of the administration, particularly in the area of wage and work norm reforms

Foreign Policy and Yugoslavia

The heavy defeat suffered by the Malenkov faction was followed by extensive commentary in *Pravda* and *Izvestia* during March that hinted at "erroneous" positions on important issues, though without attributing them explicitly to Malenkov. The following selection, typical of several articles at the time, was written by F. Konstantinov, who performed a complete about-face from the position he took in his December 21, 1954 *Izvestia* article espousing the cause of light industry.

. . . Proceeding from Lenin's teaching, J. V. Stalin repeatedly pointed out that to make the transition to communism it was necessary to ensure the uninterrupted growth of all social production, with preponderant growth of production of the means of production. . . .

As noted at the January plenum of the Party Central Committee, recently, in connection with the measures being implemented for increasing the production of consumers' goods, erroneous, anti-Marxist views on basic questions of the development of the socialist economy have gained currency among a certain section of economists, scholars and teachers in higher educational institutions. Citing the basic economic law of socialism, which they have misunderstood and have interpreted in a vulgarized manner, these would-be theoreticians attempt to prove that at some stage of socialist construction the development of heavy industry ceases to be the main task and that light industry can and should outstrip all other branches of industry. . . .

These theoretically erroneous and politically harmful views of certain economists in essence revive right-wing opportunist views on questions of a socialist economy, views long ago condemned by the Party. The Party teaches that the propagation of such anti-Leninist views is especially inadmissible in present circumstances. . . .

The Soviet people and the working people of the people's democracies, solidly united around their Communist Parties, look confidently to the future. Engaged in peaceful, constructive labor, the peoples of these countries will not permit themselves to be intimidated by the threats of imperialist warmongers. J. V. Stalin once said that the laws of artillery cannot be stronger than the laws of history.

No matter how the imperialists attempt to blackmail peace-loving peoples with atomic bombs, they cannot change the course of history. The peoples have been and remain the main force of history. It is they who have decided and will decide the fate of progress, the fate of civilization.

Theoretically erroneous and politically harmful are the assertions of the possibility of the "ruin of world civilization" if a third world war is unleashed by the imperialists. Such assertions are of advantage only to the imperialist instigators of a new war, who count on intimidating the peoples with "atomic" blackmail. . . . (F. Konstantinov, "J. V. Stalin and the Problems of Building Communism," *Pravda*, March 5, 1955)

Two aspects of this passage merit special attention. The first is the repeated citation of Stalin for authority against erroneous views. The second is the rejection of the view that atomic weapons have revolutionized warfare and international politics and have thus called into question the Marxist conception of historical development. Later, particularly after 1960, Khrushchev began to take a position on the terrible destructiveness of nuclear war that resembled Malenkov's statement of March 1954; and the Chinese Communists criticized Khrushchev with arguments like those used by Konstantinov in tacitly refuting Malenkov.

With the disagreements on economic policy and agriculture resolved, at least temporarily, the center of the leadership's attention during 1955 tended to shift to foreign affairs. After mounting warnings about the aggressiveness of "reactionary imperialist circles" in late 1954 and early 1955, during the spring of 1955 the Soviet Union began suddenly to steer a more moderate and conciliatory course in foreign policy. An Austrian peace treaty was concluded and a four-power agreement to withdraw from Austria was promulgated on May 15, 1955, followed in July by the four-power Geneva Conference of heads of state. In September the Porkkala naval base was returned to Finland. From mid-November until mid-December, Khrushchev and Bulganin, accompanied by a large entourage, paid good-will visits to India, Burma, and Afghanistan. These new directions in foreign policy were accompanied by a sharp decline in public warnings about the dangers of war; and on August 13 a reduction in the size of the armed forces by 640,000 was announced.

It seems unlikely that these various initiatives in foreign policy could have been taken without occasioning some disagreement among the leadership. As it turned out, however, leadership conflict was most visibly manifested in yet another foreign policy departure: efforts toward a rapprochement with Yugoslavia, on which Stalin had placed his anathema in 1948. The sequence of moves toward reestablishment of relations merits careful study as an instance of bargaining conducted publicly (at least in part) by two communist states. Molotov's role in the exchanges is noteworthy, as well as his absence from the Soviet delegation that finally went to Belgrade. The play began at the turn of the year:

Trade negotiations between a government trade delegation of the Federal People's Republic of Yugoslavia and the USSR Ministry of Foreign Trade were held in Moscow from December 20, 1954 to January 5, 1955.

As a result of these talks, trade and payment agreements were signed January 5 by the USSR and the Federal People's Republic of Yugoslavia. . . . (*Pravda*, January 6, 1955)

In his speech before the Supreme Soviet on February 8, Foreign Minister Molotov had made the following reference to the Yugoslav situation:

. . . As we know, progress has lately been made in the relations between the Soviet Union and Yugoslavia. We do not consider that everything has already been done in this respect, but we believe that this depends no less on Yugoslavia herself. Evidently, in these past years Yugoslavia has to some extent departed from the position which she held in the early years following the second world war. That, of course, is exclusively her internal affair. The Soviet Union is desirous of developing economic, political and cultural relations with Yugoslavia. We are also desirous of possible co-ordination of effort in so momentous a matter for all nations as safeguarding peace and international security. We are convinced that it is in the interest of both the people of the USSR and the people of Yugoslavia that Soviet–Yugoslav relations should develop propitiously. . . . (*Pravda*, February 9, 1955)

> On March 10, *Pravda* and *Izvestia* gave unusually long and thorough coverage to a March 7 speech by Yugoslav President Tito, including several sensitive statements which would have been ignored if normal Soviet reporting practices had been followed.

The Tanyug news service has transmitted the text of a report on Yugoslav foreign policy during the last year, delivered yesterday by President Tito at a session of the Yugoslav Narodna Skupshtina [Parliament].

The speaker discussed the work of the United Nations, noting that this organization "has not yet justified the hopes of mankind in all respects, although it has played an important role in many serious and critical questions." Tito sees the reason for this in "the selfish tendencies of some great powers which have shifted the center of the struggle for solution of major problems outside the U.N. framework and are being drawn ever more deeply into an arms race." Tito stated that "Yugoslavia opposes the division of the world into blocs and the arms race, for experience has shown that an arms race usually leads to war." Tito supported a policy which he called "active coexistence."

According to Tito, the most important problems which Yugoslavia has settled in the last year were the conclusion of a treaty with Greece and Turkey, the Trieste settlement with Italy, and "achievement of considerable progress in the matter of normalizing relations with the Soviet Union and other Eastern European countries — Hungary, Bulgaria, Rumania, Czechoslovakia, Poland, and Albania." . . .

As for relations with the Western countries, the speaker stressed that Yugoslavia's cooperation with these countries "is developing normally in the spirit of friendship and understanding" and that the efforts of the Yugoslav government are "concentrated on achieving the most constructive co-operation with the Western countries." . . .

In addition the speaker set forth the position of the Yugoslav government on the question of Yugoslavia's relations with the Soviet Union and the countries of Eastern Europe. Tito stated that "normalization of relations between Yugoslavia and the Soviet Union and the countries of

Eastern Europe has not only contributed to the cause of stabilizing peace in this part of Europe but has also helped to reduce world tension as a whole." . . .

Tito said that diplomatic relations have been established with the Chinese People's Republic and "soon these two countries will exchange diplomatic representatives."

Touching on relations with the countries of Eastern Europe, President Tito stated that "agreements have been concluded with them on settling border incidents so that the situation on the entire Yugoslav border is now normal. Moreover, the situation of Yugoslav minorities in these countries has improved somewhat in comparison with that of past years, but it is still not what it could and should be."

He went on to assert that in all these countries efforts are being made to explain the normalization of relations with Yugoslavia in the following manner: "Although Yugoslavia is still guilty of what she has been accused, nevertheless she has now recognized her errors somewhat and is trying to reform. This is nonsense," said Tito, "and naturally it may cause us to doubt the sincerity of the statements by responsible leaders of these countries, which were made during direct contact, about the unjust accusations against Yugoslavia in 1948. Unquestionably, Mr. Molotov's formulations about Yugoslavia in his speech to the Supreme Soviet do not correspond to reality and in some respects correspond with these assertions. We consider this an attempt to conceal the facts from the people, again at our expense. The time has come to describe things as they are and as they developed, instead of stopping halfway toward normalization and raising new doubts among the people. Manifestations of this kind do not help to improve relations, but, instead, hinder the process which, as is apparent, does not proceed easily after what was done to our country and after all the unfounded insults we have had to bear." . . .

Regarding Yugoslavia's conclusion of trade and payment agreements with the Soviet Union, Hungary, Czechoslovakia and Poland, Tito said that "Yugoslavia regards all these signs of normalization favorably and wants the initial normalization of relations . . . to lead to mutually advantageous cooperation." . . . (*Pravda*, March 10, 1955)

The publication of Tito's criticism of Molotov could hardly be considered auspicious for the Foreign Minister. However, two days later *Pravda* printed a commentary on Tito's remarks by an "Observer" (which indicates it was an authoritative statement). In addition to its importance as a pawn in the bargaining process, the reader may wish to speculate what this rejoinder did for Molotov.

President Tito of Yugoslavia touched on the present relations between Yugoslavia and the Soviet Union in his speech at the March 7 session of the Narodna Skupshtina. In so doing, he stressed the considerable progress in normalizing Soviet–Yugoslav relations. As is known, the successes achieved in this important matter were already noted at the recent session of the USSR Supreme Soviet. The improvement in relations between Yugoslavia and the Soviet Union, as well as between Yugoslavia and the people's democracies, has been received with satisfaction by all peace-loving peoples, including the peoples of the Soviet Union and Yugoslavia. There is no doubt but that such normalization contributes to peace. . . .

Referring to the question of relations between Yugoslavia and the Soviet Union, President Tito alleged that attempts were being made in the countries of the socialist camp to explain the normalization of relations with Yugoslavia in the following manner:

"Although Yugoslavia is still guilty of what she has been accused, nevertheless she has now recognized her errors somewhat and is trying to reform." The President rejected such "explanations" as "not corresponding to reality." By the way, he did not — and could not — indicate who it was that gave such strange "explanations" and where. In any case, we can only say that no one in the Soviet Union has thought of saying anything like that.

In addition the Yugoslav President asserted that V. M. Molotov's speech at the session of the USSR Supreme Soviet about Yugoslavia "in some respects corresponds with these assertions." Here it is necessary to restore the truth.

What was really said about Yugoslavia at the session of the USSR Supreme Soviet? V. M. Molotov's report stated that: "Evidently, in the last few years, Yugoslavia has to some extent departed from the position which she held in the early years following the Second World War. That, of course, is exclusively her internal affair."

As is known, in 1948 a turn occurred in the development of Yugoslavia. There are a great number of statements by Yugoslav leading figures which show in detail that after 1948 Yugoslavia embarked on a new path of development. . . .

The same thought . . . was expressed by President Tito in a

speech at a meeting in Kopar on November 21, 1954 in which he said that "Yugoslavia is not retreating from the foreign policy course which she initiated in 1948."

What else can these statements by Yugoslav leaders mean but a confirmation of the fact that "Yugoslavia in the past few years has to some extent departed from the position which she held in the early years following the second world war?"

In his report President Tito thought it necessary to raise the question of sincerity in the relations between the USSR and Yugoslavia. However, let us judge the sincerity in the policy of a state by the facts, by the concrete actions which really ensure normal relations between states. What does President Tito's speech reveal? Does it contain practical proposals for further improving Yugoslav–Soviet relations? The facts show that unfortunately there are no such proposals in his speech. Instead, President Tito turns to the past. He decided to recall for the Yugoslav people the accusations against the Yugoslav government which were put forward in the past. But, when remembering the past, he says nothing about those direct and various expressions of hostility toward the Soviet Union which took place in Yugoslavia. . . .

To any forward-looking person desirous of ensuring genuinely stable, friendly relations between Yugoslavia and the Soviet Union, it is important to expand the progress already achieved in normalizing relations and to ensure the elimination of past unfriendliness. The Soviet Union, as has been pointed out more than once in the last few years, is resolutely in favor of fully eliminating unfriendliness and building relations in a spirit of friendship and mutual respect. . . .

Improvement of the relations between the Soviet Union and Yugoslavia undoubtedly serves the interests of our peoples and the cause of strengthening peace and international security. One must keep in mind, however, that the normalization of relations depends not only on the Soviet Union but on Yugoslavia in no less degree.

As is widely known, the Soviet Union firmly adheres to the position that every state has the right to follow any course in domestic or foreign policy. Nobody in the Soviet Union thinks of "explaining" the successes achieved in the normalization of relations between the USSR and Yugoslavia by the fact that Yugoslav leaders have now "recognized their errors" or "are trying to reform." One thing is certain: the expression of unfriendliness between Yugoslavia and the Soviet Union is of advantage only to the enemies of both states and peoples — to the enemies of peace — while the elimination of unfriendliness and the improvement of relations serve the cause of strengthening peace in the Balkans and through-out Europe. . . . (*Pravda*, March 12, 1955)

After further Soviet–Yugoslav talks, on May 14, *Pravda* announced:

By mutual desire and with the aim of improving further the rela-tions between the two states and strengthening peace, the Government of the USSR and the Government of the Federal People's Republic of Yugoslavia have agreed to a meeting of their representatives on the highest level; and have appointed delegations for this purpose.

USSR – consisting of the following: Member of the Presidium of the USSR Supreme Soviet and First Secretary of the Party Central Com-mittee, N. S. Khrushchev (head of the delegation); Chairman of the Council of Ministers, N. A. Bulganin; First Deputy Chairman of the USSR Council of Ministers, A. I. Mikoyan; Chairman of the Commis-sion on Foreign Affairs of the Council of Nationalities of the USSR Su-preme Soviet, member of the Party Central Committee and chief editor of the newspaper *Pravda,* D. J. Shepilov; First Deputy Minister of For-eign Affairs, A. A. Gromyko; and Deputy Minister of Foreign Trade, P. N. Kumykin. . . .

The meeting will be held in Belgrade at the end of May 1955.

The composition of this delegation is noteworthy not only because of the absence of Foreign Minister Molotov but for the presence of Shepi-lov and the obvious effort to build up his stature by listing all his positions. It would appear that Shepilov was being groomed to play a major role in foreign relations.

The Soviet delegation remained in Yugoslavia from May 26 until June 2. The visit was given extensive coverage in the Soviet press. Khrushchev stopped off in Bulgaria and Rumania for conferences on his return to Moscow.

Upon his arrival at the Belgrade airport, Khrushchev delivered a speech in which he laid the blame for past difficulties in Soviet–Yugo-slav relations on the machinations of Beria and his police cohorts – without mentioning Stalin – and called vigorously for close relations between the two countries and two parties.

. . . The Soviet delegation has arrived in your country in order, together with the Yugoslav governmental delegation, to define the path of the further development and strengthening of friendship and co-op-eration between our peoples, to discuss our common tasks in the struggle for the well-being of our countries, for the easing of international tensions and strengthening the peace and security of all peoples.

The peoples of our countries are linked by close, long-standing, brotherly friendship and the mutual struggle against common enemies. This friendship and military co-operation were especially strengthened in the period of difficult experiences in the fight against the fascist usurpers in the years of the Second World War. . . .

We sincerely regret what has happened and are resolutely removing everything that accumulated in this period.

For our part, we undoubtedly took a provocative role in this, which was played in the relations between Yugoslavia and the USSR by the presently unmasked enemies of the people — Beria, Abakumov, and others. We have carefully studied the materials on which were based the serious accusations and insults made at that time against the Yugoslav leaders. The facts show that these materials were fabricated by enemies of the people, despicable agents of imperialism, who had by a deceptive road joined the ranks of our Party.

We are deeply convinced that the period when our relations were darkened remains in the past. We are prepared on our part to do everything necessary to eliminate all obstacles interfering with the full normalization of the relations between our countries and the strengthening of friendly relations between our peoples. . . .

The attempt of Yugoslavia to develop relations with all states, both in the West and in the East, meets with our full understanding. We consider that the strengthening of friendship and ties between our countries will promote the improvement of relations among all countries, independent of their social systems, and will promote the strengthening of world peace. . . .

We, as representatives of the Communist Party of the Soviet Union, the Party created by the great Lenin, consider as desirable a condition of mutual trust also between our Parties. Very firm ties are established among the peoples of those countries where the leading force is the Party whose entire activity is based on the teachings of Marxism–Leninism. Parties which lead according to the teachings of Marxism–Leninism achieve full mutual understanding among themselves because they have a single goal — this is the struggle for the interests of the working class, the working peasantry and for the interests of the working people. . . .

We would not fulfill our debt before our peoples and before the workers of the whole world if we did not do everything possible to establish mutual understanding between the Communist Party of the Soviet

Union and the League of Communists of Yugoslavia on the basis of the teachings of Marxism–Leninism. . . . (*Pravda,* May 27, 1955)

Tito's reception of the Soviet delegation was cool and it was obvious that Khrushchev had to eat a large dose of crow to achieve his rapprochement with the Yugoslavs. After a week of hard bargaining the Soviet delegation did wind up with a declaration pledging closer relations and friendship between the two countries. Among other things the declaration gave verbal recognition to the sovereignty, independence, and equal rights of states; the need for peaceful coexistence among nations with differing ideologies and social structures; and the inadmissibility of intervention by one state into the internal affairs of another. Both sides agreed to discontinue hostile propaganda and "misinformation" and to widen economic and cultural contacts.

Khrushchev, however, was not successful in establishing inter-party relations. And, in order to achieve his policy of closer relations with the Yugoslavs, he had to recognize the legitimacy of the Yugoslav brand of socialism and agree — tacitly at first — that there may be several paths to socialism. The rapprochement gave the Yugoslavs a new stature which permitted them to play a larger role in Eastern European affairs. These various implications of the new Soviet–Yugoslav relationship were to create difficulties for the Soviet leadership in 1956.

A Central Committeee plenum in early July devoted part of its attention to Soviet–Yugoslav relations, a subject on which Khrushchev gave the main report. A *Pravda* editorial two days after the conclusion of the plenum probably reflects Khrushchev's version of the Soviet–Yugoslav talks and their ramifications:

. . . The improvement in relations between the USSR and Yugoslavia, said Comrade N. S. Khrushchev at the meeting in Sofia on June 3, will make a new contribution to the easing of international tension and the strengthening of peace. There is no doubt that the Soviet–Yugoslav talks serve the interests of all peace-loving people and the working masses of all countries who have acclaimed with approval the announcement of the favorable results of the Soviet–Yugoslav talks. . . .

The abnormal, unhealthy relations which arose after 1948, because of the provocative role of Beria and Abakumov, have been eliminated. Firm foundations have been laid for the development of friendly relations and all-round co-operation between the USSR and the FPRY.

This corresponds to the basic interests of the peoples of both states and, at the same time, is in complete accord with the tasks of strengthening world peace and the security of the peoples of Europe. . . .

All nations will arrive at socialism, Lenin pointed out; this is inevitable, but not all will arrive there in precisely the same manner. Each one will introduce its own features into this or that form of democracy, into this or that form of the dictatorship of the proletariat, into this or that rate of socialist transformation of varying facets of the society.

The historical experience of the Soviet Union and the people's democracies shows that, given unity in the chief fundamental matter of ensuring the victory of socialism, various ways and means may be employed in different countries, depending on historical and national features, to solve the specific problems of socialist construction.

In developing and strengthening sincere and friendly relations between the Soviet Union and the Federal People's Republic of Yugoslavia, it is very important that public ownership of the basic means of production exists in Yugoslavia in large-scale and medium industry, transportation, the banking system, wholesale trade and most of retail trade. The basic classes in Yugoslavia are the working class and the toiling peasantry.

The state system of the Federal People's Republic of Yugoslavia is determined by the fact that the working class and the peasantry hold the reins of power. Yugoslavia has preserved its national independence and has resisted attempts of foreign capital to penetrate its economy. . . .

The Communist Party of the Soviet Union deems it desirable to establish contact and a rapprochement between the CPSU and the Yugoslav League of Communists on the basis of Marxist–Leninist principles. The first results have now been achieved and the foundation laid for this contact and rapprochement. It is hoped that rapprochement with the Yugoslav League of Communists will continue and develop on the basis of Marxist–Leninist principles. This corresponds to the interests of the people of the Soviet Union and Yugoslavia.

The working people of Yugoslavia realize that there is not and cannot be any threat to the Yugoslav people and Yugoslavia's national independence from the Soviet Union. . . .

On the other hand, the wide masses of working people in Yugoslavia realize that the imperialists are aiming at bringing about the restoration of capitalism in Yugoslavia and depriving her of national independence. . . . (*Pravda*, July 16, 1955)

That consensus did not reign among the leadership on the Yugoslav affair, and perhaps on other foreign policy issues at the plenum, is indicated by a strange episode of "self-criticism" indulged in by Molotov in the September issue of the Party's theoretical journal, *Kommunist*.

LETTER TO THE EDITORS OF THE JOURNAL *Kommunist* [by V. Molotov]

I request that the following letter be published in the pages of the journal *Kommunist*.

In my report to the February 8, 1955 session of the USSR Supreme Soviet I formulated incorrectly the question of the building of a socialist society in the USSR. The report said, "Side by side with the Soviet Union, where the foundations of a socialist society have already been established, there are also people's democracies that have taken only the first, though very important, steps in the direction of socialism."

This erroneous formulation leads to the incorrect conclusion that a socialist society has not yet been established in the USSR, that only the foundations, that is the basis, of a socialist society have been established; this does not correspond to the facts and conflicts with the repeated evaluations of the results of socialist construction in the USSR given in Party documents.

As early as 1932, the decision of the 17th Party conference pointed out that the building of the foundation of socialism in the USSR had been completed and that Lenin's question "who will prevail over whom?" had been decided, completely and irrevocably, against capitalism and for socialism, both in the cities and in the countryside.

On the basis of further achievements of socialist construction, the 18th Congress of the All-Union Communist Party (Bolsheviks) noted that the USSR had entered a new phase of development, the phase of completing the building of socialism and the gradual transition to a communist society.

During the period that followed, the Soviet people, under the leadership of the Communist Party, have achieved tremendous successes in the cause of completing the construction of a socialist society in the USSR. The powerful material and technical base of the socialist society has grown and been strengthened immeasurably, and socialist production relations, based on the indivisible domination of public socialist ownership and on relations of comradely co-operation that exclude all possibility of exploitation of man by man, have become completely firm and have established themselves in both industry and agriculture.

These achievements in socialist construction in the USSR are also reflected in the Party Statutes, adopted at the 19th Party Congress, in which it is pointed out that the Party has "guaranteed the building of a socialist society" and that "the principal task of the Communist Party of the Soviet Union now consists of building a communist society by means of the gradual transition from socialism to communism."

In accordance with the above, I consider my formulation on the question of the building of a socialist society in the USSR, given at the February 8, 1955 session of the USSR Supreme Soviet and from which the conclusion can be drawn that only the foundations of a socialist society have been built, to be theoretically erroneous and politically harmful.

The political harm in this formulation lies in the fact that it introduces confusion into ideological questions and contradicts the resolutions of the Party on questions of building a socialist society in the USSR, and casts doubt upon the existence in our country of a socialist society that has in the main already been built. (*Kommunist*, No. 14 (September), 1955, pp. 127-28)

> This episode suggests the importance that words have in the Soviet Union, where important differences on questions of ideology or policy may be expressed publicly by mere shadings and nuances in the words used. To a Westerner, this fine point of doctrine might seem an insignificant matter. For Molotov it meant the humiliation of a public recantation. The long editorial in the same issue of *Kommunist* drove home the seriousness of Molotov's "erroneous formulations," although it did not mention him by name; and may have hinted at other areas of "ideological deviation" by him.

. . . On the basis of a profound study of the laws of social development, Marxism arms the Communist Party, the working class, and all working people with a scientifically based program for the revolutionary reorganization of society. . . .

The Communist Party attributes great significance to the correct Marxist evaluation of the present stage of the struggle for communism. For this reason it points out the theoretical bankruptcy and the political harm of attempts to apply to the present, formulas and descriptions that are applicable only to a stage that was passed through long ago — to claim that so far only the foundations of socialism (i.e. the basis of socialism) have been built in our country. Such an assertion ignores real life and belittles the great economic, political, and ideological achievements of Soviet society, of our system. It can do our cause harm, because it distorts the perspective of development and leads to an underestimation of the socialist system's forces and potentialities. Yet these forces and potentialities are really inexhaustible. . . .

A genuinely Marxist approach to the analysis and evaluation of phenomena is particularly necessary in the sphere of international life — with its social and inter-state contradictions, its struggle between progressive and reactionary forces and the constantly changing forms and methods of this struggle. The separation of theory from life, attempts to hang fast to dogma, are especially impermissible here. The Party realized and realizes this fully, and it skillfully combines principle and flexibility in its foreign policy; this is precisely the reason for the great successes abroad in the struggle for peace and for the easing of international tensions that the Soviet Union has recently achieved. . . .

Questions about the building of communism in the USSR cannot now be considered apart from the problems connected with the existence and development of the growing camp of peace, democracy, and socialism. The formation of the mighty commonwealth of socialist states was a great, world–historic achievement of the peoples of these countries, and also of the entire world liberation movement. Social–historical practice took a new stride forward, thus posing new problems for Marxist–Leninist theory and for Party propaganda. It is a matter of fathoming, elaborating and explaining theoretically, on the basis of the new historical experience, the questions of the principal features and the international significance of the socialist camp; of the forms of economic, political, and cultural co-operation among socialist states; of the existence of common features in the principal and fundamental aspects of the social and political development of socialist states and at the same time of some originality of forms and methods, depending on historical and national peculiarities, in the solution of concrete problems of socialist construction; of the co-existence of the socialist and capitalist camps; and many other factors. . . .

Our propaganda must provide a comprehensive explanation of the question of the mutual exchange among the fraternal countries of experience in socialist construction. Each of these countries is making its contribution to the common cause of the struggle for socialism and communism. A sharing of the fundamentals, the chief features, of this cause does not prevent each of these countries from having an individual approach to the concrete forms, methods, means and also tempos of socialist transformation. . . . Stereotypes must be avoided in illuminating the life of the people's democracies — a shortcoming that has not been avoided by some books and pamphlets published in our country, and that can be found also in some lectures, reports, and newspaper and magazine articles. . . . ("The Relationship of Theory and Practice and Party Propaganda," *Kommunist,* No. 14 (September), 1955)

Toward the 20th Party Congress

The lengthy July 1955 plenum of the Party Central Committee, as made clear by the report of its proceedings, was significant not only because of its ratification of the Soviet–Yugoslav agreement:

A plenum of the Party Central Committee was held July 4–12, 1955.

The plenum discussed the following questions:

1. Comrade N. A. Bulganin's report on tasks for the further development of industry, on technical progress, and on improving the organization of production.

2. The results of spring sowing, the cultivation of crops, the execution of the harvest, and the ensuring of the fulfillment of the procurement plan for agricultural production in 1955. The plenum heard reports on this question by USSR Deputy Minister of Agriculture, Comrade V. V. Matskevich, USSR Minister of State Farms, Comrade I. A. Benediktov, USSR Minister of Procurements, Comrade L. R. Korniyets, Russian Republic Minister of Agriculture, Comrade P. I. Morozov, Russian Republic Minister of State Farms, Comrade T. A. Yurkin, and Comrade V. D. Kalashnikov, designated representative of the Russian Republic Ministry of Procurements.

3. Comrade N. S. Khrushchev's report on the result of the Soviet–Yugoslav talks.

4. The convocation of the 20th Congress of the Communist Party of the Soviet Union. . . .

The plenum of the Party Central Committee also elected Comrades A. I. Kirichenko and M. A. Suslov members of the Presidium of the Party Central Committee.

The plenum of the Party Central Committee also elected Comrades A. B. Aristov, N. I. Belyayev, and D. T. Shepilov secretaries of the Party Central Committee. (*Pravda,* July 13, 1955)

*   *   *

The resolution of the plenum of the Party Central Committee:

1. To convene the 20th regular Communist Party Congress on February 14, 1956.

2. To confirm the following agenda of the Congress:

(a) Report of the Communist Party Central Committee: speaker, Secretary of the Central Committee Comrade N. S. Khrushchev.

(b) Report of the Communist Party Central Inspection Commission: speaker, Chairman of the Inspection Commission Comrade P. G. Moskatov.

(c) Directives of the 20th Communist Party Congress on the Sixth Five-Year Plan for the development of the USSR's national economy in 1956–60: speaker, Chairman of the USSR Council of Ministers Comrade N. A. Bulganin.

(d) Elections of the central agencies of the Party. . . . (*Pravda*, July 14, 1955)

The promotion of Kirichenko and Suslov to full membership in the Party Presidium was the first alteration in the ranks of the full members of that body since the purge of Beria in July 1953. Kirichenko, First Secretary of the Ukranian Central Committee, had been an associate of Khrushchev's when the latter was in the Ukraine during the 1940's. Suslov, long occupied in ideological work, had been a member of the Central Committee Secretariat and the enlarged Presidium before Stalin's death. The appointment of Aristov, Belyayev, and Shepilov to the Secretariat doubled its size. They were the first new members on that body since Khrushchev had been named First Secretary.

The announcement of the convocation of the 20th Party Congress intensified maneuvering among the leadership. Not only would the Congress be a forum composed of the Soviet elite and leading foreign communist dignitaries at which the whole gamut of Soviet domestic and foreign policies would be definitively propounded, but it would also be the occasion on which a new Central Committee, Presidium and Secretariat would be selected.

In addition to the high-level Party appointments made at the July plenum, other important personnel changes were made in the republics and provinces in anticipation of the upcoming Congress. Some of the more important appointments to positions, whose occupants normally are elected to the Central Committee, were: Leonid Brezhnev in place of Ponomarenko as First Secretary of the Kazakh Republic in May; Nikolai Ignatov in place of Smirnov as First Secretary of the Gorki oblast committee in November; and Nuritdin Mukhitdinov in place of Nyasov as First Secretary of the Uzbek Republic in December. In addition to these three men, who within two years were to achieve membership on the top Party organs, there were many other changes in important Party secretaryships between September, 1953 and the 20th Party Congress.*

Before turning to the Congress itself, there remains to be considered the handling, in Soviet media during 1955, of Stalin and the proper methods of Party leadership. The problems of Stalin and the relationship between the top Party bodies were not only issues in their own right under contention among the leaders, but they yield clues to the balance of political forces throughout the year preceding the Congress.

On April 20, 1955, *Pravda* printed an article commemorating the anniversary of Lenin's birth, by an old Bolshevik, G. I. Petrovsky, a candidate member of the Politburo and leader in the Ukraine until his fall in 1938. (In early 1938 Khrushchev became the Ukrainian first secretary.) After personal reminiscences about Lenin's qualities, Petrovsky pointedly discussed the Leninist conception of Party leadership:

. . . Once a week and sometimes twice a week the Council of People's Commissars (predecessor of the Council of Ministers) met under the chairmanship of Lenin. At meetings of the Council of People's Commissars all the important problems of the first steps of socialist construction and the organization of Soviet power in the center and locally were considered. Questions were decided concerning the liquidation of all the bourgeois institutions. The first steps of socialist production and trade were outlined here.

Lenin taught us collectivity of work, often reminding us that all members of the Politburo are equal and that the secretary is chosen to execute the decisions of the Central Committee of the Communist Party. That was the first and only university in the entire world at that time where the People's Commissars studied how to build the worker–peasant

* According to T. H. Rigby, an authority on Soviet personnel matters, during this 2½-year period, 45 of 84 First Secretaries of republic and regional Party committees coming directly under the Central Committee were changed. T. H. Rigby, "Khrushchev and the Resuscitation of the Central Committee." *Australian Outlook,* XIII, No. 3 (September), 1959, p. 174.

power. (G. I. Petrovsky, "Under the Guidance of a Great Leader," *Pravda*, April 20, 1955)

> The moral of the Petrovsky article for contemporary leadership prac-
> tices was reinforced by an article in the April issue of *Kommunist*,
> co-authored by editors for Party affairs of *Pravda* and *Kommunist*.

. . . The Party follows strictly the principles of centralism in its organizational structure, in the governing of the state, and in all its work.
The living example of centralism in the direction of our Party is the
Central Committee which, in the period between congresses, directs the
entire ideological, political and organizational life of the Party, guides
the work of the Soviet state and all mass organizations of the working
people. The Central Committee is the brain of the Party, its combat
headquarters; the wisdom of the Party and its tremendous experience is
concentrated in it. . . .

V. I. Lenin often emphasized the significance of collectivity in the
direction of the Party and the state. "It must be emphasized from the
outset in order to avoid all misunderstanding," said V. I. Lenin in the
report of the Central Committee to the 9th Party Congress, "that only
the collegial decisions of the Central Committee adopted in the Orgburo
or the Politburo, or in a plenum of the Central Committee — exclusively
such matters — should be implemented by the secretary of the Central
Committee of the Party. Otherwise the work of the Central Committee
cannot be carried on correctly." . . . (L. Slepov and G. Shitarev,
"Leninist Standards of Party Life and the Principles of Party Leadership," *Kommunist*, No. 6 (April), 1955, pp. 65–66)

> The reader will note that the theme of these two articles is similar to
> that of the Yakovlev piece in July 1953. One can surmise that they also
> had a similarity of purpose.
> The attention given to Leninist standards of leadership raises a ques-
> tion about Stalin's leadership methods. Since Stalin had wielded power
> for so long, and since the top political organs all bore the imprint of his
> tutelage, the question of Stalin's role in Soviet history was inevitably
> connected with the proper forms and methods of leadership. Stalin's
> position posed several serious problems for his heirs. One tactic avail-
> able to a contending leader to buttress his authority was to associate
> himself closely with Stalin's name and Stalin's institutional positions and
> thus claim to be the legitimate inheritor of the old dictator's mantle.
> Malenkov, as we have seen, employed this tactic shortly after Stalin's

death. Later, Khrushchev, as First Secretary, also found occasion to make implicit comparisons between his post and Stalin's. Alternatively, public criticism of Stalin or the "cult of personality" could serve as a weapon against any leader who bid for absolute power. Moreover, because the contenders for power had served under Stalin and, hence, in varying degrees were implicated in his policies, de-Stalinization could become a potential threat to any or all of the leaders depending on who handled the criticism of Stalin and how it was presented (i.e. who was implicated in his deeds). Finally, at a more general level, de-Stalinization created a difficult problem for the Soviet leadership because to criticize him publicly might undercut the legitimacy of the regime and the institutions which he had constructed. As the events of 1956 were to demonstrate, the threat of de-Stalinization to the legitimacy of both the Soviet Union and the world communist movement was a very real one.

As it turned out, the major — though not wholly anticipated — issue which occupied the 20th Party Congress was the place of Stalin in the pantheon of Soviet history. Without tracing in detail, suffice it to say that public mention and praise of Stalin varied from one period to another between March 1953 and the 20th Party Congress. For example, Stalin's birthday on December 21 was publicly ignored in 1953 but celebrated in the press in 1954 and 1955. The entry on Stalin in the *Philosophical Dictionary* published in November 1953 was considerably shorter, and less eulogistic and absurd, than in the 1952 edition. As we have seen, as early as mid-1953, the press condemned the "cult of personality" and "underestimation of the role of the masses" but without mentioning Stalin. Obviously, the activities of Stalin had been examined and discussed behind the scenes if for no other reason than that the rehabilitation of some purge victims in 1955 had inevitably necessitated dredging up his handiwork. Nevertheless, Stalin had not been publicly criticized by name before early 1956.

After an upsurge of attention to Stalin in late 1954 and early 1955, when he was quoted against the consumers' goods program, he was somewhat neglected during most of 1955. His birthday was noted in December 1955, but the official congratulations to Voroshilov on the occasion of his seventy-fifth birthday on February 4, 1956 unexpectedly failed to describe him as a "companion of Stalin," the first time this conventional formula had been omitted. At a conference of historians on January 25–28, 1956, a group of liberal historians — led by E. N. Burdzhalov; an editor of the journal *Questions of History*, and to a lesser

extent by A. M. Pankratova, the editor-in-chief of the same journal —
launched a surprisingly candid attack on Stalinist Party history. Burdzhalov even went so far as to question the validity of the *Short Course on
the History of the VKP(b)*, theretofore the Party bible. A number of
speakers at the conference — especially Party historians — disagreed
with Burdzhalov; but the important point is that even before the Party
Congress convened, it is evident that Stalin's historical status was being
seriously reviewed. There is no firm evidence, however, that a decision
had been made by the time the Congress opened to attack Stalin for his
crimes.

The 20th Party Congress took place between February 14 and February 25. Khrushchev opened the Congress by noting that "in the period
between the 19th and 20th Congresses, we have lost outstanding leaders
of the Communist movement — Joseph Vissarionovich Stalin, Klement
Gottwald and Kyuchi Tokuda. I ask everyone to honor their memory by
standing." Thus, the Congress opened with the name of Stalin; but during the *open* sessions, he was to be mentioned by name only twice more
by Soviet speakers (Khrushchev and Mikoyan). Moreover, although his
memory was honored, the tribute was diluted by mentioning him in the
same breath with secondary figures like Gottwald and Tokuda.

Khrushchev gave the long official report of the Central Committee on
the first day. This comprehensive report set the framework for the subsequent speeches. The following excerpts from Khrushchev's report
were selected to show its major policy pronouncements, several of which
marked new departures and at one time or another may have been
in contention among the leaders. Of special interest are his statements
on the non-inevitability of war, different roads to socialism, the cult of
personality, the role of the Party apparatus, the need for new Party
histories, and still others. The reader should also give note to his
scarcely veiled criticisms of Malenkov and Molotov, his mention of the
Leningrad Case, and the passing reference to Stalin.

The possibility of preventing war in the present era. Millions of
people all over the world are asking whether another war is really inevitable, whether mankind, which has already experienced two devas-
tating world wars, must go through still a third one. Marxists must answer this question, taking into consideration the epoch-making changes
of the last decades.

As we know, there is a Marxist–Leninist precept that wars are inevitable as long as imperialism exists. This thesis was evolved at a time

when (1) imperialism was an all-embracing world system and (2) the social and political forces which did not want war were weak, insufficiently organized, and hence unable to compel the imperialists to renounce war.

People usually take only one aspect of the question; they consider only the economic basis of wars under imperialism. This is not enough. War is not merely an economic phenomenon. Whether there is to be a war or not depends in large measure on the correlation of class, political forces, the degree of organization and the awareness and resolve of the people. In certain conditions, moreover, the struggle waged by progressive social and political forces can play a decisive role. Hitherto the state of affairs was such that the forces that did not want war and came out against it were poorly organized and lacked the means to oppose their will to the schemes of the warmakers. Thus it was before World War I, when the main force fighting the threat of war — the world proletariat — was disorganized by the betrayal by the leaders of the Second International. Thus it was on the eve of World War II, too, when the Soviet Union was the only country pursuing an active peace policy; when the other great powers to all intents and purposes encouraged the aggressors, and the right-wing Social-Democratic leaders had split the workers' movement in the capitalist countries.

For that period, the above-mentioned thesis was absolutely correct. At the present time, however, the situation has changed radically. Now there is a world camp of socialism which has become a mighty force. In this camp the peace forces have not only the moral but also the material means to prevent aggression. There is a large group of other countries, moreover, with a population running into many hundreds of millions, which is actively working to avert war. The workers' movement in the capitalist countries has become a tremendous force today. The movement of peace supporters has sprung up and developed into a powerful factor.

In these circumstances, of course, the Leninist thesis remains valid: As long as imperialism exists, the economic base giving rise to wars will also remain. That is why we must display the greatest vigilance. As long as capitalism survives in the world, reactionary forces, representing the interests of the capitalist monopolies, will continue their drive toward military gambles and aggression and may try to unleash war. But war is not a fatalistic inevitability. Today there are mighty social and political forces possessing formidable means to prevent the imperialists from unleashing war and, if they try to start it, to give a smashing rebuff to the aggressors and frustrate their adventurist plans. For this it is necessary for all anti-war forces to be vigilant and mobilized; they must act as a united front and not relax their efforts in the struggle for peace. The more actively the peoples defend peace, the greater the guarantee that there will be no new war.

Forms of transition to socialism in different countries. In connection with the radical changes in the world arena, new prospects are also opening up in regard to the transition of countries and nations to socialism.

As far back as on the eve of the great October socialist revolution, V. I. Lenin wrote: "All nations will arrive at socialism — this is inevitable — but not all will do so in exactly the same way. Each will contribute something of its own in one or another form of democracy, one or another variety of the dictatorship of the proletariat, one or another rate at which socialist transformations will be effected in the various aspects of social life. There is nothing more primitive from the viewpoint of theory or more ridiculous from that of practice than to paint *this* aspect of the future in a monotonous gray 'in the name of historical materialism.' The result would be nothing more than Suzdal daubing."

Historical experience has fully confirmed this brilliant precept of Lenin's. Now, alongside the Soviet form of reorganizing society on socialist foundations, we have the form of people's democracy.

This form sprang up in Poland, Bulgaria, Czechoslovakia, Albania, and the other European people's democracies and is being employed in conformity with the specific historical social and economic conditions and peculiarities of each of these countries. It has been thoroughly tried and tested for ten years and has fully proved its worth.

Much that is unique in socialist construction is being contributed by the Chinese People's Republic, possessing an economy which was exceedingly backward and bore a semi-feudal and semi-colonial character until the triumph of the revolution. Having taken over the decisive commanding positions, the people's democratic state is pursuing a policy of peaceful reorganization of private industry and trade and their gradual transformation into components of the socialist economy in the course of the socialist revolution.

Leadership of the great cause of socialist reconstruction by the Communist Party of China and the Communist and Workers' Parties of the other people's democracies in keeping with the peculiarities and specific features of each country is creative Marxism in action. In the Federal People's Republic of Yugoslavia, where power belongs to the working people and society is founded on public ownership of the means of production, unique specific forms of economic management and organization of the state apparatus are arising in the process of socialist construction.

It is quite probable that the forms of transition to socialism will become more and more varied; moreover, achieving these forms need not be associated with civil war under all circumstances. Our enemies like to depict us Leninists as advocates of violence always and everywhere. True, we recognize the need for the revolutionary transformation of capitalist society into socialist society. It is this that distinguishes the revolutionary Marxists from the reformists, the opportunists. There is no doubt that in a number of capitalist countries violent overthrow of the dictatorship of the bourgeoisie and the sharp aggravation of class struggle connected with this are inevitable. But the forms of social revolution vary. And it is not true that we regard violence and civil war as the only way to remake society. . . .

It is impossible to manage any sector of socialist construction without a smooth-running, well organized, efficient apparatus closely linked to the people. That is why our Party organizations are required to keep close to the Soviet apparatus, to conduct organizational and ideological work among the broad stratum of workers employed in the various sectors of this apparatus.

In accordance with Lenin's principles of organization of the work of the apparatus, the Party Central Committee and the U.S.S.R. Council of Ministers have carried out important measures in the past two years to simplify this structure, reduce the staffs and improve the work of the administrative and managerial apparatus. As a result of these measures, the administrative–managerial apparatus has been reduced, according to available figures, by almost 750,000. It should be stated that the managerial apparatus is still excessively large, and the state expends enormous sums on its maintenance. Soviet society is interested in having more people working at material production — in plants and factories, in mines and at construction sites, on collective farms, MTS and state farms, wherever national wealth is produced.

It is essential to go on perfecting the administrative and managerial apparatus. This is not a mechanical matter; it should be accompanied by a simplification of the structure of the apparatus, improvement in all its practical activity, strengthening of its ties with the masses, and the enlisting of a broad *aktiv* of workers, collective farmers and intelligentsia in the management of economic and cultural work. Our state apparatus still has a great many superfluous units, duplicating each other's work. Many officials of ministries and departments, instead of occupying themselves with organizing the working masses to carry out Party and government decisions, continue to sit in their offices, killing time in paper work and bureaucratic correspondence. It is necessary to wage the most ruthless struggle against bureaucracy, that intolerable evil that is doing great harm to our common cause. . . .

The Party Central Committee has devoted and is devoting great attention to strengthening socialist justice. Experience shows that enemies of the Soviet state try to use for their own foul subversive activity the slightest weakening of socialist law observance. That is how the Beria gang, which was exposed by the Party, acted: it tried to remove the agencies of state security from the control of the Party and the Soviet regime, to place them above the Party and the government and to create in these agencies an atmosphere of lawlessness and arbitrariness. To serve hostile ends this gang fabricated false charges against honest leading officials and rank-and-file Soviet citizens.

The Central Committee has checked on the so-called "Leningrad case" and discovered that it had been rigged by Beria and his accomplices in order to weaken the Leningrad Party organization and to discredit its cadres. Having established the groundlessness of the "Leningrad case," the Party Central Committee also checked a number of other questionable cases. The Central Committee took measures to restore justice. On the recommendation of the Central Committee, innocent people who had been convicted were rehabilitated.

The Central Committee has drawn important conclusions from all this. Proper control by the Party and the government has been established over the work of the state security agencies. Considerable work has been accomplished toward strengthening the state security agencies, the courts and the prosecutor's office by putting in tested cadres. The supervisory powers of the prosecutor's office have been fully restored and strengthened.

Our Party, state and trade union organizations must vigilantly stand guard over Soviet law observance, unmask and bring into the open anyone who violates socialist law and order and the rights of Soviet citizens, and sternly call a halt to the slightest manifestation of lawlessness and arbitrariness.

It must be stated that, because a number of cases were re-examined and dismissed, some comrades began to show a certain distrust of workers of the state security agencies. This, of course, is incorrect and very harmful. We know that the overwhelming majority of our Chekists consists of honest officials, devoted to our common cause, and we trust them. . . .

Shortly after the 19th Party Congress death took Joseph Vissarionovich Stalin from our ranks. The enemies of socialism counted on the possibility of confusion in the Party ranks, of discord in the Party leadership and of hesitation in its conduct of domestic and foreign policy. Their calculations came to naught. The Communist Party rallied still more closely around its Central Committee and raised still higher the all-conquering banner of Marxism–Leninism.

The imperialists had placed special hopes on their hardened agent Beria, who had perfidiously wormed his way into leading posts in the Party and state. The Central Committee resolutely put an end to the criminal conspiratorial activity of this dangerous enemy and his accomplices. This was a big victory for the Party, a victory for its collective leadership.

The routing of this contemptible band of traitors helped further to strengthen the Party and helped toward successful solution of the problems confronting our country. The Party became still more monolithic. The Party's ideological–political and organizational unity is the guarantee of its invincibility. No enemies and no difficulties are terrifying to the Party when it is united. Any problems are within its power when it acts as a united force, knowing no fear in battle, no hesitation in the conduct of its policy and no retreat in the face of difficulties. Now our Party is united as never before, it is closely rallied around the Central Committee, and it is confidently leading the country along the path indicated by the great Lenin.

The unity of our Party has been built up over the years and decades; it grew and was strengthened in battle with a host of enemies. The Trotskyites, Bukharinites, bourgeois–nationalists and other vicious enemies of the people, men who sought to restore capitalism, tried desperately to undermine the Leninist unity of the Party ranks from within — and all of them smashed their heads against this unity.

Underlying the unity of the Communist Party and its leading core is the moral–political unity of the whole of Soviet society and the firm principles of Marxism–Leninism. People enter our Party not for personal advantage, but for the achievement of a great goal — the building of communism. The leading core of the Party is not a group bound together by personal relationships or mutual advantage, but a businesslike group of leaders whose relations are based on a foundation of principled ideas which permit neither mutual forgiveness nor personal antagonism.

Whenever it was found that one or another leading figure in the Party was making mistakes in his work, the Communist Party Central Committee unanimously took the necessary measures to correct these mistakes. The work of a number of Party organizations and personalities, among them members of the Central Committee, was subjected to Bolshevist criticism at plenary sessions of the Communist Party Central Committee, without regard for personalities. Some officials who failed to justify the high confidence placed in them by the Party were removed from the Central Committee. It is hardly necessary to point out that the unity of the Party did not suffer from this, but only gained. . . .

To further strengthen Party unity and make the Party organizations more active, it was necessary to restore the norms of Party life worked out by Lenin, which had often been violated in the past. It was of cardinal importance to restore and strengthen in every way Lenin's principle of collective leadership. The Party Central Committee tried to set an example in this respect. It is obvious to everyone how much the role of the Central Committee as the collective leader of our Party has grown in the past few years. The Presidium of the Central Committee has become a regularly functioning collective body which keeps within its field of vision all the more important questions of the life of Party and country.

Fighting for utmost development of the creative activity of the Communists and all the working people, the Central Committee took measures to explain widely the Marxist–Leninist view of the role of the individual in history. The Central Committee resolutely condemned the cult of the individual as alien to the spirit of Marxism–Leninism and as turning one or another leader into a miracle-working hero, at the same time belittling the role of the Party and the masses and tending to reduce their creative efforts. The spread of the cult of the individual diminished the role of collective leadership in the Party and sometimes led to serious defects in our work. Our Party anthem, "The Internationale," contains the words: "No one will give us deliverance, neither God, nor Tsar, nor hero! Only by our own hands shall we achieve liberation." These inspired words reflect the correct, the Marxist view of the revolutionary, creative role of the masses — the role of the collective. The people, led by the Party, armed with the Marxist theory, are a great and invincible force, the creators of a new life, the makers of history! . . .

As a result of the measures taken, local Party bodies have somewhat improved organizational work in the leading sectors of industry and agriculture. Their work in managing the economy has become more businesslike, concrete and efficient.

Unfortunately, many Party organizations draw an absurd distinction between Party political work and economic activity. One still meets so-called Party "officials" who consider Party work one thing and economic work and state administration another. One can even hear complaints from such functionaries that they are being diverted from so-called "pure Party work" and compelled to study economics, technology, farming and production.

Such a conception of the tasks of Party work is fundamentally wrong and harmful.

The Communist Party of the Soviet Union is the ruling party and everything that happens on our Soviet soil is of vital interest to the Party as a whole and to each Communist. A Communist has no right to be a detached bystander.

This is why the Party demands that Party cadres not separate Party work from economic work and that they supervise the economy in a concrete and competent manner. This, of course, does not mean confusing the functions of Party bodies with those of economic agencies or the substitution of Party bodies for economic agencies. Such substitution would obliterate personal responsibility and lead to irresponsibility in general. The idea is that Party work should be aimed at organizing and teaching the masses, at improving management of the economy, at constant growth of the socialist economy, at improving the living standard of the Soviet people and raising their cultural level. . . .

During the past 17 years our propaganda was based mainly on the "History of the Communist Party of the Soviet Union (Short Course)." The glorious history of our Party must continue to be one of the most important sources for the education of our cadres. Therefore it is essential to produce a popular Marxist textbook on the history of the Party, based on historical fact, presenting a scientific generalization of the Party's world-historic struggle for communism, and bringing the history up to our day. . . .

The Central Committee has had to correct persons who introduced disorder and confusion into certain clear issues which had been settled by the Party a long time ago. Take, for instance, the question of the building of socialism in the U.S.S.R. and the gradual transition to communism. The speeches of some people contained erroneous formulations, such as the one that so far only a basis for socialism, only the foundation of socialism has been erected in our country.

It is known that by the time the new Constitution of the U.S.S.R. was adopted in 1936 the socialist system had triumphed and been consolidated in all branches of the national economy. This means that a socialist society had been established in the main in our country even then, and since that time it has been developing on the stable basis of socialist production relations. Hence to assert that only the foundations of socialism have been erected in our country would be to disorient the Communists and all Soviet people on a most important issue of our country's long-range development.

Another extreme is sometimes observed in the interpretation of the question of the development of socialism. We also have persons who understood the thesis of the gradual transition from socialism to communism as an appeal for immediate realization of the principles of communist society at the present stage. Some hotheads decided that the building of socialism had already been fully completed and began to draw up a detailed timetable for the transition to communism. On the basis of such utopian views, a negligent attitude to the socialist principle of material incentives began to take root. There appeared unfounded proposals to speed up the substitution of direct barter for Soviet trade. In short, complacency and self-satisfaction began to spread. Some wiseacres began to counterpose light industry to heavy industry, assuring us that preponderant development of heavy industry had been essential only at the early stages of Soviet economic development, that the only task remaining is to speed up the development of light industry.

Understandably, the Party duly rebuffed the attempts to minimize the results achieved in socialist construction and corrected the dreamers and authors of these extravagant projects who disregarded reality and introduced harmful confusion in fundamental questions of development of the socialist economy. . . . (*Pravda*, February 15, 1956)

The first two-thirds of the Congress was devoted to speeches discussing Khrushchev's report. Bulganin delivered the second major report on the five-year plan on February 21 and speeches continued until February 24. The selections printed below, from several of the major speeches, are not intended to give a balanced or comprehensive coverage of the Congress proceedings — which included over 85 speeches — but rather to help the reader understand the relations among the leaders. No speaker contradicted any major point made by Khrushchev. Generally, the primary leaders reaffirmed his statements on non-inevitability of war, the cult of personality, different roads to socialism and others, depending on their major area of administrative responsibilities. However, at the 20th Congress, unlike the 19th where the speeches were stereotyped, there were some noticeable differences in tone and emphasis among the leaders. Kaganovich, for example, seemed more reserved in his criticism of the cult of personality. On the other hand, Pankratova, the editor of *Questions of History*, spoke forcefully about the need for more truthful studies of Soviet history.

Perhaps the most interesting speech was that by Mikoyan, for at several points he went well beyond Khrushchev's position — in condemnation of the cult of personality and its consequences, in advocacy of a more candid view of Western conditions and accomplishments, and in criticism of Stalinist economics and the *Short Course*. His reference to Stalin was the first public criticism by name of the old dictator since his death. His choice of Kossior to illustrate a point of distortion in historical writing — only one of a number of possible examples — is of interest because Kossior was Khrushchev's predecessor as Party boss of the Ukraine until he was purged in 1938.

Mikoyan: The principal feature of the work of the Central Committee and its Presidium in the last three years has been the fact that *after a long interval collective leadership has been established* in our Party.

Our Party now has a strongly welded directing collective, whose strength lies not only in the fact that it is made up of comrades who have worked together in the revolutionary struggle for many years — which is very important, of course — but principally in the fact that this collective, guided by Leninist ideas, the Leninist principles of building up the Party and Party leadership, has in a short period achieved the restoration of Leninist norms of Party life from top to bottom.

For a proletarian Party, a Party of the Leninist type, the principle of collective leadership is elementary. However, this old truth must be emphasized because for about twenty years we had in fact no collective leadership; the cult of the individual flourished — a cult that had been condemned by Marx and later by Lenin — and this, of course, could not fail to have an extremely negative effect on the situation of the Party and on its work. And now that collective leadership has been restored to the Communist Party in the last three years, on the basis of Leninist adherence to principle and Leninist unity, all the fruitful influence of

Lenin's methods of leadership is felt. Herein lies the chief source of the new strength that has been given to our Party in recent years. This has been the vital prerequisite of the successes Comrade Khrushchev refers to in his report and the guarantee that the Party will advance still more confidently, still more successfully along the path of the building of communism. . . .

To speak objectively, part of the blame for the unsatisfactory state of ideological work must be attributed to the atmosphere that surrounded scientific and ideological work during a number of past years. But it cannot be denied that part of the blame for our serious lag on the ideological front devolves, too, upon the workers on this front themselves.

Unfortunately, very little recourse was had in our country in the past fifteen or twenty years to the treasury of Leninist ideas for understanding and explaining the phenomena both of our country's internal life and of the international situation. Naturally, this was not because Lenin's ideas had become obsolete or were inadequate for an understanding of the contemporary setting. . . .

None of us can fail to be interested in the question of capitalism's present position, the question of whether capitalism is capable of developing at all in its period of decay and general crisis. Are technical progress and increased production possible today and tomorrow in capitalist countries?

The theory of capitalism's complete stagnation is alien to Marxism–Leninism. It cannot be held that capitalism's general crisis leads to a cessation of production growth and technical progress in capitalist countries.

Stalin's well-known pronouncement in "Economic Problems of Socialism in the U.S.S.R." concerning the U.S.A., Britain and France, to the effect that after the world market had been split up "the volume of production in these countries will contract," can hardly help us in our analysis of the condition of the economy of contemporary capitalism and is hardly correct. This assertion does not explain the complex and contradictory phenomena of contemporary capitalism and the fact that capitalist production has grown in many countries since the war.

As the Central Committee's report stated in this connection, Lenin, after giving a brilliant exposition of the logical characteristics of imperialism in his 1916 book on imperialism, pointed out that the decay of capitalism does not preclude a rapid growth of production, that individual branches of industry, and individual countries display now one, now another tendency with greater or lesser force in the epoch of imperialism.

All the facts indicate that no part of these Leninist tenets can be considered obsolete.

Incidentally, if certain other tenets in the "Economic Problems" are strictly scrutinized, it is impossible not to notice that they also need deep study and critical revision by our economists from the point of view of Marxism–Leninism.

The course of history indicates that in the present stage of imperialism, too, all Marxism–Leninism's basic tenets are invariably confirmed. But this general assertion is not enough. We must study specifically when, where, to what degree and how this takes place.

We are seriously lagging in the study of capitalism's contemporary stage; we do not study facts and figures deeply; we often restrict ourselves for agitation purposes to individual facts about the symptoms of an approaching crisis or about the impoverishment of the working people, rather than making an all-round and profound evaluation of the phenomena of life abroad. . . .

The Central Committee's report speaks out plainly on the unsatisfactory state of our *propaganda work*. A principal reason for this is that as a rule we still study Marxism–Leninism solely from the "Short Course" on the history of the Party. This is wrong, of course. The theme of our Party's history cannot accommodate in its restricted framework the wealth of ideas of Marxism–Leninism, and this is even more true of the "Short Course." What is needed is special theoretical textbooks, written for comrades at different levels of training. This is the first requirement. Secondly, we cannot be satisfied with the existing "Short Course" on the Party's history, if only because it fails to illuminate the events of almost the last twenty years of our Party's life. Is there any real justification for our lack of a comprehensive history of the Party over the last two decades?

Furthermore, if our *historians* were to make a genuine and profound study of the facts and events in the history of our Party in the Soviet period — including those that the "Short Course" deals with — if they were to delve properly into the archives and historical documents, and not only into the back issues of newspapers, they would be able to give a better explanation, from the positions of Leninism, of many of the facts and events dealt with in the "Short Course."

Another question. Is it normal that although almost 40 years have passed since October, we have neither a short nor a comprehensive

Marxist–Leninist textbook on the history of the October revolution and of the Soviet state, one that presents without embellishment not only the façade but the whole many-sided life of the Soviet fatherland? . . .

After all, until quite recently books were in vogue in our country on the history of such major Party organizations as those of Transcaucasia and Baku that stretched the facts, that arbitrarily exalted some people and failed even to mention others; indeed, these books were set up as incontrovertible standards. They exaggerated secondary events and belittled other, more important events, and they underestimated the guiding and directing role of the prerevolutionary Leninist Central Committee of the Bolshevist Party.

We also still lack genuine Marxist books on the Civil War. A number of published books have grave shortcomings and lack scholarly value, and some of them are actually capable of playing a negative role.

Certain complex and contradictory events of the 1918–1920 Civil War are explained by some historians not as changes in the correlations of class forces at a specific period of time but as alleged sabotage by some of the Party leaders of the time, who were wrongly declared enemies of the people many years after the events described.

One Moscow historian went so far as to make the following claim: Had Comrade Antonov-Ovseyenko and Comrade Kossior not been among the Ukraine Party leaders, Makhnoism and Grigoryevism might not have arisen, Petlyura might not have enjoyed his periods of success, there might have been no enthusiasm for implanting communes (which, by the way, was not merely a Ukrainian phenomenon but was common to the Party at the time) and, don't you see, the Ukraine would have straightway adopted the line to which the entire Party and country switched as a result of NEP. . . .

Comrades! The report testifies to the great work done by the Central Committee, by the entire Communist Party, by all our Soviet people between the 19th and the 20th Party Congresses. It loudly proclaims that we are on the right road in the great work of communist construction.

The Central Committee, basing itself on collective leadership and the unity of the Communist Party, has boldly unmasked the errors and shortcomings that had accumulated in past years and has resolutely set out to rectify and eliminate them in all fields of political activity and in economic, cultural and internal Party construction. Herein lies the truly Leninist feature of our Central Committee's work.

It would be no exaggeration to say that the 20th Party Congress is the most important Congress in the history of our Party since Lenin. *The Leninist spirit and Leninism permeate all our work and all our decisions,* just as if Lenin were alive and with us. . . . (*Pravda,* February 18, 1956)

Kaganovich: The period under review was a complex and difficult one in the life of our Party and country.

It must be recalled that soon after the 19th Congress the enemies of the USSR, the enemies of communism, the enemies of peace, built crafty calculations on expectations of a crisis within our Party and its leadership and discord between the working class and peasantry and among the peoples of our multinational state.

Now all the world can see how miserably — and for the nth time! — both the bosses and the fortunetellers of imperialism have failed. . . .

After the 19th Party Congress, the Central Committee boldly (I have in mind boldness of ideology, principle and theory) raised the question of the struggle against the cult of the individual. This is not an easy question. But the Central Committee gave the correct, Marxist–Leninist, Party answer to it. The cult of the individual is a harmful cult; it belittles the masses, the Party and its leading cadres.

The exposure of the cult of the individual, the correct Marxist–Leninist concept of the role of the masses, the role of the Party and its leading cadres and the role of the leaders, is of exceptional importance for strengthening the Party's unity. The struggle against the cult of the individual has proved to be a most important factor in the formation and consolidation of the collective leadership of our Party.

Collective leadership of the Party guarantees correct leadership, thorough and deep analysis and Leninist solution of the most important problems in the life of the Party and state.

The most important thing is that the Party's collective leadership is united and consolidated on a Party, principled, Marxist–Leninist basis. . . . (*Pravda*, February 21, 1956)

Pankratova: . . . The Central Committee's instructions on the need to combat the survivals of the subjectivist–idealist views on the role of the individual in history have played and still play a very important role in developing the Party's ideological work and in the ideological and political training of our cadres. We know that the Marxist–Leninist classics viewed the cult of the individual as a serious and harmful deviation from the materialist concept of history, as one of the widespread forms of idealism. The theory of "heroes and the crowd" means belittling the creative role of the masses.

The Central Committee, carying out Lenin's injunctions on the decisive role of the masses as the true maker and motive force of history, has naturally demanded a struggle against the cult of the individual. It must be said outright that we Communists, whom the Party has entrusted with ideological work, are far from keeping up with the Central Committee's very important instructions. The serious lag in the development of the social sciences must be admitted. . . .

Immense satisfaction greeted the injunction by Comrade N. S. Khrushchev in the Party Central Committee report that concrete facts should be studied well, that truthful evaluations should be made without embellishment and glossing over, that all our ideological work should develop on a high theoretical level, in vigorous struggle against dogmatism and pedantry. Untruthful elucidation of historical reality can prevent our cadres and our friends abroad from making proper use of the priceless experience of the struggle of the Communist Party of the Soviet Union. Unfortunately, we are not waging a consistent and vigorous struggle against deviation from the Leninist appraisal of historical events, against elements of antihistoricism and oversimplification, against the subjectivist approach to history, against the modernization of history and turning facts to suit the current situation. . . . (*Pravda*, February 22, 1956)

At the conclusion of the early session on the 24th, it was announced that at 6 P.M. there would be a closed evening meeting of the Congress, limited to Soviet delegates. The stenographic report of the Congress, however, indicates that this closed meeting (at which Khrushchev delivered his "Secret Speech") was not held until February 25. Western reports indicate that this closed session convened around midnight.

Khrushchev's Secret Speech has never been published in the Soviet Union. On June 4, 1956, the United States Department of State released a text of the speech which it had somehow obtained. Although the State Department did not vouch for its authenticity, there is little reason to doubt that it is genuine. It was accepted as authentic by Communist Parties everywhere and the Soviets never claimed it was fabricated. Moreover, material presented at the 22nd Party Congress in October 1961 supports the authenticity of the Secret Speech.

Western specialists have disagreed on a number of questions relating to the Secret Speech. Was it prepared well in advance, or only at the last minute? Who authorized it and when? Was it approved just as Khrushchev delivered it, or did the authorizing body merely approve it in general terms? There is substantial agreement, however, that Khrushchev used the occasion to advance his own fortunes. He subtly linked his rivals with Stalin's errors while defending his own innocence. In reading the speech, it is interesting to observe which of Stalin's major policies are explicitly approved and which condemned; and to recall important actions of Stalin, particularly in foreign affairs, about which the Secret Speech, as we have it, is silent. This speech is a highly significant document from a number of perspectives. It reveals much about the political conditions under Stalin. Khrushchev's efforts to explain how the Stalinist cult came about and why he and his colleagues were unable to control Stalin are important in their own right. For our purposes, however, of special interest are the ramifications of the speech for the leadership struggle. The reader should notice carefully the contexts in which Khrushchev refers to himself and the other top leaders; and how he obviously attempts to link himself with Lenin's style of leadership. The repeated, almost self-conscious, assertions that the secret police and Stalin were responsible for the death of Kossior are particularly noteworthy, especially after Mikoyan's reference to Kossior eight days before. Khrushchev's description of Stalin's talents as a military chief and strategist and his praise for Marshal Zhukov suggest he was playing up to the military. Careful reading of the following portions of the Secret Speech may yield yet other clues to the course of elite politics in early 1956.

Comrades! In the report of the Central Committee of the Party at the Twentieth Congress, in a number of speeches by delegates to the Congress, as also earlier during the plenary sessions of the Party Central Committee, quite a lot has been said about the cult of the individual and about its harmful consequences.

After Stalin's death the Party Central Committee began to implement a policy of explaining concisely and consistently that it is impermissible and foreign to the spirit of Marxism–Leninism to elevate one person, to transform him into a superman possessing supernatural characteristics akin to those of a god. Such a man supposedly knows everything, sees everything, thinks for everyone, can do anything, is infallible in his behavior.

Such a belief about a man, and specifically about Stalin, was cultivated among us for many years.

The objective of the present report is not a thorough evaluation of Stalin's life and activity. Concerning Stalin's merits an entirely sufficient number of books, pamphlets and studies had already been written in his lifetime. The role of Stalin in the preparation and execution of the Socialist Revolution, in the Civil War, and in the fight for the construction of Socialism in our country is universally known. Everyone knows this well. At present we are concerned with a question which has immense importance for the Party now and for the future — with how the cult of the person of Stalin has been gradually growing, the cult which became at a certain specific stage the source of a whole series of exceedingly serious and grave perversions of Party principles, of Party democracy, of revolutionary legality.

Because not all as yet realize fully the practical consequences resulting from the cult of the individual leader, the great harm caused by the violation of the principle of collective direction of the Party, and because immense and limitless power was gathered in the hands of one person, the Party Central Committee considers it absolutely necessary to make the material pertaining to this matter available to the 20th Congress of the Communist Party of the Soviet Union. . . .

During Lenin's life the Party Central Committee was a real expression of collective leadership of the Party and the country. Being a militant Marxist revolutionist, always unyielding in matters of principle, Lenin never imposed by force his views upon his co-workers. He tried to persuade; he patiently explained his opinions to others. Lenin always diligently saw to it that the norms of Party life were realized, that the Party Statutes were enforced, that the Party Congresses and Central Committee plenary sessions took place at the proper intervals.

In addition to V. I. Lenin's great accomplishments for the victory of the working class and working peasants, for the victory of our Party and for the application of the ideas of scientific communism to life, his keen mind expressed itself also in that he detected in Stalin in time those negative characteristics which resulted later in grave consequences. Fearing the future destiny of the Party and of the Soviet country, V. I. Lenin gave a quite correct characterization of Stalin, pointing out that it was necessary to consider the question of transferring Stalin from the position of Secretary-General because Stalin was excessively rude, did not have a proper attitude toward his comrades, was capricious and abused his power. . . .

Stalin acted not through persuasion, explanation and patient cooperation with people, but by imposing his concepts and demanding absolute submission to his opinion. Whoever opposed this concept or tried to prove his viewpoint and the correctness of his position was doomed to removal from the leading collective and to subsequent moral and physical annihilation. This was especially true during the period following the 17th Party Congress, when many prominent Party leaders and rank-and-file Party workers, honest and dedicated to the cause of communism, fell victim to Stalin's despotism.

We must affirm that the Party fought a serious fight against the Trotskyites, rightists and bourgeois–nationalists, and that it disarmed ideologically all the enemies of Leninism. This ideological fight was carried on successfully, and as a result the Party was strengthened and tempered. Here Stalin played a positive role.

The Party led a great political ideological struggle against those in its own ranks who proposed anti-Leninist theses, who represented a political line hostile to the Party and to the cause of socialism. This was a stubborn and a difficult fight but a necessary one, because the political line of both the Trotskyite–Zinovievite bloc and of the Bukharinites led actually toward the restoration of capitalism and capitulation to the world bourgeoisie. Let us consider for a moment what would have happened if in 1928–1929 the political line of right deviation had prevailed among us, or orientation toward "cotton-dress industrialization," or toward the kulak, etc. We would not now have a powerful heavy industry, we would not have the collective farms, we would find ourselves disarmed and weak in a capitalist encirclement.

It was for this reason that the Party led an inexorable ideological fight and explained to all Party members and to the non-Party masses the harm and the danger of the anti-Leninist proposals of the Trotskyite opposition and the rightist opportunists. And this great work of explaining the Party line bore fruit; both the Trotskyites and the rightist opportunists were politically isolated; the overwhelming Party majority supported the Leninist line and the Party was able to awaken and organize the working masses to apply the Leninist Party line and to build socialism.

Worth noting is the fact that even during the progress of the furious ideological fight against the Trotskyites, the Zinovievites, the Bukharinites and others, extreme repressive measures were not used against them. The fight was on ideological grounds. But some years later, when socialism in our country had been fundamentally established, when the exploiting classes had been generally liquidated, when the Soviet social structure had radically changed, when the social base for political movements and groups hostile to the Party had shrunk sharply, when the ideological opponents of the Party had long since been defeated politically, then the repression directed against them began.

It was precisely during this period (1935–1937–1938) that the practice of mass repression through the state apparatus was born, first against the enemies of Leninism — Trotskyites, Zinovievites, Bukharinites, long since politically defeated by the Party — and subsequently also against many honest Communists, against those Party cadres which had borne the heavy burden of the Civil War and the first and most difficult years of industrialization and collectivization, which had fought actively against the Trotskyites and the rightists for the Leninist party line.

Stalin originated the concept "enemy of the people." This term automatically rendered it unnecessary that the ideological errors of a man or men engaged in a controversy be proved; this term made possible the use of the most cruel repression, violating all norms of revolutionary legality, against anyone who in any way disagreed with Stalin, against those who were only suspected of hostile intent, against those who had bad reputations. This concept, "enemy of the people," actually eliminated the possibility of any kind of ideological fight or the making of one's views known on this or that issue, even issues of a practical nature. In the main, and in actuality, the only proof of guilt used, contrary to all norms of current law, was the "confession" of the accused himself; and, as subsequent investigation has proved, "confessions" were obtained through physical pressures against the accused. . . .

Arbitrary behavior by one person encouraged and permitted arbitrariness in others. Mass arrests and deportations of many thousands of people, execution without trial and without normal investigation created conditions of insecurity, fear and even desperation.

This, of course, did not contribute toward unity of the Party ranks and of all strata of the working people, but, on the contrary, brought about annihilation and the expulsion from the Party of workers who were loyal but inconvenient to Stalin. . . .

Lenin used severe methods only in the most necessary cases, when the exploiting classes were still in existence and were vigorously opposing the revolution, when the struggle for survival was decidedly assuming the sharpest forms, even including a civil war.

Stalin, on the other hand, used extreme methods and mass repressions at a time when the revolution was already victorious, when the Soviet state was strengthened, when the exploiting classes were already liquidated and socialist relations were rooted solidly in all phases of national economy, when our party was politically consolidated and had strengthened itself both numerically and ideologically. It is clear that here Stalin showed in a whole series of cases his intolerance, his brutality and his abuse of power. Instead of proving his political correctness and mobilizing the masses, he often chose the path of repression and physical annihilation, not only against actual enemies, but also against individuals who had not committed any crimes against the Party and the Soviet government. Here we see no wisdom but only a demonstration of the brutal force which had once so alarmed V. I. Lenin.

Lately, especially after the unmasking of the Beria gang, the Central Committee has looked into a series of cases fabricated by this gang. This disclosed a very ugly picture of brutal willfulness connected with the incorrect behavior of Stalin. As facts prove, Stalin, using his unlimited power, allowed himself many abuses. He acted in the name of the Central Committee, not asking for the opinion of the Committee members or even of the members of the Central Committee's Political Bureau; often he did not inform them about his personal decisions concerning very important Party and government matters. . . .

During the first few years after Lenin's death Party Congresses and Central Committee plenary sessions took place more or less regularly, but later, when Stalin began increasingly to abuse his power, these principles were brutally violated. This was especially evident during the last 15 years of his life. Was it a normal situation when 13 years elapsed between the 18th and 19th Party Congresses, years during which our Party and our country experienced so many important events? These events demanded categorically that the Party should have adopted decisions pertaining to the country's defense during the patriotic war [World War II] and to peacetime construction after the war. Even after the end of the war a Congress was not convened for more than seven years.

Central Committee plenary sessions were hardly ever called. Suffice it to mention that during all the years of the patriotic war not a single Central Committee plenary session took place. It is true that there was an attempt to call a Central Committee plenary session in October 1941, when Central Committee members from the whole country were called to Moscow. They waited two days for the opening of the plenary session, but in vain. Stalin did not even want to meet and to talk to the Central Committee members. This fact shows how demoralized Stalin was in the first months of the war and how haughtily and disdainfully he treated the Central Committee members. . . .

Having numerous data showing brutal willfulness toward Party cadres, the Central Committee created a Party commission under the control of the Central Committee Presidium; it was charged with investi-gating what had made possible the mass repressions against the majority of the Central Committee's members and candidates elected at the 17th Congress of the All-Union Communist Party (Bolsheviks).

The commission has familiarized itself with a large amount of ma-terials in the NKVD archives and with other documents and has estab-lished many facts pertaining to the fabrication of cases against Commu-nists, to false accusations, to glaring abuses of socialist legality which resulted in the death of innocent people. It became apparent that many Party, Soviet and economic activists who were branded in 1937–1938 as "enemies" were actually never enemies, spies, wreckers, etc., but were always honest Communists; they were only so stigmatized, and often, no longer able to bear barbaric tortures, they charged themselves (at the order of the investigating judges — falsifiers) with all kinds of grave and unlikely crimes. The commission has presented to the Central Committee Presidium lengthy and documented materials pertaining to mass repressions against delegates to the 17th Party Congress and against members of the Central Committee elected at that Congress. These materials have been studied by the Central Committee Presidium.

It was determined that of the 139 members and candidates of the Party Central Committee who were elected at the 17th Congress, 98 persons, i.e., 70 per cent, were arrested and shot (mostly in 1937–1938). . . .

The same fate befell not only the Central Committee members but also the majority of the delegates to the 17th Party Congress. Of 1966 delegates with either voting or advisory powers, 1108 persons were arrested on charges of counterrevolutionary crimes, i.e., decidedly more than a majority. This very fact shows how absurd, wild and contrary to common sense were the charges of counterrevolutionary crimes made, as we now see, against a majority of the participants in the 17th Party Congress. . . .

What is the reason that mass repressions against activists increased more and more after the 17th Party Congress? It was because at that time Stalin had so elevated himself above the Party and above the na-tion that he ceased to consider either the Central Committee or the Party. While he still reckoned with the opinion of the collective before the 17th Congress, Stalin in even greater measure ceased to reckon with the views of the members of the Party's Central Committee and even the members of the Political Bureau after the complete political liquidation of the Trotskyites, Zinovievites and Bukharinites, when the Party had achieved unity as a result of that fight and socialist victories. Stalin thought that now he could decide all things alone and all he needed were statisticians; he treated all others in such a way that they could only listen to and praise him. . . .

Mass repressions grew tremendously from the end of 1936 after a telegram from Stalin and Zhdanov, dated from Sochi Sept. 25, 1936, was addressed to Kaganovich, Molotov and other members of the Political Bureau. The content of the telegram was as follows:

"We deem it absolutely necessary and urgent that Comrade Yezhov be nominated to the post of People's Commissar for Internal Affairs. Yagoda has definitely proved himself to be incapable of unmasking the Trotskyite–Zinovievite bloc. The OGPU is four years behind in this matter. This is noted by all Party workers and by the majority of the representatives of the NKVD." Strictly speaking we should stress that Stalin did not meet with and therefore could not know the opinion of Party workers. . . .

The majority of the Central Committee members and candidates elected at the 17th Congress and arrested in 1937–1938 were expelled from the Party illegally through gross violation of the Party Statutes, since the question of their expulsion was never studied at a Central Committee plenary session.

Now when the cases of some of these so-called "spies" and "saboteurs" were examined it was found that all their cases were fabricated. Confessions of guilt of many arrested and charged with enemy activity were gained with the help of cruel and inhuman tortures.

At the same time Stalin, as we have been informed by members of the Political Bureau of that time, did not show them the statements of many accused political activists who retracted their confessions before the military tribunal and asked for an objective examination of their cases. There were many such declarations, and Stalin doubtless knew of them.

The Central Committee considers it absolutely necessary to inform the Congress of many such fabricated "cases" against the members of the Party Central Committee elected at the 17th Party Congress. . . .

The way in which the former NKVD workers manufactured various fictitious "anti-Soviet centers" and "blocs" with the help of provocatory methods is seen from the confession of Comrade Rozenblum, Party member since 1906, who was arrested in 1937 by the Leningrad NKVD.

During the examination in 1955 of the Komarov case Rozenblum revealed the following fact: When Rozenblum was arrested in 1937 he was subjected to terrible torture, during which he was ordered to confess false information concerning himself and other persons. He was then brought to the office of Zakovsky, who offered him freedom on condition that he make before the court a false confession fabricated in 1937 by the NKVD concerning "sabotage, espionage and diversion in a terroristic center in Leningrad." With unbelievable cynicism Zakovsky told about the vile "mechanism" for the crafty creation of fabricated "anti-Soviet plots."

"In order to illustrate it to me," stated Rozenblum, "Zakovsky gave me several possible variants of the organization of this center and of its branches. After he detailed the organization to me, Zakovsky told me that the NKVD would prepare the case of this center, remarking that the trial would be public.

"Before the court were to be brought four or five members of this center: Chudov, Ugarov, Smorodin, Pozern, Shaposhnikova (Chudov's wife) and others, together with two or three members from the branches of this center. . . .

"The case of the Leningrad center has to be built solidly and for this reason witnesses are needed. Social origin (of course, in the past) and the Party standing of the witness will play more than a small role.

"You yourself," said Zakovsky, "will not need to invent anything. The NKVD will prepare for you a ready outline for every branch of the center; you will have to study it carefully and to remember well all questions and answers which the court might ask. This case will be ready in four or five months or perhaps a half year. During all this time you will be preparing yourself so that you will not compromise the investigation and yourself. Your future will depend on how the trial goes and on its results. If you begin to lie and to testify falsely, blame yourself. If you manage to endure it, you will save your head and we will feed and clothe you at the government's cost until your death."

This is the kind of vile thing which was then practiced. . . .

Many thousands of honest and innocent Communists have died as a result of this monstrous falsification of such "cases," as a result of the practice of forcing accusations against oneself and others. In the same manner were fabricated the "cases" against eminent Party and State workers — Kossior, Chubar, Postyshev, Kosarev, and others. . . .

The vicious practice was condoned of having the NKVD prepare lists of persons whose cases were under the jurisdiction of the Military

Collegium and whose sentences were prepared in advance. Yezhov would send these lists to Stalin personally for his approval of the proposed punishment. In 1937–1938, 383 such lists, containing the names of many thousands of Party, Soviet, Young Communist League, army and economic workers were sent to Stalin. He approved these lists.

A large part of these cases are being reviewed now and a great part of them are being voided because they were baseless and falsified. Suffice it to say that from 1954 to the present time the Military Collegium of the Supreme Court has rehabilitated 7679 persons, many of whom were rehabilitated posthumously. . . .

We justly accuse Yezhov of the degenerate practices of 1937. But we have to answer these questions: Could Yezhov have arrested Kossior, for instance, without the knowledge of Stalin? Was there an exchange of opinions or a Political Bureau decision concerning this? No, there was not, as there was none regarding other cases of this type. Could Yezhov have decided such important matters as the fate of such eminent Party figures? No, it would be a display of naïveté to consider this the work of Yezhov alone. It is clear that these matters were decided by Stalin, and that without his orders and his sanction Yezhov could not have done this.

We have examined the cases and have rehabilitated Kossior, Rudzutak, Postyshev, Kosarev and others. For what causes were they arrested and sentenced? The review of evidence shows that there was no reason for this. They, like many others, were arrested without the prosecutor's knowledge. In such a situation there is no need for any sanction, for what sort of sanction could there be when Stalin decided everything? He was the chief prosecutor in these cases. Stalin not only agreed to, but on his own initiative issued arrest orders. We must say this so that the delegates to the Congress can clearly understand and themselves assess this and draw the proper conclusions.

Facts prove that many abuses were committed on Stalin's orders without reckoning with any norms of Party and Soviet legality. Stalin was a very distrustful man, sickly suspicious; we knew this from our work with him. He could look at a man and say: "Why are your eyes so shifty today?" or "Why are you turning so much today and avoiding looking me directly in the eyes?" The sickly suspicion created in him a general distrust even toward eminent Party workers whom he had known for years. Everywhere and in everything he saw "enemies," "double-dealers" and "spies."

Possessing unlimited power, he indulged in great willfulness and strangled a person morally and physically. A situation was created in which one could not express one's own will.

When Stalin said that one or another should be arrested, it was necessary to accept on faith that he was an "enemy of the people." Meanwhile, Beria's gang, which ran the organs of state security, outdid itself in proving the guilt of the arrested and the truth of materials which it had falsified. And what proofs were offered? The confessions of the arrested, and the investigative judges accepted these "confessions." And how is it possible that a person confesses to crimes which he has not committed? Only in one way — because of application of physical methods of pressuring him, tortures, bringing him to a state of unconsciousness, depriving him of his judgment, taking away his human dignity. In this manner were "confessions" acquired. . . .

Not long ago, only several days before the present Congress, we summoned to the Central Committee Presidium session and interrogated the investigative judge Rodos, who in his time investigated and interrogated Kossior, Chubar and Kosarev. He is a vile person with a bird brain, and morally completely degenerate. And it was this man who decided the fate of prominent Party workers; he made judgments also concerning the politics in these matters, because, having established their "crime," he provided therewith materials from which important political implications could be drawn.

The question arises whether a man with such an intellect could alone conduct the investigation in a manner to prove the guilt of people such as Kossior and others. No, he could not have done it without proper directives. At the Central Committee Presidium session he told us: "I was told that Kossior and Chubar were enemies of the people and for this reason I, as an investigative judge, had to make them confess that they were enemies."

He could do this only through long tortures, which he did, receiving detailed instructions from Beria. We must say that at the Central Committee Presidium session he cynically declared: "I thought that I was executing the orders of the Party." In this manner Stalin's orders concerning the use of methods of physical pressure against the arrested were in practice executed. . . .

During the war and after the war Stalin put forward the thesis that the tragedy which our nation experienced in the first part of the war was the result of the "unexpected" attack of the Germans against the Soviet Union. But, comrades, this is completely untrue. As soon as Hitler came to power in Germany he undertook the task of liquidating communism.

The fascists said this openly; they did not hide their plans. To attain this aggressive end all sorts of pacts and blocs were created, such as the famous Berlin-Rome-Tokyo Axis. Many facts from the prewar period clearly showed that Hitler was going all out to begin a war against the Soviet state and that he had concentrated large armed units, together with armored units, near the Soviet borders.

Documents which have now been published show that by April 3, 1941, Churchill, through his Ambassador to the USSR, Cripps, personally warned Stalin that the Germans had begun regrouping their armed units with the intent of attacking the Soviet Union. It is self-evident that Churchill did not do this at all because of his friendly feeling toward the Soviet nation. He had in this his own imperialist goals — to bring Germany and the USSR into a bloody war and thereby to strengthen the position of the British Empire. Just the same, Churchill affirmed in his writings that he sought to "warn Stalin and call his attention to the danger which threatened him." Churchill stressed this repeatedly in his dispatches of April 18 and in the following days. However, Stalin took no heed of these warnings. What is more, Stalin ordered that no credence be given to information of this sort, in order not to provoke the initiation of military operations.

We must state that information of this sort concerning the threat of German armed invasion of Soviet territory came in also from our own military and diplomatic sources; however, because the leadership was conditioned against such information, such data were dispatched with fear and assessed with reservation. . . .

Had our industry been mobilized properly and in time to supply the army with the necessary matériel, our wartime losses would have been decidedly smaller. Such mobilization had not been, however, started in time. And already in the first days of the war it became evident that our army was badly armed, that we did not have enough artillery, tanks and planes to throw the enemy back.

Soviet science and technology produced excellent models of tanks and artillery pieces before the war. But mass production of all this was not organized and as a matter of fact we started to modernize our military equipment only on the eve of the war. As a result, at the time of the enemy's invasion of the Soviet land we did not have sufficient quantities either of old machinery which was no longer used for armament production or of new machinery which we had planned to introduce into armament production. The situation with antiaircraft artillery was especially bad; we did not organize the production of antitank ammunition.

Many fortified regions had proved to be indefensible as soon as they were attacked because the old arms had been withdrawn and new ones were not yet available there.

This pertained, alas, not only to tanks, artillery and planes. At the outbreak of the war we did not even have sufficient rifles to arm the mobilized manpower. I recall that in those days I telephoned to Comrade Malenkov from Kiev and told him, "People have volunteered for the new army and demand arms. You must send us arms."

Malenkov answered me, "We cannot send you arms. We are sending all our rifles to Leningrad, and you will have to arm yourselves." . . .

Very grievous consequences, especially in reference to the beginning of the war, ensued from Stalin's annihilation of many military commanders and political workers in 1937–1941 because of his suspiciousness and through slanderous accusations. During these years repressions were instituted against certain parts of the military cadres, beginning literally at the company and battalion commander level and extending to the higher military centers; during this time the cadre of leaders who had gained military experience in Spain and in the Far East was almost completely liquidated.

The policy of large-scale repressions against the military cadres led also to undermined military discipline, because for several years officers of all ranks and even soldiers in the Party and Young Communist League cells were taught to "unmask" their superiors as hidden enemies. . . .

It would be incorrect to forget that after the first severe disaster and defeats at the front Stalin thought that this was the end. In one of his speeches in those days he said: "All that Lenin created we have lost forever."

After this, Stalin for a long time actually did not direct the military operations and ceased to do anything whatever. He returned to active leadership only when some members of the Political Bureau visited him and told him that it was necessary to take certain steps immediately in order to improve the situation at the front.

Therefore, the threatening danger which hung over our motherland in the first period of the war was largely due to the faulty methods of directing the nation and the Party by Stalin himself. . . .

When there developed an exceptionally serious situation for our army in the Kharkov region in 1942, we correctly decided to drop an operation whose objective was to encircle Kharkov, because the actual situation at that time would have threatened our army with fatal consequences if this operation were continued.

We communicated this to Stalin, stating that the situation demanded changes in operational plans so that the enemy would be prevented from liquidating a sizable concentration of our army.

Contrary to common sense, Stalin rejected our suggestion and issued the order to continue the operation aimed at the encirclement of Kharkov, despite the fact that at this time many army concentrations were themselves actually threatened with encirclement and liquidation.

I telephoned to Vasilevsky and begged him, "Alexander Mikhailovich, take a map" (Vasilevsky is present here) "and show Comrade Stalin the situation which has developed." We should note that Stalin planned operations on a globe. Yes, comrades, he used to take the globe and trace the front line on it. I said to Comrade Vasilevsky: "Show him the situation on a map; in the present situation we cannot continue the operation which was planned. The old decision must be changed for the good of the cause."

Vasilevsky replied that Stalin had already studied this problem and that he, Vasilevsky, would not see Stalin further concerning this matter because the latter did not want to hear any arguments on the subject of this operation.

After my talk with Vasilevsky I telephoned to Stalin at his villa. But Stalin did not answer the telephone and Malenkov was at the receiver. I told Comrade Malenkov that I was calling from the front and that I wanted to speak personally to Stalin. Stalin informed me through Malenkov that I should speak with Malenkov. I stated for the second time that I wished to inform Stalin personally about the grave situation which had arisen for us at the front. But Stalin did not consider it convenient to raise the phone and again stated that I should speak to him through Malenkov, although he was only a few steps from the telephone.

After "listening" in this manner to our plea, Stalin said, "Let everything remain as it is!"

And what was the result of this? The worst that we had expected. The Germans surrounded our army concentrations, and consequently we lost hundreds of thousands of our soldiers. This is Stalin's military "genius"; this is what it cost us.

On one occasion after the war, during a meeting of Stalin with members of the Political Bureau, Anastas Ivanovich Mikoyan mentioned that Khrushchev must have been right when he telephoned concerning the Kharkov operation and that it was unfortunate that his suggestion had not been accepted.

You should have seen Stalin's fury! How could it be admitted that he, Stalin, had not been right! He is, after all, a "genius," and a genius cannot help but be right! Everyone can err, but Stalin considered that he never erred, that he was always right. He never acknowledged to any-one that he made any mistake, large or small, despite the fact that he made not a few mistakes both in the matter of theory and in his practical activity. After the Party Congress we shall probably have to re-evaluate many wartime military operations and to present them in their true light. . . .

All the more shameful was the fact that after our great victory over the enemy, which cost us so much, Stalin began to downgrade many of the commanders who had contributed so much to the victory over the enemy, because Stalin excluded every possibility that services rendered at the front should be credited to anyone but himself.

Stalin was very much interested in the assessment of Comrade Zhukov as a military leader. He asked me often for my opinion of Zhu-kov. I told him then, "I have known Zhukov for a long time; he is a good general and a good military leader."

After the war Stalin began to relate all kinds of nonsense about Zhukov, among other things the following: "You praised Zhukov, but he does not deserve it. It is said that before each operation at the front Zhukov used to behave as follows: He used to take a handful of earth, smell it and say, 'We can begin the attack,' or the opposite, 'The planned operation cannot be carried out.'" I stated at that time, "Comrade Stalin, I do not know who invented this, but it is not true."

It is possible that Stalin himself invented these things for the pur-pose of minimizing the role and military talents of Marshal Zhukov.

In this connection Stalin very energetically popularized himself as a great leader; in various ways he tried to implant among the people the fiction that all victories gained by the Soviet people during the great patriotic war were due to the courage, daring and genius of Stalin and of no one else. . . .

But it was precisely at this time that the so-called "Leningrad Case" was born. As we have now proved, this case was fabricated. Those who innocently lost their lives included Comrades Voznesensky, Kuznetsov, Rodionov, Popkov and others.

As is known, Voznesensky and Kuznetsov were talented and emi-nent leaders. Once they stood very close to Stalin. Suffice it to mention that Stalin made Voznesensky first assistant to the Chairman of the Council of Ministers and Kuznetsov was elected Secretary of the Central Committee. The very fact that Stalin entrusted Kuznetsov with the supervision of the state security agencies shows the trust Kuznetsov enjoyed.

How did it happen that these persons were branded enemies of the people and liquidated?

Facts prove that the "Leningrad Case" is also the result of willfulness which Stalin exercised against Party cadres.

Had a normal situation existed in the Party Central Committee and in the Central Committee Political Bureau, cases of this nature would have been examined there in accordance with Party practice, and all pertinent facts assessed; as a result, such a case, as well as others, would not have happened.

We must state that after the war the situation became even more complicated. Stalin became even more capricious, irritable and brutal; in particular, his suspicion grew. His persecution mania reached unbelievable dimensions. Many workers were becoming enemies before his very eyes. After the war Stalin separated himself from the collective even more. He decided everything alone, without any consideration for anyone or anything.

The arrant provocateur and vile enemy, Beria, who had murdered thousands of Communists and loyal Soviet people, cleverly took advantage of this incredible suspicion. The elevation of Voznesensky and Kuznetsov alarmed Beria. As we have now proved, it was Beria who "suggested" to Stalin the fabrication by him and by his confidants of materials in the form of declarations and anonymous letters, and in the form of various rumors and talk.

The Party Central Committee has examined this so-called "Leningrad Case"; persons who suffered innocently are now rehabilitated and the glorious Leningrad Party organization has been restored to honor. Abakumov and others who fabricated this affair were brought before a court; their trial took place in Leningrad and they received their just deserts.

The question arises: Why is it that we see the truth of this case only now, and why did we not do something earlier, during Stalin's lifetime, to prevent the loss of innocent lives? It was because Stalin personally supervised the "Leningrad Case," and the majority of the Political Bureau members at that time did not know all of the circumstances in these matters, and could not therefore intervene.

When Stalin received certain materials from Beria and Abakumov, without examining these slanderous materials he ordered an investigation of the "case" of Voznesensky and Kuznetsov. With this their fate was sealed. . . .

The July plenary session of the Central Committee studied in detail the reasons for the development of conflict with Yugoslavia. It was a shameful role that Stalin played there. The "Yugoslav affair" contained no problems that could not have been solved through Party discussions among comrades. There was no substantial basis for the development of this "affair"; it was entirely possible to have prevented the rupture of relations with that country. This does not mean, however, that the Yugoslav leaders did not make mistakes or did not have shortcomings. But these mistakes and shortcomings were monstrously magnified by Stalin, which resulted in the breaking of relations with a friendly country.

I recall the first days when the conflict between the Soviet Union and Yugoslavia began artificially to be blown up. Once, when I came from Kiev to Moscow, I was invited to visit Stalin, who, pointing to the copy of a letter lately sent to Tito, asked me, "Have you read this?" Not waiting for my reply, he answered: "I will shake my little finger — and there will be no more Tito. He will fall."

We have paid dearly for this "shake of the little finger." This statement reflected Stalin's mania for greatness, but he acted just that way: "I will shake my little finger — and there will be no Kossior"; "I will shake my little finger once more, and Postyshev and Chubar will be no more"; "I will shake my little finger again — and Voznesensky, Kuznetsov and many others will disappear."

But this did not happen to Tito. No matter how much or how little Stalin shook not only his little finger, but everything else that he could shake, Tito did not fall. Why? The reason was that, in this case of disagreement with the Yugoslav comrades, Tito had behind him a state and a people who had gone through a severe school of fighting for liberty and independence, a people who gave support to their leaders.

You see to what Stalin's mania for greatness led. He had completely lost a sense of reality; he demonstrated his suspicion and haughtiness not only in relation to individuals in the USSR, but in relation to whole parties and nations.

We have carefully examined the case of Yugoslavia and have found a proper solution which is approved by the peoples of the Soviet Union and of Yugoslavia, as well as by the working masses of all the people's democracies and by all progressive humanity. The liquidation of the abnormal relationship with Yugoslavia was done in the interest of the whole camp of socialism, in the interest of strengthening peace in the whole world.

Let us also recall the "case of the doctor-plotters." Actually there was no "case" outside of the declaration of the woman doctor Timashuk, who was probably influenced or ordered by someone (after all, she was an unofficial collaborator of the agencies of state security) to write Stalin a letter in which she declared that the doctors were applying allegedly improper methods of medical treatment.

Such a letter was sufficient for Stalin to reach an immediate conclusion that there were doctor-plotters in the Soviet Union. He issued orders to arrest a group of eminent Soviet medical specialists. He personally issued advice on the conduct of the investigation and the method of interrogation of the arrested persons. He said Academician Vinogradov should be put in chains, another one should be beaten. Present at this Congress as a delegate is the former Minister of State Security, Comrade Ignatyev. Stalin told him curtly, "If you do not obtain confessions from the doctors we will shorten you by a head."

Stalin personally summoned the investigative judge, gave him instructions, advised him on the investigative methods to be used; these methods were simple — beat, beat and, once again, beat.

Shortly after the doctors were arrested, we members of the Political Bureau received transcripts of the doctors' confessions of guilt. After distributing these, Stalin told us, "You are blind as young kittens; what would happen without me? The country would perish because you do not know how to recognize enemies."

The case was so presented that no one could verify the facts on which the investigation was based. There was no possibility of trying to verify the facts by contacting those who had made the confessions of guilt.

We felt, however, that the case of the arrested doctors was questionable. We knew some of these people personally, for they had once treated us. When we examined this "case" after Stalin's death, we found it to be fabricated from beginning to end.

This ignominious "case" was set up by Stalin; he did not, however, have the time in which to bring it to a conclusion (as he conceived that conclusion), and for this reason the doctors are still alive. Now all have been rehabilitated. They are working in the same places they were working before; they treat top individuals, not excluding members of the government; they have our full confidence; and they execute their duties honestly, as they did before. . . .

Were there any signs that Beria was an enemy of the Party? Yes, there were. As far back as in 1937, at a Central Committee plenary session, the former People's Commissar of Public Health, Kaminsky, said that Beria had worked for the Mussavat intelligence service. But the Central Committee plenary session had barely concluded before Kaminsky was arrested and then shot. Did Stalin examine Kaminsky's statement? No, because Stalin believed in Beria, and that was enough for him. And when Stalin believed in anyone or anything, then no one could say anything that was contrary to his opinion; anyone who would have dared to express opposition would have met the same fate as Kaminsky.

There were other signs also. The declaration which Comrade Snegov made to the Party Central Committee is interesting. (Incidentally, he was also rehabilitated not long ago, after seventeen years in prison camps.) In this declaration Snegov writes:

"In connection with the proposed rehabilitation of the former Central Committee member, Lavrenti Kartvelishvili, I have entrusted to the hands of the representative of the Committee on State Security a detailed deposition concerning Beria's role in the disposition of the Kartvelishvili case and concerning the criminal motives by which Beria was guided.

"In my opinion it is indispensable to recall an important fact pertaining to this case and to communicate it to the Central Committee, because I did not consider it suitable to include in the investigation documents.

"On Oct. 30, 1931, at the session of the Organizational Bureau of the All-Union Communist Party Central Committee, Kartvelishvili, Secretary of the Transcaucasus Territory Committee, delivered a report. All members of the Executive of the territory committee were present; of them I alone am alive.

"During this session J. V. Stalin made a motion at the end of his speech concerning the organization of the Secretariat of the Transcaucasus Territory Committee composed of the following: First Secretary, Kartvelishvili; Second Secretary, Beria. (This was the first time in the Party's history that Beria's name was mentioned as a candidate for a Party position.)

"Kartvelishvili answered that he knew Beria well and for that reason refused categorically to work with him. Stalin proposed then that this matter be left open and that it be settled in the process of the work itself. Two days later a decision was arrived at that Beria would receive the Party post and that Kartvelishvili would be deported from the Transcaucasus."

This fact can be confirmed by Comrades Miyokan and Kaganovich, who were present at that session. . . .

Beria also cruelly treated the family of Comrade Ordzhonikidze. Why? Because Ordzhonikidze had tried to prevent Beria from realizing his shameful plans. Beria had cleared from his way all persons who could possibly interfere with him. Ordzhonikidze was always an opponent of Beria, which he told Stalin. Instead of examining this matter and taking appropriate steps, Stalin permitted the liquidation of Ordzhonikidze's brother and brought Ordzhonikidze himself to such a state that he was forced to shoot himself. Such was Beria.

Beria was unmasked by the Party Central Committee shortly after Stalin's death. The particularly detailed legal proceedings established that Beria had committed monstrous crimes, and Beria was shot.

The question arises why Beria, who had liquidated tens of thousands of Party and Soviet workers, was not unmasked during Stalin's lifetime. He was not unmasked earlier because he had very skillfully utilized Stalin's weaknesses; feeding him with suspicions, he assisted Stalin in everything and acted with his support.

Comrades, the cult of the individual acquired such monstrous proportions chiefly because Stalin himself, using all conceivable methods, supported the glorification of his own person. This is confirmed by numerous facts. One of the most characteristic examples of Stalin's self-glorification and of his lack of even elementary modesty is the edition of his "Short Biography," which was published in 1948.

This book is an expression of the most dissolute flattery, an example of making a man into a godhead, of transforming him into an infallible sage, "the greatest leader," "sublime strategist of all times and nations." Finally, no other words could be found with which to exalt Stalin to the heavens.

We need not give here examples of the loathsome adulation filling this book. All we need to add is that they all were approved and edited by Stalin personally and some of them were added in his own handwriting to the draft text of the book.

What did Stalin consider essential to write into this book? Did he want to cool the ardor of his flatterers who were composing his "Short Biography"? No! He marked the very places where he thought that the praise of his services was insufficient. . . .

Stalin loved to see the film, "Unforgettable 1919," in which he was shown on the steps of an armored train and where he practically vanquished the foe with his own saber. Let Kliment Yefremovich [Voroshilov], our dear friend, find the necessary courage and write the truth about Stalin; after all, he knows how Stalin fought. It will be difficult for Comrade Voroshilov to undertake this, but it would be good if he did. Everyone will approve of it, both the people and the Party. Even his grandsons will thank him. . . .

Stalin's reluctance to consider life's realities and the fact that he was not aware of the real state of affairs in the provinces can be illustrated by his direction of agriculture.

All those who interested themselves even a little in the national situation saw the difficult situation in agriculture, but Stalin never even noted it. Did we tell Stalin about this? Yes, we told him; but he did not support us. Why? Because Stalin never travelled anywhere, did not meet city and collective farm workers; he did not know the actual situation in the provinces.

He knew the countryside and agriculture only from films. And these films had dressed up and beautified the existing situation in agriculture.

Many films pictured collective farm life as if the tables bent under the weight of turkeys and geese. Evidently Stalin thought that it was actually so.

Vladimir Ilyich Lenin looked at life differently. He was always close to the people; he used to receive peasant delegates, and often spoke at factory gatherings; he used to visit villages and talk with the peasants.

Stalin cut himself off from the people and never went anywhere. This lasted tens of years. The last time he visited a village was in January 1928, when he visited Siberia in connection with grain deliveries. How then could he have known the situation in the provinces?

And when he was once told during a discussion that our situation on the land was a difficult one and that the likestock situation was especially bad, a commission was formed and charged with drafting a resolution entitled "Means Toward Further Development of Livestock Raising on Collective and State Farms." We worked out this draft.

Of course, our proposals of that time did not contain all possibilities, but we did chart ways in which livestock raising on the collective and state farms could be improved. We proposed then to raise the prices of animal products to create material incentives for the collective farmers and MTS and state farm workers in the development of livestock. But our draft was not accepted and in February 1953 was laid aside entirely.

What is more, while reviewing this draft Stalin proposed that the taxes paid by the collective farms and by the collective farmers should be raised by 40,000,000,000 rubles. According to him, the peasants were well-off and the collective farmer would need to sell only one more chicken to pay his tax in full.

Imagine what this would have meant. Certainly 40,000,000,000 rubles is a sum which the collective farmers did not realize for all the products which they sold to the government. In 1952, for instance, the collective farms and the collective farmers received 26,280,000,000 rubles for all their products delivered and sold to the government.

Did Stalin's position rest, then, on data of any sort whatever? Of course not. . . .

Some comrades may ask us: Where were the members of the Political Bureau of the Central Committee? Why did they not assert themselves against the cult of the individual leader in time? Why is this being done only now?

First of all we have to consider the fact that the members of the Political Bureau viewed these matters in a different way at different times. Initially, many of them backed Stalin actively because Stalin was one of the strongest Marxists and his logic, his strength and his will greatly influenced the cadres and Party work.

It is known that Stalin, after Lenin's death, especially during the first years, fought actively for Leninism against the foes of Leninist theory and against those who deviated. Basing itself on Leninist theory, the Party, headed by its Central Committee, started on a great scale the work of socialist industrialization of the country, agricultural collectivization and the cultural revolution.

At that time Stalin gained great popularity, sympathy and support. The Party had to fight those who attempted to lead the country away from the correct Leninist path; it had to fight Trotskyites, Zinovievites and rightists, and the bourgeois–nationalists. This fight was indispensable. Later, however, Stalin, abusing his power more and more, began to fight eminent Party and government leaders and to use terroristic methods against honest Soviet people. As we have already shown, Stalin thus treated such eminent Party and government leaders as Kossior, Rudzutak, Eikhe, Postyshev and many others.

Attempts to oppose groundless suspicions and charges resulted in the opponent falling victim of the repression. This characterized the fall of Comrade Postyshev.

In one of his speeches Stalin expressed his dissatisfaction with Postyshev and asked him, "What are you actually?"

Postyshev answered clearly, "I am a Bolshevik, Comrade Stalin, a Bolshevik."

This assertion was at first considered to show a lack of respect for Stalin; later it was considered a harmful act, and consequently resulted in Postyshev's annihilation and in his being branded without reason as an "enemy of the people."

In the situation which then prevailed I talked with Nikolai Alexandrovich Bulganin. Once when we two were traveling in a car, he said: "It has happened sometimes that a man goes to Stalin by invitation, as a friend. And when he sits with Stalin, he does not know where he will be sent next, home or to jail."

It is clear that such conditions put every member of the Political Bureau in a very difficult situation. And when we also consider the fact that in the last years Central Committee plenary sessions were not convened and that the sessions of the Political Bureau occurred only occasionally, from time to time, then we shall understand how difficult it was for any member of the Political Bureau to take a stand against one or another unjust or improper procedure, against serious errors and shortcomings in the practice of leadership.

As we have already shown, many decisions were taken either by one person or in a roundabout way, without collective discussions. The sad fate of Political Bureau member Comrade Voznesensky, who fell victim to Stalin's repressions, is known to all. It is characteristic that the decision to remove him from the Political Bureau was never discussed, but was reached in a devious fashion. The same is true of the decision to remove Kuznetsov and Rodionov from their posts.

The importance of the Central Committee Political Bureau was reduced and its work was disorganized by the creation within the Political Bureau of various committees — the so-called "quintets," "sextets," "septets" and "novenaries." Here is, for instance, a resolution of the Political Bureau of Oct. 3, 1946:

"Stalin's Proposal:

"1. The Political Bureau Committee for Foreign Affairs ('sextet') is to concern itself in the future, in addition to foreign affairs, with matters of internal construction and domestic policy.

"2. The sextet is to add to its roster the Chairman of the USSR State Economic Planning Commission, Comrade Voznesensky, and is to be known as a septet.

"Signed: Secretary of the Central Committee, J. Stalin."

What a card-player's terminology! It is clear that the creation within the Political Bureau of such committees — "quintets," "sextets," "septets" and "novenaries" — was against the principle of collective leadership. The result of this was that some members of the Political Bureau were thus kept from participation in the most important state matters.

One of the oldest members of our Party, Kliment Yefremovich Voroshilov, found himself in an almost impossible situation. For several years he was actually deprived of the right of participation in Political Bureau sessions. Stalin forbade him to attend the Political Bureau sessions and to receive documents. When the Political Bureau was in session and Comrade Voroshilov heard about it, he telephoned each time and asked whether he would be allowed to attend. Sometimes Stalin permitted it, but always showed his dissatisfaction. Because of his extreme suspicion, Stalin toyed also with the absurd and ridiculous suspicion that Voroshilov was a British agent. It's true, a British agent. A special tapping device was installed in his home to listen to what was said there.

By unilateral decision Stalin had also cut off another man from the work of the Political Bureau — Andrei Andreyevich Andreyev. This was one of the most unbridled acts of willfulness.

Let us consider the first Central Committee plenary session after the 19th Party Congress when Stalin, in his talk at the plenary session, characterized Vyacheslav Mikhailovich Molotov and Anastas Ivanovich Mikoyan and suggested that these old workers of our Party were guilty of some baseless charges. It is not excluded that, had Stalin remained at the helm for another several months, Comrades Molotov and Mikoyan would probably not have delivered any speeches at this Congress.

Stalin evidently had plans to finish off the old members of the Political Bureau. He often stated that Political Bureau members should be replaced by new ones.

His proposal after the 19th Congress concerning the selection of

25 persons to the Central Committee Presidium was aimed at removing the old Political Bureau members and bringing in less experienced persons, so that these would extol him in all sorts of ways.

We can assume that this was also a design for future annihilation of the old Political Bureau members and in this way a cover for all the shameful acts of Stalin which we are now considering. . . .

Comrades! Lenin often stressed that modesty is an absolutely integral part of a real Bolshevik. Lenin himself was the living personification of the greatest modesty. We cannot say that we have been following this Leninist example in all respects. Suffice it to point out that we have called many cities, factories and industrial enterprises, collective and state farms, Soviet institutions and cultural institutions after the private names — as if they were the private property, if I may express it so — of various government or Party leaders who were still active and in good health. Many of us participated in the act of assigning our names to various cities, districts, factories and collective farms. We must correct this.

But this should be done calmly and slowly. The Central Committee will discuss this matter and consider it carefully to prevent errors and excesses. I can remember how the Ukraine learned about Kossior's arrest. The Kiev radio used to start its programs thus: "This is Radio Kossior." When one day the programs began without naming Kossior, everyone was quite certain that something had happened to Kossior, that he had probably been arrested.

Thus, if today we begin to remove the signs everywhere and to change names, people will think that the comrades in whose honor the given enterprises, collective farms or cities are named also met some bad fate and that they have also been arrested.

How is the prestige and importance of this or that leader judged? By the number of cities, industrial enterprises, factories, collective and state farms that bear his name. Is it not time we ended this "private property" and "nationalized" the factories, the industrial enterprises, the collective and state farms? This will benefit our cause. After all, the cult of the individual leader is manifested also in this way.

We should consider the question of the cult of the individual leader quite seriously. We cannot let this matter get out of the Party, especially not to the press. It is for this reason that we are considering it here at a closed Congress session. We should know the limits; we should not give ammunition to the enemy; we should not wash our dirty linen before

their eyes. I think that the delegates to the Congress will understand and assess all these proposals properly. . . .

At the conclusion of the Secret Speech, the Congress is recorded as having unanimously adopted the following resolution "Concerning the Cult of Personality and Its Consequences":

Having heard the report of Comrade N. S. Khrushchev concerning the cult of personality and its consequences, the Congress of the Communist Party of the Soviet Union approves the statements of the report of the Central Committee and charges the CPSU Central Committee consequently to carry out measures ensuring the complete suppression of the cult of personality, which is foreign to Marxism–Leninism, the liquidation of its consequences in all branches of Party, state and ideological work, the strict execution of the norms of Party life and the principles of collective Party leadership which were worked out by the great Lenin. (*The CPSU in Resolutions and Decisions of Congresses, Conferences, and Plenums of the Central Committee*, Volume IV, 1954–1960, Moscow, 1960, p. 208)

The 20th Congress increased the size of the Central Committee from 125 full and 111 candidate members to 133 full and 122 candidate members. According to long-established custom, the Central Committee included the power elite from the various bureaucratic hierarchies — Party, governmental, military, and industrial — and representatives from all walks of life. However, among the full members, the numerically dominant group was the central and regional Party functionaries.

More than a third of both the full and candidate members were newly elected. Many of these, especially from the Party apparatus, could reasonably be expected to owe their first loyalty to First Secretary Khrushchev, who was strategically placed to influence appointments in the Party. However, while Khrushchev's support in the Central Committee was undoubtedly increased, there is no reason to believe that he alone was able to manipulate its selection.

The new Central Committee Presidium and Secretariat were announced on February 28:

A plenum of the Party Central Committee, elected by the 20th Party Congress, was held on February 27, 1956.

The plenum elected the following Presidium of the Party Central Committee:

Members of the Presidium: Comrades N. A. Bulganin, K. Ye Voroshilov, L. M. Kaganovich, A. I. Kirichenko, G. M. Malenkov, A. I. Mikoyan, V. M. Molotov, M. G. Pervukhin, M. Z. Saburov, M. A. Suslov, and N. S. Khrushchev.

Candidate Members: Comrades G. K. Zhukov, L. I. Brezhnev, N. A. Mukhitdinov, D. T. Shepilov, Ye. A. Furtseva, and N. M. Shvernik.

The Presidium elected the following Secretariat of the Party Central Committee: Comrades N. S. Khrushchev, First Secretary of the Party Central Committee, A. B. Aristov, N. I. Belyayev, L. I. Brezhnev, P. N. Pospelov, M. A. Suslov, Ye. A. Furtseva, and D. T. Shepilov.

The plenum elected Comrade N. M. Shvernik Chairman of the Party Control Committee of the Central Committee and Comrade P. T. Komarov Deputy Chairman of the Party Control Committee. (*Pravda*, February 28, 1956)

> Thus, the full members of the Presidium remained unchanged, while at the candidate level Ponomarenko was dropped and five new faces were added. The new candidate members, except for Defense Minister Zhukov, were Party functionaries who appeared to be indebted to Khrushchev for their appointments. Shepilov, former editor of *Pravda*, had been named to the Secretariat the previous July, while Furtseva (the first woman on the Presidium), Brezhnev, and Mukhitdinov were heads of the Moscow, Kazakhstan, and Uzbek Party organizations respectively. The elevation of Furtseva and Brezhnev to the Central Committee Secretariat simultaneously with their appointment as candidate members of the Presidium increased the number of Central Committee secretaries to eight, five of whom had been appointed within eight months and appeared to be close to Khrushchev.
>
> Of the fifteen Union Republics in the USSR, all but the Russian Republic — by far and away the most important — had their own central committees and republic Party staffs. Immediately after the 20th Congress, this organizational anomaly was partially rectified, and in a manner which strengthened Khrushchev's organizational base.

To bring about more concrete leadership of the work of republic organizations and oblast and krai Party, Soviet and economic agencies and more effective resolution of problems of economic and cultural construction in the Russian Republic, the Party Central Committee has created a Russian Republic Bureau of the Party Central Committee.

Comrade N. S. Khrushchev, First Secretary of the Party Central

Committee, has been appointed Chairman of the Party Central Committee's Russian Republic Bureau and Comrade N. I. Belyayev, Secretary of the Party Central Committee, has been appointed Deputy Chairman.

Comrades M. A. Yasnov, Chairman of the Russian Republic Council of Ministers; I. V. Kapitonov, First Secretary of the Moscow Oblast Party Committee; F. R. Kozlov, First Secretary of the Leningrad Oblast Party Committee; V. M. Churayev, Director of the Party Central Committee's Department of Party Organs for the Russian Republic; A. M. Puzanov, First Deputy Chairman of the Russian Republic Council of Ministers; N. G. Ignatov, First Secretary of the Gorky Oblast Party Committee; and A. P. Kirilenko, First Secretary of the Sverdlovsk Oblast Party Committee have been appointed members of the Russian Republic Bureau. (*Pravda*, February 29, 1956)

V · THE FRUITS OF DE-STALINIZATION AND INDUSTRIAL REORGANIZATION

The year 1956 witnessed great flux and tension in both the Soviet Union and the entire communist world. The directions established at the 20th Party Congress gathered momentum as the year progressed, and threatened to get out of hand in the closing months of 1956. Khrushchev emerged from the Congress with his position considerably strengthened; but by late autumn both the man and his policies came under attack. De-Stalinization, a policy with which Khrushchev's name was most closely associated after the Secret Speech, opened a Pandora's box, the results of which were not always predictable — especially in Eastern Europe.

If Eastern Europe was the dominating concern of the Soviet leadership during the last half of 1956, by the turn of the year domestic economic problems took the center stage. During the late winter and spring of 1957 the regime was preoccupied with economic growth

March 1956 to May 1957

rates and industrial management. Khrushchev, with characteristic dynamism, grabbed the initiative with a radical scheme for reorganization of industrial management.

The First Results of De-Stalinization

Following the 20th Party Congress, the contents of the Secret Speech were conveyed to Party meetings throughout the Soviet Union, and the word soon spread to the entire Soviet population. The damning criticism of Stalin came as a shock to many Soviet citizens who since childhood had been bombarded with praises of Stalin portraying him as a demigod and the chief architect of Soviet society. The drastic downgrading of Stalin hit a tender nerve, particularly in Georgia, Stalin's birthplace, where open protests and rioting broke out among students. The criticism of Stalin, which contradicted 25 years of Soviet propaganda, threatened to erode public confidence in the entire edifice of Stalinist institutions and values.

The months following the 20th Congress showed the Soviet leadership divided and uncertain as to how far and how fast to go in eliminating what were regarded as the "harmful" consequences of Stalin's rule. Within a few weeks the press had brought the campaign against Stalin into the open, at the same time warning that de-Stalinization must not be used as a vehicle for criticizing the Party itself or its leaders. Moreover, the press attempted to delineate what was beneficial and what was harmful in Stalin's record.

. . . There is no doubt that J. V. Stalin performed great tasks for our Party, the working class and the international workers' movement. His role in the preparation and conduct of the socialist revolution, the civil war, and the struggle for the construction of socialism is well known. Occupying the major post of General Secretary of the Party Central Committee, J. V. Stalin became one of the number of leading workers of the Party and the Soviet state. Together with other members of the Central Committee, he actively fought for Leninism against distorters and enemies of Lenin's teaching — particularly in the first years after Lenin's death. Stalin was one of the strongest Marxists, and his works, his logic, and his will had a great influence on the cadres and work of the Party. . . .

However, little by little those features and qualities of Stalin's leadership became manifested which later led to the cult of the individual. The cult of the individual originated and developed against the background of great historical conquests by Marxism-Leninism, great achievements of the Soviet people and the Communist Party in the construction of socialism, the valiant conclusion of the Great Patriotic War, the further strengthening of our social and state system, and the growth of its authority on the international scene. Slighting a correct Marxist interpretation, these gigantic successes in the construction of a new society, achieved by the Soviet people under the leadership of the Communist Party on the basis of its knowledge of the laws of Marxism–Leninism, were consistently attributed to the work of one man — Stalin — and were explained by some sort of special qualities which he had as a leader. Lacking modesty, he not only did not stop these eulogies and glorifications addressed to him but supported and assisted them in every way. With the passage of time this cult of personality took on increasingly uglier forms and considerably damaged our work. . . .

Giving what is due to J. V. Stalin, soberly evaluating that major contribution made by him to the work of the revolution and the construction of socialism, the Party, at the same time, resolutely posed the question concerning the liquidation of the cult of the individual in Stalin's case in order to re-establish Lenin's principles and norms of Party and state work in full and thereby create the best possible conditions for our great creative work in the construction of Communism. . . . ("Why the Cult of Personality Is Foreign to the Spirit of Marxism–Leninism," *Pravda,* March 28, 1956)

*   *   *

. . . It is well known that the cult of the individual, which became widespread in the latter part of J. V. Stalin's life and work, inhibited the development of initiative and creativity, led to a downgrading of the role of the Party and the masses, contributed in no small measure to the difficulties in our constructive work, and was very damaging to our cause. The resolute struggle against survivals of the cult of the individual has aroused new political and labor enthusiasm among the broad masses. The re-establishment and development of Lenin's norms and principles in Party and state life by the Party and its Central Committee are of tremendous significance for the cause of the construction of communism. . . .

Increasingly apparent are the beneficial results of the measures being implemented by the Party Central Committee to re-establish and develop further democratic principles of Party life and activity, to fight against naked rule by command and bureaucratic leadership methods, to fight the practice of smoothing over shortcomings and garnishing reality, to eradicate bureaucratic self-satisfaction and complacency, and to encourage businesslike, principled criticism and self-criticism. . . .

At the same time, we cannot ignore cases when individual rotten elements attempt to use criticism and self-criticism for all kinds of slanderous fabrications and anti-Party statements. For example, at a meeting of the Party organization of one of the scientific laboratories, members of the staff, Avalov, Orlov, Nesterov, and Shchedrin, employed inner-Party democracy to make slanderous speeches against Party policy and its Leninist foundations. The Communists in the Party organization did not show proper militant, Bolshevik intolerance of these attacks against the Party. Provocative, anti-Party statements were also made by L. Yaroshenko at a Party meeting of the Moscow Oblast Statistical Administration. Such speeches are in essence the refrains of another's voice, the reiteration of the worn-out, slanderous lies of reactionary foreign propaganda.

Under the cloak of condemning the cult of the individual, certain rotten elements try to cast doubt on the correctness of the Party's policy. . . . ("The Communist Party Continues Victorious through Loyalty to Leninism," *Pravda,* April 5, 1956)

A comparison of these two articles with the Secret Speech demonstrates the variation between confidential criticism of Stalin for the Party elite and open criticism for the masses.

As should be abundantly clear to the reader, de-Stalinization was coupled with increased attention to Leninism. By asserting that Lenin, and not Stalin, was the architect of the Soviet system and by pledging fidelity to "Leninist principles," the leadership attempted to avoid the discredit that might fall on itself and Soviet institutions as a result of the criticism of Stalin. As a part of the "return to Leninism," during the spring of 1956, a number of documents from Lenin's last years were published for the first time. For the Soviet reader these must have been revealing and, perhaps, unsettling since several of them were critical of Stalin and they shed new light on the first years of the Soviet regime which dashed some of the standard stereotypes.

In the first months after the Congress, a series of policies were adopted to improve living and working conditions, to reform and cautiously to continue the decentralization of the Party and state bureaucracies, and, in general, to get rid of some of the worst abuses of the Stalinist era. Some of these practices had already lapsed. By publicly legislating their abolition, the regime sought to assure the population that it was breaking with the "consequences of the cult of personality."

On April 19, the Presidium of the Supreme Soviet officially decreed:

That the December 1, 1934 Decree of the USSR Central Executive Committee "On the Legal Procedure for Trying Cases of the Preparation or Execution of Terrorist Acts" and the December 1, 1934 and September 14, 1937 Decrees of the USSR Central Executive Committee "Concerning the Amendment of the Criminal Codes Presently in Operation in the Union Republics," which created an exceptional procedure for investigating and trying cases concerning crimes defined by Articles 58-7, 58-8 and 58-9 of the Russian Republic Criminal Code and by corresponding articles in the criminal codes of the other Union republics, be rescinded.

That it be established that henceforth the agencies of investigation and justice, in investigating and trying the crimes defined in the criminal code articles mentioned above, shall follow the trial procedures established by the criminal codes of the Union republics. (*Bulletin of the USSR Supreme Soviet,* No. 9, April 1956, p. 229)

> By this act, the dreaded administrative boards of the secret police, which had arbitrarily pronounced sentence on thousands of persons during the Stalinist purges, were officially abolished. Two weeks before, another decree had revised the structure of the Procuracy, apparently with the intent, in part, of strengthening its supervision of the police and legal agencies. At about the same time, M. D. Bagirov, former strongman of Azerbaidzhan, who had fallen from power in July 1953, was sentenced to death allegedly for criminal intrigues with Beria, particularly against the famous Bolshevik, Sergo Ordzhonikidze. Finally in late May a commission was created to study a revision of the criminal codes.
>
> In late April, workers were given more employment flexibility by the repeal of the Stalinist decree of June 26, 1940, which prohibited unauthorized changes of jobs and criminal prosecution for absenteeism and repeated tardiness. Under the new ruling, workers could change jobs legally by giving two weeks' notice. This decree of April 25 was only one of several issued during the spring and summer of 1956 directly affecting the working man and woman. On March 26, maternity

leave was extended from 77 to 112 days. On May 26, a six-hour work-day, without reduction in pay, was instituted for youths under 18. On July 14, the minimum old age pension for those qualifying was set at 300 rubles per month, with a maximum of 1200 rubles per month. Up to that time the maximum pension had been 210 rubles per month. On September 8, a new minimum wage law set a floor of 300–350 rubles per month in the cities and 270 rubles for wage-earners in the country-side (excluding collective farmers).

On May 26 increased decentralization in economic management was decreed with the transfer of certain enterprises from the light and textile industries and shipping to the jurisdiction of the Union Republics. The Party structure, also, was streamlined to give more authority to the lower territorial–administrative Party organizations by reducing central control through the use of Central Committee plenipotentiaries.

CONCERNING PARTY ORGANIZERS OF THE PARTY CENTRAL COMMITTEE

1. In order to widen to the greatest possible degree internal Party democracy and to raise the responsibility of local Party organizations for the work of large enterprises and the most important institutions, [it has been resolved] to abolish the post of Party organizer of the Party Central Committee in all industrial enterprises, transportation, scientific institutes and other organizations.

2. To establish in the Party organizations of enterprises and insti-tutions, where the post of Party organizer of the Central Committee is abolished, the position of freed [i.e. full-time, Party-paid] secretaries of Party organizations, reserving for them the pay established for the Party organizer of the Central Committee. (Decree of the Central Committee, CPSU, August 17, 1956, *The Party Worker's Handbook,* Moscow, 1957, p. 429).

At the height of this wave of reforms two important personnel changes took place:

The Presidium of the USSR Supreme Soviet has satisfied the re-quest of First Deputy Chairman of the Council of Ministers, Vyacheslav Mikhailovich Molotov, for release from his duties as USSR Minister of Foreign Affairs.

The Presidium of the USSR Supreme Soviet has appointed Com-rade Dmitri Trofimovich Shepilov USSR Minister of Foreign Affairs. (*Pravda,* June 2, 1956)

*   *   *

The Presidium of the USSR Supreme Soviet has satisfied the request of First Deputy Chairman of the USSR Council of Ministers, Lazar Moiseyevich Kaganovich, for release from his duties as Chairman of the State Committee of the USSR Council of Ministers on Questions of Labor and Wages.

The Presidium of the USSR Supreme Soviet has appointed Alexander Petrovich Volkov Chairman of the State Committee of the USSR Council of Ministers on Questions of Labor and Wages. (*Pravda*, June 9, 1956)

Unrest in Eastern Europe

Domestically, the public criticism of Stalin and the apparent decision of the regime to break openly with some of Stalin's more repressive policies resulted in considerable ferment. There are indications that demands for radical reforms were sometimes voiced in 1956 (e.g. that workers' councils in plants be created to further workers' control of industry). Such proposals were resolutely rejected by the leadership. During the autumn, as we shall later see, Soviet writers began to get out of hand.

It was above all among the foreign communist parties, especially in Eastern Europe, that de-Stalinization created the greatest uncertainties and confusion. The revelation of Stalin's crimes was a psychological blow to communist parties throughout the world. Leaders in some communist countries, who could be considered Stalin's lieutenants and who had patterned their rule after his — particularly Ulbricht in East Germany and Rakosi in Hungary — attempted to minimize the impact of de-Stalinization. On the other hand, the Polish and Italian communist parties, as well as some others, warmly welcomed the relaxation and began to call for a more thorough inquiry into the nature of the Stalinist system and for a Marxist explanation of how the "cult of personality" arose.

On April 18, the Cominform (Communist Information Bureau), which was created in 1947 to lay down the line for the world communist movement and from which Yugoslavia was expelled in 1948, was abolished. It was liquidated in part because it was tainted as a Stalinist instrument for controlling foreign communist parties, in part because it was an obstacle to improving Soviet-Yugoslav relations and, perhaps, also because it was hoped that this would facilitate a rapprochement between the communists and social democrats in Western Europe. This latter objective, however, received a serious setback as a result of the unfavorable outcome of the Bulganin and Khrushchev talks with British labor leaders during their visit to Great Britain on April 18-27.

Not only did probes of the attitudes of Western European social democrats prove unfruitful, the uprisings in the Polish city of Poznan on June 28 presented compelling evidence of the serious deterioration in the situation of the communist regimes in Eastern Europe. Largely because of the confusion arising from de-Stalinization in foreign communist parties, as well as at home, on June 30 the Central Committee adopted a lengthy resolution, "On Overcoming the Cult of the Individual and its Consequences." Notable for its defensive tone, this declaration attempted to answer some of the embarrassing questions which had been raised by communist parties abroad: How did the cult of personality arise in a Marxist country? Why was not Stalin controlled by the other members of the Politburo? Did Stalinism include a fundamental change in the Soviet system? The resolution's implication that those communists who were probing too deeply into the causes and results of Stalinism were undermining the communist movement, and its obvious attempt to squelch further discussion of the issue, as well as its characterization of the Poznan uprising as "anti-popular demonstrations" financed by American monopolies, evidenced a growing concern about the course of events in Eastern Europe and a general hardening of policy in foreign and domestic affairs, including retrenchment on the issue of Stalinism. In contrast to statements of five months before, the consequences of Stalinism were now regarded as having been already removed. As such, this resolution may mark the beginning of a policy change that became more evident in the autumn.

. . . Recently, the bourgeois press has embarked on a widespread, slanderous anti-Soviet campaign which reactionary circles are attempting to base on certain facts connected with the condemnation of the cult of J. V. Stalin by the Communist Party of the Soviet Union. The managers of this campaign are exercising every effort to obfuscate the issue and to hide the fact that this stage in the life of the country of Soviets is past; they also want to gloss over or distort the fact that during the years since Stalin's death, the Communist Party and government of the Soviet Union have been very persistent and determined in eradicating the consequences of the cult of the individual and are successfully implementing the new tasks in the interest of strengthening peace and constructing communism, and for the benefit of the broad masses. . . .

The fraternal Communist and Workers' Parties have also seen through in time this maneuver of the enemies of socialism and are repulsing it accordingly. Nevertheless, it would be incorrect to shut our eyes to the fact that certain of our friends abroad are not entirely clear on the question of the cult of the individual and its consequences and sometimes give incorrect interpretations of certain points related to it. . . .

In raising the question of fighting the cult of J. V. Stalin, the Party Central Committee proceeded from the fact that the cult of the individual contradicts the nature of the socialist system and had become a brake on the development of Soviet democracy and the advance of socialist society toward communism.

The 20th Party Congress, on the initiative of the Central Committee, judged it necessary to speak boldly and frankly about the grave consequences of the cult of the individual and the serious mistakes made during the latter period of Stalin's life, and to summon the whole Party to unite its efforts in ending everything that resulted from the cult of the individual. At the same time, the Central Committee was aware that the frank admission of mistakes made would be connected to certain shortcomings and losses which might be exploited by enemies. The brave and relentless self-criticism in the case of the cult of the individual was new and striking proof of the might and strength of our Party and the Soviet socialist system. . . .

How could the cult of Stalin, with all its negative consequences, have arisen and become widespread under conditions of the Soviet socialist system?

In examining this question, it is necessary to keep in mind both the objective, concrete historical conditions under which socialism was built in the USSR and certain subjective factors connected with Stalin's personal qualities. . . .

This complicated international and internal situation [the danger of imperialism and fascism, the struggle against hostile domestic elements — Trotskyites, right-wing opportunists and bourgeois–nationalists, and the difficulties of collectivization and industrialization] demanded iron discipline, constantly growing vigilance and strict centralization of leadership, which inevitably had an adverse effect on the development of certain democratic forms. In the course of an intense struggle against the entire imperialist world, our country had to submit to certain restrictions on democracy, justified by the logic of our people's struggles for socialism under conditions of capitalist encirclement. However, these restrictions were at that time considered temporary by the Party and the people, subject to removal as the Soviet state grew stronger and the forces of democracy and socialism developed the world over. . . .

As General Secretary of the Party Central Committee, a position which he long held, J. V. Stalin, together with other leaders, struggled actively to carry out Lenin's biddings. He was devoted to Marxism–Leninism and, as a theoretician and good organizer, headed the Party's struggle against the Trotskyites, right-wing opportunists and bourgeois–nationalists, against the intrigues of the capitalist encirclement. In this political and ideological struggle, Stalin achieved great authority and popularity. But, all our great victories came to be incorrectly associated with his name. The successes achieved by the Communist Party and the Soviet land and the praise of Stalin went to his head. In this atmosphere the cult of Stalin gradually began to develop.

The development of the cult of the individual was promoted to a great degree by certain individual traits of J. V. Stalin, the negative character of which had already been pointed out by V. I. Lenin. . . .

The 20th Party Congress and the whole policy of the Central Committee since Stalin's death are clear evidence that there has been within the Party Central Committee a Leninist core of leaders who correctly understood the urgent needs of both domestic and foreign policy. It cannot be said that there was no resistance to the negative manifestations connected with the cult of the individual and which retarded the advance of socialism. There were, moreover, certain periods during the war, for example, when unilateral actions by Stalin were sharply curtailed and when the negative consequences of lawlessness, arbitrariness, etc., were considerably reduced.

It is known that during the war period members of the Central Committee, and also outstanding Soviet military leaders, took over certain sectors of activity on the domestic front and at the fighting front, took independent decisions and, through their organizational, political, economic, and military work with local Party and Soviet organizations, ensured the victory of the Soviet people in the war. . . .

The question might arise why, then, did these people not take an open stand against Stalin and remove him from leadership. This could not be done in the conditions prevailing at that time. . . .

It was not at all a question of lack of personal courage. It was apparent that if anyone had taken action against Stalin in this situation, he would not have been supported by the people. Moreover, such a stand under these conditions would have been considered a stand against the cause of socialist construction, against the unity of the Party and the entire state, which would have been extremely dangerous in light of the capitalist encirclement. . . .

It should also be remembered that many facts about the wrong actions by Stalin, particularly those regarding the violation of Soviet law, have become known only recently — since Stalin's death — and chiefly in connection with the exposure of the Beria gang and the establishment of Party control over state security agencies. . . .

The cult of the individual has undoubtedly caused great harm to the cause of the Communist Party and to Soviet society. However, it would be a serious mistake to conclude from the existence of the cult of the individual in the past that the social system in the USSR has somehow changed, or to seek the sources of this cult in the nature of the Soviet social system. Both alternatives are completely incorrect, for they do not match reality and contradict the facts.

Despite the evil which the Stalin cult brought to the Party and the people, it could not and did not change the nature of our social system. No cult of an individual could change the nature of the socialist state, which is based on public ownership of the means of production, the alliance of the working class and peasantry, and the friendship of peoples. . . .

A number of fraternal Communist Parties have issued statements endorsing and suporting our Party's measures against the cult of the individual and its consequences. . . .

At the same time, it should be noted that in discussing the question of the cult of the individual, a correct interpretation has not always been given of the causes which gave rise to the cult of the individual and of the consequences it has had for our social system. For example, the detailed and interesting interview given by Comrade Togliatti [Italian Communist Party leader] to the magazine *Nuovi Argomenti* contains incorrect propositions along with many very important and correct conclusions. In particular, one cannot agree with the question raised by Comrade Togliatti about whether Soviet society has not reached "certain forms of degeneration." There are no possible grounds for this question. . . .

As is now recognized by everyone, while the Soviet Union has done and is doing much to ease international tension, American monopoly capital continues to appropriate large sums for intensifying subversive activities in the socialist countries. . . . It is clear, for example, that the antipopular demonstrations in Poznan were financed from this source. However, the provocateurs and saboteurs, who were paid from abroad, had courage enough for only a few hours. The working people of Poznan repelled the enemy attacks and provocations. . . .

Let the bourgeois ideologists make up myths about the "crisis" of communism, about "confusion" in the ranks of the communist parties. We are used to hearing such incantations by enemies. Their predictions have always burst like soap bubbles. These unlucky prophets have come and gone, but the communist movement, the immortal and live-giving ideas of Marxism–Leninism, have triumphed and will continue to triumph. . . . (*Pravda,* July 2, 1956)

> Following up this declaration, *Pravda,* on July 16, again warned, in even more militant fashion, against imperialist attempts to undermine the Soviet bloc by sowing the seeds of national discord. In its emphasis on the overriding need for bloc solidarity, *Pravda* watered down noticeably the formula about "different roads to socialism" which the Soviet Union, under Yugoslav prodding, had propounded the previous year.

. . . Using their network of agents, relying on the remnants of the defeated exploiting classes which are antagonistic to communism, and attempting to draw into their clutches certain people who are honest but not politically tested, they are trying to arouse chauvinistic feelings, to destroy the ties among socialist countries and to sow discord. Proceeding in this manner, the imperialists count on weakening the socialist countries so that they can launch extensive subversive operations against the rule of the people and the socialist system. . . .

Since the 20th Party Congress, the struggle for the creative application of Marxism in conditions peculiar to each country has become more intensive in fraternal communist and workers' parties of the people's democracies. . . .

Creatively applying Marxism–Leninism in the conditions of their own countries, free people, under the leadership of communist parties, are moving *toward one goal,* toward communism. It is impossible to move separately or haphazardly toward such a great goal. The working people of all socialist countries are marching toward this goal in unison, holding each other firmly by the hand. No one will succeed in destroying this unity. The necessary consideration of national peculiarities does not lead to estrangement among the countries building socialism, but, on the contrary, contributes to their solidarity. . . . (*Pravda,* July 16, 1956)

> Tensions continued to mount in Eastern Europe during the late summer and early fall. The danger of a clash between Soviet troops and the Polish population or of Soviet loss of control over developments in Poland under the newly elevated Polish Communist Party leader, Gomulka, led to the sudden flight of a Soviet delegation to Poland on October 19. The composition, as well as the Russian alphabetical listing and the manner of identification, of this delegation are noteworthy.

A delegation of the Party Central Committee arrived in Warsaw on October 19, 1956 to discuss with the Politburo of the Central Committee of the Polish United Workers' Party vital questions of interest to both parties. Comrades L. M. Kaganovich, A. I. Mikoyan, V. M. Molotov, and N. S. Khrushchev, members of the Presidium of the CPSU Central Committee, comprised the delegation of the Party Central Committee. . . . (*Pravda,* October 21, 1956)

> The Hungarian uprising began on October 24. After the withdrawal of Soviet troops from Budapest on October 31, four days later Soviet military forces again intervened, crushed the revolution and installed the Kadar regime after overthrowing the Nagy government.
>
> The course of events in Eastern Europe deeply influenced the newly established Soviet–Yugoslav rapprochement. On June 2, the day Molotov was removed as Foreign Minister, Marshal Tito had arrived in Moscow. His visit ended with a joint Soviet–Yugoslav declaration marked by amicability:

. . . The discussions, which were held in a cordial and friendly atmosphere, in a spirit of frankness and full mutual understanding, provided an opportunity for a wide exchange of views on the development of the international situation over the past year, and also on questions of the further development of relations and all-round co-operation between the two countries. This exchange of views revealed a broad similarity in the points of view of the two governments on the development of the international situation and on existing international problems, as well as their common desire to develop even more profound mutual understanding and friendship between the USSR and the FPRY in the future. . . . (*Pravda,* June 21, 1956)

In late September Khrushchev had another series of meetings with Tito in Yugoslavia and Yalta, apparently to enlist Tito's assistance in dampening the growing ferment in Eastern Europe before it coalesced into a revolutionary explosion. Because of his independence from, and yet newly-formed friendly relations with, Moscow, Tito was regarded by many Eastern European communists as a key figure for advice and moral support. In late September and October, Tito had conferences with communist delegations from Poland, Hungary, Bulgaria, Czechoslovakia, Rumania, and Italy.

Whatever Tito's actual role, the unrest in Eastern Europe — culminating in the Gomulka regime in Poland and the Hungarian uprising — and the subsequent Soviet actions and explanations of these events, as well as Soviet backtracking on positions expressed at the 20th Party Congress concerning relations among communist regimes, could not but strain Soviet–Yugoslav relations. After Soviet military intervention in Hungary, Tito delivered a speech in Pula which was critical of several — but not all — Soviet actions. The Yugoslavs were especially upset by the blatant Soviet intervention in Eastern Europe and the resulting setback to a looser arrangement between the Soviet Union and the Eastern European regimes for which they had been working, and by the arrest of Nagy, the former head of the Hungarian Government, by Soviet troops after he had been guaranteed asylum by the Yugoslav government.

At this point there must have been considerable doubt among the Soviet leadership about the wisdom of the policy of rapprochement with Yugoslavia, which had been pursued so ardently during the previous eighteen months. The Yugoslav example had proved unsettling for its neighbors. On November 23, *Pravda* answered Tito and also gave the Soviet version of events in Hungary and their implication for Soviet policy and communist relations.

. . . The course of events in Hungary reveals that the reaction attempted to exploit for its antipopular purposes the accumulated discontent of the working masses, who were correctly demanding improvement in the country's leadership and an increase in the people's living standard.

Without doubt the blame for the Hungarian events lies with Hungary's former state and Party leadership, headed by Rakosi and Gero, who, in the solution of problems of socialist construction, committed flagrant mistakes both in general political affairs and in the area of economic policy and cultural work. . . .

Some workers participated in these demonstrations with good intentions in an attempt to express their legitimate dissatisfaction caused by the mistakes of the former leadership. But counter-revolutionary forces exploited this spontaneous discontent. It has now been definitely confirmed that counter-revolutionary elements had been organized in advance, that they had their own central military command, that their forces had been trained and deployed for a coup d'état, that men had been assigned to seize arsenals, that it had been decided which objectives would be attacked, that means of transportation had been mobilized to carry arms and that places for the distribution of arms had been chosen. This is the reason the bloody events in Budapest, caused by the provocational actions of fascist-Horthy bands, took place.

Western bourgeois newspapers state quite openly that the Hungarian events were carefully prepared for a long time by the reaction both inside and outside the country and that the skillful hand of the conspirators was evident everywhere from the first. Allen Dulles, head of American intelligence, stated bluntly that "we knew" about the Hungarian events beforehand. . . .

The composition of Imre Nagy's government changed several times over seven or eight days, and each day it slipped further and further to the right. The Imre Nagy government became a screen for the activities of the counter-revolutionary forces. The conspiratorial military center put increasing pressure on it.

Under these conditions, the best people, such as Comrades Janos Kadar, Ferenc Munnich and Imre Horvath, who were members of the Imre Nagy government, broke with this government.

The newly organized government — the Revolutionary Workers and Peasants Government of Janos Kadar — resolved to end the bloodshed and to rebuff the reactionary fascist forces, and it turned for help to the Soviet Union.

In these conditions, the decision of the Soviet Union to come to the assistance of Hungary's revolutionary forces was the only correct one. A socialist state could not remain an indifferent bystander to the bloody violence of the fascist reaction in people's democratic Hungary. . . .

Of the foreign reactions to the Hungarian events, Comrade Tito's recent speech in Pula attracts attention. It devotes a great deal of attention to the Hungarian events and correctly notes that counter-revolutionary elements played a provocative role in them. . . .

As Tito noted, the Hungarian events assumed such proportions that it became clear that a terrible massacre, a terrible civil war, would take place there, the result of which might have been the end of socialism and matters might have ended in a third world war. Although we are against intervention, Tito declared, the Soviet intervention was necessary. Of course, this is a correct evaluation of the Hungarian events. However, in the same speech Tito terms the assistance of Soviet troops to the Hungarian government a "mistake" and asserts: "We never advised them to resort to the help of the army." It is impossible to judge such a position consistent and true to reality. . . .

The fate of socialism in Hungary was being decided during the last few weeks. If a fascist Hungary had appeared in the center of Europe, the political position of a number of countries in Eastern and Central Europe would have changed substantially, and the international situation on the whole European continent would doubtless have deteriorated. . . .

This makes all the more amazing, therefore, certain propositions in Tito's speech which do not at all contribute either to unifying all supporters of socialism or to a correct understanding of a number of important problems of the international situation and current tasks of the world Communist movement.

To begin with, Tito's speech contains, together with correct evaluations of the Hungarian events, judgments which cannot but cause legitimate objections. "See," said Tito to his audience, "how strongly a people can resist, bare-handed and badly armed, if they have before them the single goal — to free themselves and to be independent. They are no longer interested in what kind of independence this would be or whether the bourgeoisie and the reactionary system would be restored in the country. Their only concern is to be independent as a nation. This is what was mainly in their minds." In the first place, Comrade Tito obviously exaggerates when he speaks in this case of "the people." Secondly, Marxism–Leninism teaches us to examine such phenomena another way. If a section of the working people is indifferent whether or not the yoke of exploitation is put on their necks . . . whether or not they are plunged into a new war like the fascist-Hitlerite clique of Horthy plunged the Hungarian people into a war in 1941–1944, this means that this section of the working people has fallen into a trap set by the reaction. . . .

Discussing the Hungarian events, Comrade Tito also makes a number of critical comments about the Communist Party of the Soviet Union. . . .

Let us take the main proposition put forward by Tito about the Soviet system. He persistently emphasizes that the "cult of the individual leader was essentially the product of a specific system." He states that one must talk of the "system which gave rise to the creation of the cult of the individual." In reality, however, the cult of the individual was a flagrant contradiction of our entire Soviet socialist system. . . .

How, then, can we interpret Tito's comments about our system except as an attempt to cast a shadow on the Soviet people's system of social life? How can we fail to ask if this is not a repetition of previous attacks on the Soviet Union, which were in vogue in the past when relations between the USSR and Yugoslavia were deteriorating? . . . One cannot help but see that the idea is appearing more and more often in the Yugoslav press that the "Yugoslav road to socialism" is the most correct, or even the only possible, road for almost all countries of the world. . . .

It is quite apparent what great importance aid from the capitalist states, above all the USA, has for Yugoslavia's economy. As a result of a situation that came about, Yugoslavia had for many years the opportunity to exploit the aggravated contradictions between imperialism and the socialist countries. But if aid from the capitalist countries constitutes a substantial part of its economy, it cannot be considered that this road has any special advantages. After all, all countries in the socialist camp cannot count on such aid; they cannot base their policy on the assumption of aid from the imperialists. Consequently, such a road is by no means universal. . . .

In his speech Comrade Tito puts forth the slogan of "independence" of the socialist countries and communist parties from the Soviet Union and the Communist Party of the Soviet Union. However, everyone knows that the Soviet Union does not demand any dependence or subordination of anyone. . . .

While making an on-the-whole favorable evaluation of the development of Soviet–Yugoslav relations and of the agreements concluded between the USSR and Yugoslavia, Tito reprimands the Soviet leaders for allegedly not wanting to extend the principles set forth in these agreements to the other socialist countries. Tito required this strange and entirely absurd assertion in order to ascribe to the Soviet Union "insufficient confidence" in the socialist forces of the people's democracies. . . .

What does Comrade Tito advocate in his speech? To go it alone? But, it may be asked, what does this road promise; what advantages does it have for the socialist countries? There are no such advantages. The call to break with the other socialist states, with the entire fraternal family of socialist countries, cannot be of any benefit to the cause of constructing a socialist society. Fidelity to the great banner of socialist internationalism, solidarity and unity of all fighters for socialism — this is a major condition for the success of our great cause. . . .

Domestic Problems

On the home front, spurred on by relaxation of controls and uncertainties over the extent to which de-Stalinization might be carried, Soviet writers vigorously tested the boundaries of orthodoxy in literature. Works by Granin, Dudintsev, and Yashin, among others, were highly critical of many aspects of Soviet society and officialdom, especially the bureaucracy and the pervasive bureaucratic mentality. November saw publication of *Literaturaya Moskva,* a collection of miscellaneous writings which went further than anything previously in attacking restrictions on creative work.

The events of 1956 shook particularly the values and attitudes of the younger generation. During the late autumn, university students were openly demanding to know the truth about Hungary and were circulating heretical materials. Clearly, from the leadership's point of view, things were getting out of hand.

The Party press in late November began to censure the more radical "revisionist" views expressed by artists, writers, and historians. At meetings of intellectuals and of students, Party leaders gave clear warning that continuation of such activities would lead to reprisals. On November 10, *Pravda* reported on a speech given by Khrushchev to a meeting of young people in Moscow:

. . . It is necessary to improve organizational work, said N. S. Khrushchev, to develop criticism and self-criticism more widely, and to observe consistently the principles of democracy. In improving educational work among young people, it is necessary to correct wrong views and to eliminate unhealthy phenomena.

Comrade Khrushchev related how a while ago Rumanian comrades explained their errors to groups of young students, and, at the same time, noted the great responsibility of the youth to their people.

After noting certain unhealthy attitudes among students in one educational institution, the Rumanian comrades decided to have a frank talk with these students and some of their parents. During the talk, they asked them the following questions:

"Do you study in the institute and receive a grant?"

"Yes," these student representatives answered.

"Do you have a dormitory and good professors?"

"We do," the students answered.

"Do you want to learn?" they were asked.

"We do," they answered.

"Then study better and learn more about life. If some do not want to study well, let them go and work. Then they will probably understand the life of the working people better."

This frank talk was of great educational importance for the youth. . . . (*Pravda,* November 10, 1956)

The implied threat to Soviet students in this story is clear enough. At another point in this speech, Khrushchev had a curious interchange with Mikoyan:

. . . I once spoke from Alma Ata with Anastas Ivanovich Mikoyan. We exchanged views on the possibilities of providing the country with grain. When I told him that Kazakhstan would produce a billion poods of grain in 1956, he did not say a word. I said to him:

"Why are you silent?"

He replied:

"I am not arguing, but I do not visualize quite a billion. Maybe 750,000,000, instead of the 650,000,000 under the plan, but a billion?"

"Do you recall that conversation, Anastas Ivanovich? Is that what you said?"

"That is what I said."

"And what did Kazakhstan say?"

"It kept its word."

"Did it produce a billion?"

"Yes, a billion!"

This indicates that even some of us leaders who raised the question of developing the virgin and idle lands did not expect such wonderful results, particularly in Kazakhstan, which had previously produced little grain. This is why Anastas Ivanovich's surprise at the time was understandable. . . .

> In addition to whatever relevance this published interchange has for elite politics, it is an obvious effort by Khrushchev to claim personal credit for the bumper grain harvest of 1956, one area where his policies at that time seemed to be a resounding success.
>
> Of special interest in this endeavor to quell, or at least limit, the growing radicalism among the intelligentsia was a conference held in mid-November by the Ministry of Culture.

. . . The USSR Ministry of Culture has held a conference on problems of the development of the fine arts. It was attended by representatives of Moscow's art community, artists, sculptors, art critics, and officials of the USSR Academy of Arts, the USSR Soviet Artists' Union's organizational committee, and the Moscow Artists' Union. V. M. Molotov, First Deputy Chairman of the USSR Council of Ministers, participated in the conference. . . .

Criticizing elements of rule by administrative order and bureaucracy in the guidance of the fine arts, V. M. Molotov, at the same time, stressed the need for thorough-going day-to-day Party leadership in the field of art. "We are opposed to replacing guiding ideas in the field of art by pure administrative measures, but we strive for high, Bolshevik ideas in the creative work of our artists," said Molotov. . . . (*Soviet Culture,* the triweekly organ of the USSR Ministry of Culture, November 20, 1956)

> Two days after this report, *Pravda* carried the following announcement:

The Presidium of the USSR Supreme Soviet has appointed Comrade Vyacheslav Mikhailovich Molotov, First Deputy Chairman of the USSR Council of Ministers, as USSR Minister of State Control. . . . (*Pravda,* November 22, 1956)

> The Ministry of State Control had broad powers and responsibilities to check on the efficiency and honesty of the far-flung governmental bureaucracy. Although this post had not been held by an official of the first rank for some time, it was a potentially powerful position. Molotov's appointment to head state control may have indicated a heightened concern about the performance of the economic bureaucracy and a determination to tighten its operations. During the previous three

years, the press had given primary emphasis to the responsibility of the Party in keeping the state administration under control.

Two and a half months before, yet another important appointment in the industrial administration had been announced:

The Presidium of the USSR Supreme Soviet has appointed Comrade Lazar Moiseyevich Kaganovich, First Deputy Chairman of the USSR Council of Ministers, to the post of USSR Minister of Building Materials Industry. (*Pravda,* September 4, 1956)

In the aftermath of the upheaval in Eastern Europe and the rising tide of ferment among the Soviet intelligentsia, new limitations were placed on the scope of the de-Stalinization campaign. Soviet propaganda now denied that Stalin had developed a special teaching of his own, and continued to speak of mistakes made by him "on a number of occasions," instead of more thoroughgoing criticism. The more positive aspects of Stalin's regime were also given greater attention. *Pravda,* on December 23, noted:

. . . The author of an article from the [Polish] newspaper, *Nova Kul'tura,* writes about the need for correct relations among communist and workers parties and among socialist states. This position, of course, cannot be argued. One cannot, however, agree with his definition of the "base" on which he proposes to consolidate these relations; the author thinks that socialist internationalism should rely on the struggle with "Stalinism."

First of all, it must be said that we do not know what the teaching of "Stalinism" is. It must be clear to everyone who understands Marxism that Stalin did not leave any kind of his own special teaching. He was an important Marxist and in his work he was guided by the teachings of Marx and Lenin. His services in the revolutionary movement are well known. It is also known that on a number of occasions he made serious errors, of both a theoretical and practical kind, but these errors did not create some sort of special direction of Marxism–Leninism. The essence of these errors and their harmful consequences were bravely criticized in front of the whole world by the Communist Party of the Soviet Union in a number of documents known to everyone. We are fighting and will go on fighting resolutely against the harmful consequences of Stalin's cult of the individual. Under the guise of struggling with so-called "Stalinism," an offensive is being conducted by the imperialistic reactionary forces against the most sacred property of the working class, against its revolutionary world outlook — Marxism–Leninism . . . (*Pravda,* December 23, 1956)

> Khrushchev, in a speech during a reception at the Chinese Embassy in Moscow in mid-January, 1957 made the following observations about Stalin:

. . . Recently in the West we have been accused of being "Stalinists." In answer to this we have stated more than once that in our understanding, Stalinist, just as Stalin himself, is inseparable from the great name of communist. When it was a matter of revolution, of the protection of the class interests of the proletariat in the revolutionary struggle against our class enemies, Stalin bravely and irreconcilably protected Marxism–Leninism. We criticized Stalin not because he was a poor communist. We criticized him for certain deviations, for negative qualities, and for committing serious errors. These negative qualities were noticed first of all by Lenin. Vladimir Ilyich pointed out these shortcomings and errors of Stalin. However, the latter forgot Lenin's warnings in the last years of his life. It is, of course, bad that Stalin deviated and committed errors which damaged our work. But, even when he was committing errors, breaking the law, Stalin was quite certain that he did this in the interests of the defense of that which was won by the revolution — socialism. This was Stalin's tragedy. In the fundamental and important things — the fundamental and important things to Marxist–Leninists are the protection of working-class interests, the work of socialism, the struggle with enemies of Marxism–Leninism — in these fundamental and important things, as they say, let God help every communist to fight as Stalin fought.

Enemies of communism deliberately invented the word "Stalinist" and are trying to make it into a swear word. To all of us Marxist–Leninists, who have dedicated our lives to the struggle for the interests of the working class and to its vanguard — Lenin's party — the name of Stalin is inseparable from Marxism–Leninism. Because of this, every one of us, members of the Communist Party of the Soviet Union, wants to be as loyal to Marxism–Leninism, to the struggle for the interests of the working class as was Stalin. . . .

The enemies of communism tried to capitalize on our criticism of Stalin's shortcomings and errors and utilize this criticism for their own purposes. They wanted to direct the criticism of Stalin's cult of personality against the foundations of our system, against the basis of Marxism–Leninism, but nothing came of it and nothing will come of it, gentlemen! You won't be able to do that just as you cannot see your ears without a mirror. . . . (*Pravda,* January 19, 1957)

> If Molotov and Kaganovich appeared to gain new prominence in the autumn of 1956, still another member of the presidium, who had been previously downgraded, turned up at important talks in early January in Hungary to work out new post-rebellion relationships between the Soviet Union and several of the Eastern European regimes.

At the invitation of the Hungarian Revolutionary Worker–Peasant Government and the leaders of the Hungarian Socialist Workers Party, on January first the following representatives arrived in Budapest: representatives of the Bulgarian Communist Party . . . , representatives of the Rumanian Workers Party and the Rumanian People's Republic . . . , representatives of the Soviet Union and the Soviet Government, Comrades Khrushchev and Malenkov; representatives of the Communist Party of Czechoslovakia and the Government of the Czechoslovakian Republic. . . . (*Pravda,* January 6, 1957)

Planning and Industrial Management

> Endeavors to work out new relationships within the Communist Bloc and difficulties with writers and other members of the creative intelligentsia continued to occupy the attention of the Soviet leadership during the first half of 1957. However, by the beginning of the new year, questions of economic planning and industrial management increasingly absorbed the energies of the regime. A new round of debate over the economy was launched at a Central Committee plenum in late December 1956.

On December 20–24, a plenum of the Party Central Committee was held. The Central Committee plenum discussed the following questions:

(1) Reports by Comrades N. K. Baibakov and M. Z. Saburov on completion of the work of drawing up the Sixth Five-Year Plan and on the policy of working out more specific control figures for 1956–60 and the national economic plan for 1957.

(2) The report by Comrade N. A. Bulganin on questions of improving guidance of the national economy. . . .

In connection with the designation of Comrade D. Y. Shepilov as USSR Minister of Foreign Affairs, the plenum freed Comrade Shepilov from the responsibilities of Secretary of the Party Central Committee. (*Pravda,* December 25, 1956)

> Although the published reports indicate that only the economic situation was discussed at the plenum, given the current difficulties in other areas of domestic and foreign policy, one may reasonably suppose that additional subjects were also broached. Although this was a plenum of the Party Central Committee, the published accounts of the plenum do not indicate that Khrushchev or any other member of the Secretariat played a major role in its proceedings. Moreover, the membership of the Secretariat was reduced by the release of Shepilov; and the role of the Party in industrial administration was minimized in the plenum's resolutions.

. . . The 1956 plan for industrial output as a whole will be overfulfilled. Industrial output will increase approximately 11 per cent over 1955 output, including more than 11 per cent in production of the means of production and more than 9 per cent in the production of consumer goods. The goals for many major types of industrial output will be overfulfilled. . . .

At the same time, the plenum of the Party Central Committee notes that while the output of coal, metal, cement and lumber has increased as compared to 1955, the 1956 production plan for these products is not being met; the plan for enlarging production capacity both in these and in certain other industries of the national economy is also not being fulfilled. Housing construction plans are not being completely met. . . .

To eliminate these shortcomings swiftly and to utilize all reserves and possibilities correctly for ensuring the continued planned development of the national economy, the plenum of the Party Central Committee resolves: . . .

In order to eliminate excessive strain in the plans for some industries and to bring production goals and the volume of capital investment into line with material resources, to recognize the necessity of making more specific the individual approximate quotas foreseen by the five-year-plan directives and by the draft plan for 1957. . . .

To condemn attempts by some executives to hide their unsatisfactory work in managing enterprises and construction projects by stortcomings in planning, and to condemn the desire of such managers to have plans lowered. Plans must be realistic, but not too low. . . .

It is essential to continue to increase the role of the Union republics in economic work and to develop and support their initiative in discovering and making better use of local resources and possibilities for increasing the output of industrial and consumers' goods. This requires that all administrative agencies of Union republics be given greater responsibility for fulfillment of state plans and a larger organizational role in mobilizing the masses for achieving the tasks set by the Party and government. . . .

The plenum of the Party Central Committee deems it necessary to note that there are substantial shortcomings in state planning and, above all, in current planning. The State Planning Commission, the State Economic Commission and the ministries are not doing an adequate job of studying conditions in individual branches of production, are maintaining poor contact with the Union and autonomous republics, krais, oblasts, enterprises and scientific institutions, are allowing serious omissions and errors in the drafting of production plans, capital construction plans and equipment and supply plans and are not coping with their duties in checking on fulfillment of state plans. . . .

The plenum of the Central Committee resolves:

To regard it essential to carry out measures for a fundamental improvement in the work of the USSR State Economic Commission for Current Planning of the National Economy and to entrust it with the function of operative solution of current questions connected with fulfillment of the state plan and responsibility for ensuring that necessary material resources are provided for assignments foreseen in the plan. . . .

For the purpose of eliminating excessive centralization in administration of the economy, to regard it necessary:

to carry out measures for considerably expanding the range of economic and cultural questions which the Union republic Councils of Ministers should decide and which are connected with fulfillment of Union republic state plans, including questions of capital construction, equipment and supplies, labor productivity, unit costs, marketing of goods and finance;

to ensure a further expansion of the powers of ministries, chief administrations of ministries, Soviets and economic enterprises;

to eliminate unnecessary links of the apparatus which duplicate each other's work for the purpose of simplifying and lowering the cost of the administrative apparatus. . . . (*Pravda,* December 25, 1956, extracted from the "Resolution of the Party Central Committee Plenum on Completing the Work of Drafting the Sixth Five-Year Plan and on

Policy in Drawing Up More Specific Control Figures for 1956–1960 and the Economic Plan for 1957" and the "Resolution of the Party Central Committee Plenum on Questions of Improving Guidance of the USSR National Economy")

These resolutions mark the beginning of a serious and far-reaching search, which has continued until today, for new means to manage an increasingly sophisticated and complex economy. The leadership by 1956 had become increasingly aware that the economy had reached a stage of development where merely single-minded devotion to ever higher production of basic industry by forced-draft methods was no longer appropriate. Questions of proportionate development, incentives, the introduction of new technology, costs, more finely calibrated indicators on which plant managers could base production decisions, and still others had come to the fore. While there was general consensus on the necessity of rationalizing the economic administration, as we shall see, there was disagreement on the methods.

The resolution's emphasis on de-centralization by increasing the operative powers of the Union republics and ministries was one such means. It was consistent with several measures which had been taken since 1953 and with the discussion of the July 1955 plenum. A second means, hinted at in the resolutions' statements on planning, was made more explicit in a decree published on December 26:

In connection with the resolution of the USSR Council of Ministers on the tasks and reorganization of the work of the USSR State Economic Commission, the Presidium of the USSR Supreme Soviet has adopted the following decisions:

(a) It has appointed Comrade M. G. Pervukhin, First Deputy Chairman of the USSR Council of Ministers, Chairman of the USSR State Economic Commission and has released from this post Comrade M. Z. Saburov, First Deputy Chairman of the USSR Council of Ministers.

(b) It has appointed Comrades A. N. Kosygin and V. A. Malyshev USSR Ministers and First Deputy Chairmen of the USSR State Economic Commission and Comrades M. V. Khrunichev and V. A. Kucherenko USSR Ministers and Deputy Chairmen of the USSR State Economic Commission. In addition, the Presidium has appointed Comrades V. V. Matskevich, USSR Minister of Agriculture, and I. A. Benediktov, USSR Minister of State Farms, as Deputy Chairmen of the USSR State Economic Commission.

In this connection, the Presidium of the USSR Supreme Soviet has released Comrades A. N. Kosygin, V. A. Malyshev, M. V. Krunichev, V. A. Kucherenko and V. V. Matskevich of their duties as Deputy Chairmen of the USSR Council of Ministers. (*Pravda,* December 26, 1956)

> Thus, from all appearances, the State Economic Commission for current planning, which had been separated from the State Planning Commission in mid-1955, was strengthened to serve as a powerful, high-level committee of the governmental apparatus to co-ordinate the economy. In becoming Chairman of this Commission, Pervukhin was promoted to a very powerful position.
>
> On February 5, Pervukhin delivered a report on the revised 1957 plan to the Supreme Soviet. Although this speech did not indicate any additional structural changes in the economic administration beyond those made at the December plenum, in one respect it did vary from the line taken a month and a half earlier. The December plenum resolutions touched upon difficulties in the economy, but, at the same time, claimed continuing high rates of industrial growth and did not indicate that these rates would, or should, be slackened. The official report of the Central Statistical Administration on January 31 officially claimed that compared to 1955, in 1956 heavy industrial output was up 11.4 per cent and consumers' goods output up 9.4 per cent. Yet, Pervukhin stated:

. . . On the basis of the goals established for developing various branches of industry in 1957, gross industrial output will be 7.1 per cent higher than 1956; 7.8 per cent higher in the production of the means of production . . . and 5.9 per cent in the production of consumers' goods. . . .

In drafting the plan for 1957, the USSR Council of Ministers was guided by the instructions of the December plenum of the Central Committee not to set goals too high for production and construction. The plan submitted for your consideration does set high goals, but goals that are completely realistic and materially sound for industry. . . . (*Pravda,* February 6, 1957)

> Whether these lowered growth projections reflected some padding in the officially claimed rates in 1956 or a belief by the industrial planners in the State Economic Commission that economic difficulties made necessary some slackening in the tempo of growth to permit

measures for rationalizing the economy, at any rate they marked a basic deviation from traditional Soviet economic policy. Within one year after the Sixth Five-Year Plan had been launched with great fanfare at the 20th Party Congress, it was publicly revealed that this plan was unrealistic and would not be met. This revelation could not but cause great concern.

The day after the conclusion of the Supreme Soviet session, the Party Central Committee convened for a short two-day session.

A plenum of the Party Central Committee was held on February 13 and 14. It heard and discussed Comrade N. S. Khrushchev's report on further improving organization in the management of industry and construction and adopted a resolution on the report which is published today.

The plenum elected Comrade F. R. Kozlov Candidate Member of the Presidium of the Party Central Committee and Comrade D. T. Shepilov Secretary of the Party Central Committee. (*Pravda,* February 16, 1957)

These personnel actions suggest some alterations in the balance of political power. Shepilov again joined the Party Secretariat after having been removed from that body only the previous December. The professional diplomat, A. A. Gromyko, replaced Shepilov as Minister of Foreign Affairs. The already high ratio of candidates to members in the Party Presidium was further increased by the elevation of Frol Kozlov, Leningrad First Secretary, as the seventh candidate as against eleven full members. In Stalin's day, such a high ratio usually presaged the replacement of some members by candidates.

The policy direction on questions of economic administration set by the plenum, although as usual presented as merely a continuation and extension of the previous line, largely nullified the decisions of the December Central Committee plenum and the February session of the Supreme Soviet. Moreover, in contrast to the situation in either December or February, the resolution on industrial management was based not on the reports of governmental functionaries, but on the speech of Khrushchev.

. . . The 20th Party Congress blueprinted a magnificent program for the further development of the national economy; its fulfillment would mark an important advance toward the solution of the USSR's major economic task — to overtake and surpass the most developed countries in per-capita production in an historically brief period. The most important condition for achieving this goal is the rapid growth of labor productivity based on steady improvement in the techniques and organization of production along with further improvement in the forms and methods of planning and managing the national economy.

We have every possibility of achieving this task successfully. The results of 1956, the first year of the Sixth Five-Year Plan, show that the Soviet Union is advancing at an ever-increasing rate. The 1956 plan for gross industrial output was substantially overfulfilled, the production of the means of production increased 11.4 per cent for the year and the production of consumers' goods increased 9.4 per cent. Major successes were achieved in agriculture — 1956 grain procurements exceeded those of 1955 by more than 1,000,000,000 poods . . .

The Party Central Committee Plenum resolves:

1. To consider it necessary to implement measures for further improving the management of industry and construction in order to bring it in line with the tasks and requirements of the national economy at the present stage of communist construction, with the aim of bringing management closer to economic areas, expanding the rights of Union and autonomous republics, enhancing the role of local Party and Soviet organizations as well as of trade unions and other public organizations, in economic development, and enlisting the masses on a broader scale in the management of industry.

In consideration of the fact that present forms of management of industry and construction through specialized ministries lead to departmental barriers that prevent the full utilization of the tremendous reserves and potentialities of our economy and fail to ensure concrete and efficient management of enterprises and construction projects, it is necessary to work out new forms of management of economic construction that will more fully combine concrete and efficient management in economic areas with strict observance of the basic principle of centralized planning on an all-Union scale.

2. To instruct the Presidium of the Party Central Committee and the USSR Council of Ministers to draft concrete proposals for the reorganization of management of industry and construction in the direction indicated above and — being aware of the great nationwide significance of the question — to submit them for the examination of the USSR Supreme Soviet.

In formulating practical measures, the need to enlarge the role of the State Planning Commission in planning and managing the country's national economy must be taken into account . . .

In continuing to strengthen in every way possible the principle of planning in the development of the nation's economy, it is necessary to reorganize radically the work of the USSR State Planning Commission so that it will base its work on the agencies established in the economic areas and will submit major long-term questions of future economic development in time for review by the government and the Party Central Committee. . . .

It is necessary to reorganize the work of the State Economic Commission, to simplify its structure and to make it less unwieldy. The State Economic Commission must not duplicate the work of the State Planning Commission and other agencies and must not interfere with the functions of the administration. Its duty, in addition to current planning, is to co-ordinate the work of administration of economic areas in fulfilling annual plans. . . .

Reorganization of the management of industry and the national economy requires a radical change in the scope and methods of state control. It is necessary to concentrate the principal control functions in the economic areas, with a view to uncovering and eliminating shortcomings in the work of the government and economic apparatus in the localities. . . . (*Pravda*, February 16, 1957)

Although its policy recommendations were not precise (these were to be formulated by the "Party Presidium and the Council of Ministers") the objects of the resolution's concern and the drift of its recommendations were clear enough – and politically loaded. "Decentralization" was apparently not to be carried out within the confines of the ministerial system, but through its abolition. The State Planning Commission was to be strengthened at the expense of the recently refurbished State Economic Commission. Molotov's Ministry of State Control was to be reorganized. Finally, in place of the relatively sombre and cautious projections of economic growth voiced during the previous two months, the resolution reverted to the old slogans of rapidly catching up with the West and in fulfilling the "magnificent" Sixth Five-Year Plan.

Khrushchev's speech to the February plenum, on which this resolution was based, was not published. A month and a half elapsed before Khrushchev's "Theses" on reorganizing the industrial administration were publicized, on March 30. These Theses made more specific the policy recommendations implied by the resolution of the February plenum and, in some instances, went beyond those recommendations — as in the case of the State Economic Commission. It is not clear whether the Theses of March 30 are substantially the same as Khrushchev's speech to the February plenum or whether they represent a new version of his scheme for reorganization of industrial management.

The form in which Khrushchev's plan for industrial reorganization was announced was highly unusual in the Soviet Union at that time:

. . . The Presidium of the Party Central Committee and the USSR Council of Ministers are submitting the question of further improving organization in the management of industry and construction to the next session of the USSR Supreme Soviet. Comrade N. S. Khrushchev is to give the report on this question. . . .

The Party Central Committee and the USSR Council of Ministers have decided to publish the Theses of the report in the press and to hold a nationwide discussion of this question so that a widespread exchange of opinions and a broad consideration of available experience may be used as a basis for working out the most practical forms of administration of the country's national economy. The Theses set out the main lines along which the management of industry and construction should be reorganized. It is not the task of the Theses to present final recommendations on all concrete questions involved in the new structure of management of the economy at the center and locally. A nationwide discussion will make it possible to discover the best organizational forms of management of industry and construction in present conditions.

In organizing a nationwide discussion of the Theses, the Union-republic Party Central Committees, the krai and oblast Party committees, the Union-republic Councils of Ministers and the executive committees of krai and oblast Soviets must waste no time in drafting measures for the reorganization of management and in drawing up concrete proposals for the structure of the economic councils. It is also necessary to give thorough consideration to the rational distribution of personnel in order to promote to leading posts in the economic councils and planning agencies highly skilled specialists and experienced production organizers able to cope effectively with the guidance of industrial enterprises and construction projects. . . . (*Pravda*, March 30, 1957)

The attribution of the plan for industrial reorganization to Khrushchev personally is highly reminiscent of the personal credit given to him in early 1954 for the Virgin Lands scheme. With the publication of his Theses, Khrushchev staked out a new claim as spokesman on industrial organization and production.

. . . In the postwar years, when our industry and the entire national economy have risen to a higher stage of development, when new qualitative changes are taking place in the development of production, tendencies to create more and more branches of industry and construction, to implement further specialization and to establish new specialized branches, ministries and administrations have become increasingly evident. . . .

The Soviet Union presently has over 200,000 state industrial enterprises and over 100,000 construction sites distributed throughout the vast area of the country. In these circumstances it is difficult to provide concrete and efficient leadership to the vast number of industrial enterprises and construction projects from a single ministry or administration. . . .

It has become necessary in this connection to abandon some outdated organizational forms of industrial management in order to end the policy of further fragmentation of technical, economic, and administrative management in favor of more flexible forms of directing the national economy — forms which take into account more fully the specific features of the particular oblast, krai or republic.

The question of radically reorganizing the management of industry and construction has not arisen because some shortcomings have been revealed in the fulfillment of national economic plans. The industry of the Soviet Union has advanced confidently and is continuing to do so at present, as convincingly demonstrated by the results of the fulfillment of the national economic plans. The organizational structure of management should be reorganized primarily to give greater scope to the development of the country's productive forces . . .

A major shortcoming in the practice of managing industry and construction today is the presence of departmental barriers which often impede the solution of important questions of economic development. There are numerous facts to show that the narrow departmental approach of some industrial executives considerably damages the state and delays for a long time the solution of urgent economic problems. . . .

A departmental approach weakens and not infrequently upsets normal economic ties between enterprises of different branches of industry located in a single economic administrative area. Narrow departmental approaches make it impossible to utilize fully opportunities for solving economic problems efficiently on the spot, to distribute more rationally available material resources, manpower and finances, and to take specific measures for timely elimination of shortcomings revealed in the course of fulfilling plans. . . .

Under the present system of industrial and construction management, each ministry frequently attempts to manufacture for itself everything it needs, disregarding costs and ignoring the fact that the production area and equipment are not fully utilized and that there is considerable cross-shipping, long-distance and other irrational transportation of goods. . . .

In keeping with the further growth of the national economy at the present stage of its development, it is necessary to transfer the center of gravity of the operational leadership of industry and construction to the localities, nearer to the enterprises and construction sites. To this end it is apparently necessary to switch from earlier organizational forms of management through branch ministries and administrations to new forms of management on the territorial principle. One form of such management might be, for example, economic councils. Reorganization in this direction will be in the interests of further implementation of the Leninist principle of democratic centralism in the field of economic construction . . .

If it is found advantageous to adopt the proposal to establish agencies of territorial management of industry and construction in the form of economic councils in the republics, krais and oblasts, there will be no further need to have Union and republic ministries controlling industry and construction. . . .

The economic councils should be organized, as a rule, in correspondence with the existing administrative division, taking into consideration the level of industrial development in the oblast, krai, or republic. Such economic administrative areas are, for example, Sverdlovsk Oblast, Chelyabinsk Oblast, and the Bashkir Autonomous Republic, each of which has highly developed industry. . . .

There is no need to have economic councils in all oblasts, krais and autonomous republics; but they should be created wherever industry is sufficiently developed. . . . In a number of instances the organization of councils may prove to be justified in oblasts where industry, even if not strongly developed, nevertheless requires local management agencies because of their remoteness and the dispersion of their territory. . . .

The economic council of an oblast, krai, or republic will represent the basic link of industrial and construction management; guided by the tasks of the general state plan for the development of the national economy, it will exercise direct management of the enterprises and construction sites subordinated to it. . . .

Some comrades have put forward proposals to establish under the Council of Ministers special economic agencies in the form, for example, of Committees under the USSR Council of Ministers, which, they suggest, will be entrusted with leadership of key branches of heavy industry. This means that some branches of heavy industry will have to be managed from the center as before.

Such proposals in effect mean the preservation of the old form of management under a new name and of a worse nature. . . .

Comrades who make such proposals apparently are worried that various operational problems will arise during the fulfillment of the annual and five-year plans which some agency will have to decide. Questions not foreseen in the process of compiling the plan will, of course, arise. But it will be expedient to submit them to the State Planning Commission for consideration since no other parallel agency will be able to settle them without the State Planning Commission at any rate. . . .

It is obviously necessary to grant the USSR State Planning Commission concrete and effective powers to resolve questions of co-ordinating the work of the economic councils in fulfilling their national economic plans. The USSR State Planning Commission should be involved in consolidated planning on the basis of plans formulated by the economic councils. . . .

Analyzing the plans drawn up by the economic administrative areas, the State Planning Commission should abort trends toward autarchy and localism so that the interests of a given area will not be counterposed to the interests of the state as a whole. . . .

In connection with the projected reorganization of the management of the Soviet Union's economy, when the chief task of planning, both operational and long-term, is to be concentrated in the economic administrative areas, when the work of consolidated planning of the Soviet Union's economy is to be concentrated in the State Planning Commission and the latter is entrusted with powers to co-ordinate the activities of the economic councils in plan fulfillment, the existence of the State Economic Commission becomes inexpedient at the present stage and it should be dissolved. . . .

The content and methods of work of the USSR Ministry of State Control and the Union republic Ministries of State Control evidently should be radically reorganized. The Ministry of State Control now has an unwieldy apparatus based on the departmental principle which attempts to cover literally all matters, even the control of the level of technical development of the various industries and the level of science and technology . . .

Some comrades express fears that the organization of industrial and construction management on the territorial principle and the transfer of enterprises from all-Union to republic subordination may weaken the centralized planning principle in the development of our Soviet economy. This is incorrect, of course, . . . The national economy of the Soviet Union is managed on the basis of an integrated national economic plan consolidating the plans of all the Union republics and approved by the USSR Supreme Soviet. . . .

The reorganization of the management of the economy on the territorial principle will increase immeasurably the responsibility of the Party agencies in the republics, krais and oblasts, of all Party organizations, for the development of production and the condition of construction in each economic–administrative area, and confronts Party organizations with the need to study more thoroughly the economics of industry and construction, to guide efficiently and concretely industrial enterprises and construction jobs, to increase their organizational work among the masses.

Under existing forms of leadership, where plans are drafted and implemented through the specialized ministries and departments, the local Party units are in a number of cases denied the possibility of more actively influencing the work of the enterprises, of more fully utilizing the economic potentials of each raion and oblast, or eliminating harmful departmental barriers, of implementing on a wider scale co-operation in production among enterprises of a given raion, oblast, krai, or republic.

New forms of industrial and construction management will give republic, krai, and oblast Party organizations greater powers and opportunities to influence the fulfillment of state plans, the production activities of enterprises and construction projects, to promote the implementation of Party and governmental decisions on the development of the economy and continued improvement in the living standards of the working people. . . . (*Pravda*, March 30, 1957)

Khrushchev's plan of industrial reorganization was directed toward alleviating a number of genuine problems in the economic administration, several of which he mentioned in his Theses. Indications of a slackening in the economic growth rate spurred him to drastic action. It has been a hallmark of Khrushchev's modus operandi that when faced with a serious problem in Soviet society he has reacted by ordering a major overhaul of the pertinent bureaucratic structure. Although highly critical of the "bureaucrat," he himself has tended to take an organizational view of the world and has attempted to cope with difficulties by altering the forms of organization.

Nevertheless, Khrushchev's particular plan of attack on administrative shortcomings was also shaped by personal and political motivations and had far-reaching political consequences. Not only did it bring under fire Molotov's Ministry of State Control and Pervukhin's powerful State Economic Commission, it directly and personally threatened a number of important and powerful ministerial officials and diluted the significance of the Council of Ministers. Many of the industrial ministries had been powerful fiefdoms over which the ministers ruled as lords. Suddenly, these men found themselves reorganized out of a job and faced with the unhappy prospect either of finding a lesser job in Moscow, such as in the State Planning Commission, or of heading a regional economic council, oftentimes far from Moscow, the center of power, patronage, and promotions. On the other hand, as Khrushchev frankly stated, by regionalizing industrial administration, the influence of the provincial and republic Party first secretaries over the economy was greatly enhanced.

Aside from these bald political considerations, there were other grounds on which some members of the power elite — "some comrades" — viewed his plans with skepticism. If regionalization were carried too far, it would make difficult the imposition and enforcement of a detailed, centrally determined economic plan. Regional authorities, if vested with too much authority, might run afoul of the sin of "localism," i.e. promoting the interests of their own bailiwick at the expense of co-ordinated national development. Khrushchev did take cognizance of these protestations and attempted to pull their sting. In actual fact, developments in the late 1950's and early 1960's justified these fears in part; and the industrial administration was never decentralized to the extent visualized by Khrushchev in his Theses. By 1963 much of the 1957 reorganization had been reversed.

Beginning the day after the publication of Khrushchev's Theses, a widespread propaganda campaign was launched in support of his plan to reorganize the administration of industry. *Pravda, Izvestia* and other newspapers were filled with articles and letters discussing the scheme and how it should be implemented. According to Khrushchev's report to the May session of the Supreme Soviet, "between March 30 and May 4 over 514,000 meetings were held at enterprises and construction sites, in scientific organizations and institutes, collective farms, machine and tractor stations and state farms, in units of the Soviet Army and in educational establishments. These meetings were attended by 40,820,000 working people, of whom more than 2,300,000 made comments and proposals on the question of improving management of industry and construction." This, according to Khrushchev, was "vivid proof of Soviet democracy."

Although there was no opposition expressed to the plan in general, largely because the Theses had not laid down the details of the reform, there was a surprising breadth of views publicly aired about how the reorganization should be carried out and what additional measures might be taken to make it more effective. Several enterprise managers argued for an expansion of the rights of managers. There were differences expressed on the precise relations which should pertain between the State Planning Commission and the regional economic councils and on the concrete structure and responsibilities of the councils.

Khrushchev and his supporters in the Party apparatus campaigned vigorously for the plan. Similar to his actions in rallying support for the Virgin Lands program in 1954, Khrushchev personally took to the hustings, making numerous speeches from various parts of the country, which were reported in the press. One may conjecture that he spent much of his time appealing for backing and rapid action from regional officials whose interests were favored by his scheme. In fact, already in early April a number of oblast, city, and republic Party organizations held plenums to draw up plans for the reorganization. *Pravda,* on April 5, featured an article by Furtseva, First Secretary of the Moscow City Party Committee, in which she provided some specific details on the structure of the proposed Moscow economic council. Significantly, apart from Khrushchev and Kirichenko, no full member of the Party Presidium was reported to have spoken publicly on the reorganization plan.

Shortly before the Supreme Soviet session, which was to discuss and ratify the reorganization, several significant personnel alterations were decreed:

The Presidium of the USSR Supreme Soviet has appointed Comrade Mikhail Georgiyevich Pervukhin, First Deputy Chairman of the USSR Council of Ministers, to the post of USSR Minister of Medium Machine Building. (*Pravda*, May 3, 1957)

* * *

The Presidium of the USSR Supreme Soviet has appointed Comrade Iosif Iosifovich Kuzmin to the posts of Chairman of the USSR State Planning Commission and First Deputy Chairman of the USSR Council of Ministers.

The Presidium of the USSR Supreme Soviet has released Comrade Nikolai Konstantinovich Baibakov from his duties as Chairman of the USSR State Planning Commission in connection with his transfer to another post.

By decree of the Presidium of the Russian Republic Supreme Soviet, Comrade N. K. Baibakov has been appointed Chairman of the Russian Republic State Planning Commission and First Deputy Chairman of the Russian Republic Council of Ministers. (*Pravda*, May 5, 1957)

Prior to his appointment as head of the State Planning Commission, Kuzmin was an unknown both in the West and in the Soviet Union, although, in fact, he had had considerable experience in the Party apparatus and in extra-ordinary governmental bodies. In recent years he had worked in the apparatus of the Central Committee as head of the Department of Machine Building of the Central Committee.

On May 7, Khrushchev delivered to the Supreme Soviet the major address, on the industrial reorganization. Aside from the customary smattering of speeches by worker and peasant delegates, the major participants in the discussion of the report were provincial and republic Party secretaries; except for Khrushchev no full member of the Party Presidium addressed the session. On May 11, the newspapers carried Khrushchev's concluding remarks and the resolution of the Supreme Soviet on the industrial reorganization.

The provisions of the reorganization plan as they emerged from the Supreme Soviet session appeared to diverge in several minor respects from Khrushchev's original Theses. For example, several of the industrial ministries were retained, particularly those relating to defense industry. Khrushchev gave the Supreme Soviet the following explanation for these exceptions:

. . . Speeches on behalf of the Union ministries, and particularly the defense ministries, should be mentioned. Comrade Zasyadko said in his speech that he did not consider it expedient to retain those all-Union ministries that direct enterprises of the defense industry. These proposals are not appropriate.

During the initial discussion of the reorganization of industrial and construction management, proposals were advanced to abolish all industrial ministries. However, during the course of the discussion, after a broad exchange of views, the need to retain some of the Union ministries was recognized.

Enterprises of the ministries concerned with defense will be placed under the regional economic councils. The economic councils will manage these enterprises. As already indicated in the report and in the speeches of some Deputies, these ministries should be retained so that in implementing the reorganization of industrial and construction management a more systematic change-over to the new system can be made without weakening centralized control over the development of these branches of our industry. . . . (*Pravda*, May 11, 1957)

This modification must have assuaged any misgivings which the military may have harbored about the reorganization.

A second modification was the increased number of regional economic councils created. Although the Theses were vague on this point, from the initial discussions it appeared that originally many fewer councils were projected than the 105 finally established. Even at the early May session of the Supreme Soviet a deputy from Kazakhstan indicated that only one council was planned for the entire Kazakh Republic; by mid-May the number had jumped to nine. While the larger number of councils may in part have resulted from a need to mesh the new structure of industrial management in with existing Party and governmental provincial boundaries, this development may also have been influenced by a desire to avoid jurisdictional disputes among oblast and krai Party bosses and to build support for the program in the political hinterlands. During the discussions of the reorganization, it was made abundantly clear that powerful provincial officials wanted their own economic councils unshared with other provinces.

As suggested by the increase in the number of councils even after the Supreme Soviet meeting, the May 10 decree left a number of details on the reorganization unresolved. Nevertheless, it ordered that the reorganization "must be carried out by July 1, 1957." This deadline set a breakneck pace for such a vast undertaking.

VI · THE ROUT OF THE OPPOSITION

Khrushchev and his scheme of industrial reorganization had won the day at the May session of the Supreme Soviet. During the remainder of the month he continued aggressively to pursue his advantage. He gave three interviews to foreign journalists from Poland, Yugoslavia, and the U.S.; reports of these were prominently featured in the press. In addition, Khrushchev dominated the spotlight of publicity with speeches to conferences and workers' gatherings. Radiating ebullience, he confidently predicted great economic achievements. In his speech to the Supreme Soviet in May he had claimed that "we now have at our disposal everything required for solving . . . the main economic problem of the USSR – to catch up with and surpass the most developed capitalist countries in per capita output." During a speech to a conference of agricultural workers, in Leningrad on May 22, he more specifically predicted that "the strength of the collective farm system,

June 1957 to March 1958

the patriotism of the Soviet people and socialist competition will enable us to solve this problem in the near future and to catch up with the United States in per capita output of meat, milk, and butter during the present five-year plan [by 1960]."

While Khrushchev received the lion's share of publicity during the spring, other leaders did not go entirely unnoticed. Of particular interest was an article by Molotov, entitled "On Lenin," which appeared in *Pravda* on April 22. Purporting to be a discussion of Lenin's ideas expressed before and during the Bolshevik Revolution, this piece was, in fact, a bold polemical attack by Molotov on his political opponents and their policies.

To speak about Lenin — this is a difficult business. . . .

Perhaps it is especially difficult to do this for someone who met Lenin personally and knew him closely in this or that period. In any case, to speak about Lenin — this means to speak also about our Party and about Leninism.

It is possible to say that at the beginning of 1902, when Lenin's well-known book, *What Is To Be Done? The Pressing Questions of Our Movement,* appeared, the revolutionary genius of Lenin was already in blossom. In this remarkable book — more precisely, brochure — Lenin put forth a brilliant defense of revolutionary Marxism, revealing the roots, the ideological sources of opportunism (the current "revisionism"); providing the necessary foundation for the creation of a Marxist party of a new type; and giving a general elaboration of its ideological foundation. In *The History of the All-Union Communist Party (Bolshevik),* the "Short Course," it is correctly said that the theoretical position developed in *What Is To Be Done* provided the basis of the ideology of our Communist Party. . . .

Of all the questions of the 20th century for the working class — and, consequently, for the communist movement — especially significant is the question concerning the attitude toward imperialist wars. It is known that imperialism cannot live without war, because its existence is linked with the pursuit after monopolistic profits, with the development of sharp contradictions in the camp of imperialism, with the struggle for colonies . . . Only other, anti-imperialist forces may prevent new imperialist wars. . . .

Lenin's ideas of the struggle against imperialist wars, as they were set forth by him in the years of the first world war and later, are also now the guiding star for communists and all conscious workers in all countries. In the light of these great ideas, we consider also the decisions of the 20th Congress of our Party about the possibilities of averting wars. . . .

The camp of the socialist states grows and recruits all new forces. We, of course, should take into consideration the fact that we do not have a level road ahead and that in our path lies not a few obstacles, not to mention any undermining tactics which imperialism employs against the USSR and the whole socialist camp. . . .

A socialist country may not stand aside from this fraternal co-operation of the socialist countries. This would be a rejection, not only of co-operation in strengthening the socialist camp — in which only our class enemies, the imperialists, may rejoice — but would also danger-ously weaken the position of our countries. All attempts to prove the contrary are empty sophistry, having nothing in common with the in-terests of the working class and all working people. . . .

There is little doubt but that the sophists Molotov had in mind were Khrushchev and his followers, for this article implicitly condemned their major policies. Claiming unique authority as an ideological spokesman because he alone of the top leaders had known Lenin per-sonally, Molotov cited Lenin to emphasize the dangers of the imperial-ist threat and the need for discipline in the socialist camp — a thinly veiled slap at Yugoslavia. He ignored the "cult of personality" and soft-pedalled the ideological innovations of the 20th Party Congress concerning peaceful co-existence and different roads to socialism, even going so far as to imply that these ideas were unwarranted revisions of Leninism. He stressed the difficulties ahead for the Soviet Union rather than propounding the optimistic line current at that time. Fi-nally, he gave tacit support for the Stalinist history of the Party (the "Short Course") which was under official attack.

The June Crisis

During the spring and early summer of 1957 the leadership struggle was reaching a new level of intensity. In addition to the personality clashes and policy issues in dispute already reviewed, there was an-other contentious matter exacerbating elite politics — a matter which was not visible at the time and was only hinted at later. This was the issue of rehabiliating the purge victims of the Stalin era. Since a num-ber of the older leaders had been in high positions during the Stalinist

"The return of N. A. Bulganin and N. S. Khrushchev from a trip to Finland. In the photograph: Reception at the Leningrad Station." (*Pravda*, June 15, 1957, page 1)

purges, they in one way or another were inevitably implicated in his crimes. Thus, the review of the cases of those purged with a view to their rehabilitation posed a grave threat to these leaders if some faction were powerful enough to use these materials to condemn its Presidium opponents while suppressing derogatory information about its own past activities.

Between June 5 and June 14, Khrushchev and Bulganin visited Finland. Upon their return, they were given a royal reception which was pictorially presented in *Pravda* on June 15.

An announcement of a Presidium reception for a group of Hungarian journalists on June 18 provides a guide for identifying which Presidium members were in Moscow on what turned out to be a fateful date:

On June 18 the delegation of Hungarian journalists were received by the Presidium of the Party Central Committee. Comrades N. A. Bulganin, K. Ye. Voroshilov, L. M. Kaganovich, G. M. Malenkov, A. I. Mikoyan, V. M. Molotov, M. G. Pervukhin, N. S. Khrushchev, G. K. Zhukov, L. I. Brezhnev, D. T. Shepilov and Ye. A. Furtseva warmly greeted the Hungarian journalists. (*Pravda,* June 19, 1957)

Only on July 2 was there public hint of serious difficulties among the leadership. The outcome of this new leadership struggle, just as in the purge of Beria in 1953, was revealed in stages. On July 2, *Pravda* listed those leaders in attendance at a concert:

. . . The following were present at the final concert of the Kabardino-Balkar Autonomous Republic collective art show: N. A. Bulganin, K. Ye. Voroshilov, A. I. Mikoyan, M. A. Suslov, N. S. Khrushchev, L. I. Brezhnev, N. M. Shvernik, N. I. Belyayev, P. N. Pospelov, First Secretary of the Kabardino-Balkar Party Committee, J. K. Mal'bakhov, and Chairman of the Presidium of the Kabardino-Balkar Supreme Soviet, K. J. Jlostanov. (*Pravda,* July 2, 1957)

The following day, a *Pravda* editorial emphasized the monolithic unity of the Party and justified purges in the leadership as a Leninist precept.

. . . The great Lenin taught the Party to protect the unity of its ranks with great care, to struggle relentlessly against those who under various pretexts strive to undermine this unity. The 10th Party Congress, discussing the question of Party unity, upon a proposal from Lenin, directed the immediate dissolution of all factional groups and instructed all organizations to see to it that no factional actions of any kind were taken. Noncompliance with the decree of the Congress would lead to certain and immediate dismissal from the Party. The Congress vested the Central Committee with authority to take all kinds of Party punitive measures, even including expulsion from the Central Committee and the Party, in the event that Central Committee members violated discipline or in the event that factionalism was revived or tolerated. . . .

When it was discovered that some Party figure did not comply with its decisions and allowed mistakes in his work, the Party Central Committee adopted measures for the correction of these mistakes. In the period before the 20th Party Congress, at the Central Committee plenum, the activity of a number of Party organizations was subjected to severe criticism, as was also the activity of members of the Central Committee. Some Party workers, who had not justified the trust placed in them, were excluded from Central Committee membership.

The 20th Party Congress noted in particular that the Central Committee had taken timely action against attempts to retreat from the Party's general line on the preponderant development of heavy industry and had also acted against confusion about the question of building socialism in our country and some other theoretical questions. . . .

The unity of the Party and its closely united ranks have made possible the rapid implementation of the plan for a radical reorganization of industrial management, the achievement of great successes in the progress of agriculture, and the formulation of a very important task: to catch up with the United States in the per capita production of milk, meat, and butter in the near future. . . .

The Party's Statutes obligate every Party member to safeguard Party unity in every way because it is the principal condition of its strength and might. This requirement concerns equally the rank-and-file and the leadership of the Party. . . . (*Pravda,* July 3, 1957)

> Only on the next day, July 4, was the public notified that a Central Committee plenum of far-reaching consequences for the nation's leadership had concluded its deliberations five days before.

A plenum of the Party Central Committee was held from June 22 to June 29, 1957.

The plenum discussed the question of the anti-Party group of G. M. Malenkov, L. M. Kaganovich, and V. M. Molotov.

The plenum adopted an appropriate resolution which is published today.

The plenum removed Comrades Malenkov, Kaganovich, and Molotov from membership in the Presidium of the Central Committee and from membership in the Party Central Committee and removed Comrade Shepilov from his post as Secretary of the Party Central Committee and from the list of candidate members of the Presidium of the Central Committee and from membership in the Central Committee.

The plenum elected the following PRESIDIUM of the PARTY CENTRAL COMMITTEE:

Members of the Presidium: Comrades A. B. Aristov, N. I. Belyayev, L. I. Brezhnev, N. A. Bulganin, K. Ye. Voroshilov, G. K. Zhukov, N. G. Ignatov, A. I. Kirichenko, F. R. Kozlov, O. V. Kuusinen, A. I. Mikoyan, M. A. Suslov, Ye. A. Furtseva, N. S. Khrushchev, and N. M. Shvernik.

Candidate members of the Presidium: Comrades N. A. Mukhitdinov, P. N. Pospelov, D. S. Korotchenko, J. E. Kalnberzin, A. P. Kirilenko, A. N. Kosygin, K. T. Mazurov, V. P. Mzhavanadze, and M. G. Pervukhin.

The plenum filled out the Secretariat by electing Comrade O. V. Kuusinen a Secretary of the Party Central Committee. (*Pravda,* July 4, 1957)

The published resolution of the Central Committee "On the Anti-Party Group" threw the book at Malenkov, Kaganovich, Molotov and, to a lesser degree, at "Shepilov who joined them"; but, with the exception of several more specific accusations levelled against Molotov, the charges are vague and generalized. Similarly, no precise ideological charges are made against them, only that they were "conservative," "dogmatic," "sectarian," and "scholastic." Finally, they are charged with attempting "to change the composition of the Party's leading bodies," but we are left in ignorance of what changes they wanted to make.

. . . Striving to alter the Party's political line, this group [Malenkov, Kaganovich, and Molotov] used anti-Party, factional methods in an endeavor to change the composition of the Party's leading bodies, elected by the plenum of the Party Central Committee.

This was not accidental.

In the last three or four years, during which the Party has been setting a determined course toward correcting the errors and short-comings engendered by the cult of personality and waging a successful struggle against revisionists of Marxism–Leninism, both on the international front and within the country — years during which the Party has done considerable work to correct past distortions of Leninist nationality policy — the members of the anti-Party group, now stripped and completely exposed, have been giving continual opposition, both direct and indirect, to the course approved by the 20th Party Congress.

This group attempted, in effect, to oppose the Leninist course toward peaceful co-existence among states with different social systems, to oppose the relaxation of international tension and the creation of friendly relations between the USSR and all the peoples of the world.

They were against enlarging the powers of the Union republics in the area of economic and cultural development and in the area of legislation and also against enhancing the role of local Soviets in carrying out these tasks. Thus, the anti-Party group opposed the Party's firm course toward more rapid economic and cultural development in the national republics. . . . Not only did the anti-Party group fail to understand the Party's measures directed toward fighting bureaucracy and reducing the inflated state apparatus, it opposed them. . . .

This group persistently opposed and tried to upset such an extremely important measure as the reorganization of industrial management and the establishment of economic councils in the economic regions, a measure approved by the whole Party and the people. . . . This group even continued its struggle against the reorganization of industrial management after the approval of these measures during the course of the nationwide discussion and subsequent adoption of the law at the session of the USSR Supreme Soviet.

With regard to agricultural questions, the members of this group failed to understand the new and vital tasks. They did not recognize the need to increase material incentives for the collective farm peasantry in enlarging the output of agricultural products. They opposed the elimination of the old bureaucratic system of planning on the collective farms and the introduction of the new planning system which unfetters the initiative of the collective farms in managing their own affairs. . . .

They conducted a completely unjustified struggle against the Party's appeal, which was actively supported by the collective farms, oblasts and republics, to overtake the USA in per capita output of milk, butter, and meat in the next few years. Thus, the members of the anti-Party group demonstrated a lofty indifference to the vital interests of the broad masses of the people and a lack of faith in the tremendous potentialities inherent in the socialist economy. . . .

It cannot be regarded as accidental that Comrade Molotov, a participant in the anti-Party group, showing conservatism and a stagnant attitude, not only failed to realize the need for developing the virgin lands but even opposed the plowing up of 35,000,000 hectares of virgin land, which has been of such tremendous importance for our country's economy.

Comrades Malenkov, Kaganovich, and Molotov stubbornly opposed those measures which the Central Committee and our entire Party carried out to eliminate the consequences of the cult of the individual leader, to eliminate the violations of revolutionary legality which had occurred and to create conditions which would preclude their recurrence. . . .

As Minister of Foreign Affairs, Comrade Molotov for a long time not only failed to take any measures through the Ministry of Foreign Affairs to improve relations between the USSR and Yugoslavia but repeatedly came out against those measures which the Presidium of the Central Committee carried out to improve relations with Yugoslavia. Comrade Molotov's incorrect position on the Yugoslav question was unaimously condemned by the July 1955 plenum of the Party Central

Committee as "not corresponding to the interests of the Soviet state and the socialist camp and not conforming to the principles of Leninist policy."

Comrade Molotov raised obstacles to the conclusion of the state treaty with Austria and the improvement of relations with this state in the center of Europe. . . . He was also against normalizing relations with Japan, whereas this normalization has played an important part in relaxing international tension in the Far East. He opposed the fundamental propositions worked out by the Party on the possibility of different roads of transition to socialism in different countries, on the necessity of strengthening contacts between the Communist Party of the Soviet Union and the progressive parties of foreign countries. . . .

He denied the advisability of establishing personal contacts between the leaders of the USSR and the statesmen of other countries, which is essential in the interests of achieving mutual understanding and improving international relations.

On many of the aforementioned questions Comrade Molotov's opinion was supported by Comrade Kaganovich and in a number of cases by Comrade Malenkov. The Presidium of the Central Committee and the Central Committee as a whole patiently corrected them and fought against their errors, assuming that they would learn from their errors, that they would not persist in them and would fall into line with the entire guiding collective of the Party. However, they continued to hold to their erroneous non-Leninist positions.

What is at the basis of the position of Comrades Malenkov, Kaganovich, and Molotov — which is at odds with the Party line — is that they were, and still are, bound up by old attitudes and methods, that they have become divorced from the life of the Party and the country and fail to see the new conditions, the new situation, that they take a conservative attitude and hang stubbornly to outdated forms and methods of work . . .

In questions of both domestic and foreign policy they are sectarian and dogmatic and they employ a scholastic, lifeless approach to Marxism–Leninism. . . .

Seeing that their incorrect statements and actions were constantly rebuffed in the Presidium of the Central Committee, which has been consistently carrying out the line of the 20th Party Congress, Comrades Molotov, Kaganovich, and Malenkov launched a group struggle against the Party leadership. Reaching agreement among themselves on an anti-Party basis, they set out to alter the policy of the Party, to return the Party to those erroneous methods of leadership which were condemned by the 20th Party Congress. They resorted to methods of intrigue and reached a secret agreement against the Central Committee. The facts revealed at the Central Committee plenum show that Comrades Malenkov, Kaganovich, and Molotov, along with Comrade Shepilov who joined them, having embarked on the path of factional struggle, violated the party Statutes and the decision of the 10th Party Congress "On Party Unity" drafted by Lenin . . .

This Leninist resolution makes it obligatory for the Central Committee and all Party organizations constantly to strengthen Party unity, to rebuff resolutely any signs of factional or group activity . . .

Confronted with the unanimous condemnation of the anti-Party activity of the group by the Central Committee plenum, in a situation where the members of the Central Committee plenum unanimously demanded the removal of the members of the group from the Central Committee and their expulsion from the Party, they admitted the existence of collusion and the harmful nature of their anti-Party activity and obligated themselves to comply with the Party's decisions. . . .

The Party Central Committee summons all Communists to rally still more closely around the invincible banner of Marxism–Leninism, to direct all their strength toward the successful solution of the tasks of communist construction. (Adopted on June 29, 1957 by unanimous vote of all the members of the Central Committee, candidate members of the Central Committee and members of the Central Inspection Commission, with one abstention in the person of Comrade Molotov.) (*Pravda,* July 4, 1957)

> Before examining the evidence bearing on the issues under dispute and the procedural course of the in-fighting in late June, let us review the upheaval in the membership of the leading Party and governmental bodies which transpired at that time. In addition to the changes in the membership of the top Party organs announced by the Central Committee resolution, there were also alterations in the Council of Ministers.

The Presidium of the USSR Supreme Soviet has relieved Comrade G. M. Malenkov of the posts of Deputy Chairman of the USSR Council of Ministers and USSR Minister of Power Plants, Comrade L. M. Kaganovich of the post of First Deputy Chairman of the USSR Council of Ministers, and Comrade V. M. Molotov of the posts of First Deputy Chairman of the USSR Council of Ministers and USSR Minister of State Control. . . . (*Pravda,* July 5, 1957)

* * *

The Presidium of the USSR Supreme Soviet has appointed Comrade Alexei Nikolayevich Kosygin Deputy Chairman of the USSR Council of Ministers.

The Presidium of the USSR Supreme Soviet has relieved Comrade Mikhail Georgiyevich Pervukhin, USSR Minister of Medium Machine Building, of the responsibilities of First Deputy Chairman of the USSR Council of Ministers.

The Presidium of the USSR Supreme Soviet has relieved Comrade Maxim Zakharovich Saburov of the responsibilities of First Deputy Chairman of the USSR Council of Ministers. (*Pravda,* July 6, 1957)

Subsequently, Molotov was sent to Ulan Bator as Ambassador, Kaganovich was made director of a cement plant in the Urals, and Malenkov was designated head of a power station in Kazakhstan.

The Party Presidium was now composed of fifteen full members, nine of whom were new. The majority of them were from the Party apparatus and had only recently made their appearance at the top under the aegis of Khrushchev. There were now nine candidate members of the Presidium, five of whom were republic or provincial Party officials. The Central Committee Secretariat membership remained at eight, with Kuusinen replacing Shepilov. Reinforcing the dramatically increased representation of the Party apparatus in the Party Presidium and the enhanced stature of the Central Committee Secretariat was the decimation of the ranks of the Presidium of the Council of Ministers. Four First Deputy Chairmen and one Deputy Chairman of the Council of Ministers were dismissed, while only one new Deputy Chairman was appointed. Besides Chairman Bulganin, there were only First Deputy Chairmen Mikoyan and Kuzmin and Deputy Chairman Kosygin.

Although only Malenkov, Kaganovich, Molotov, and Shepilov were listed in the Central Committee resolution as members of the anti-Party group, it should not be overlooked that Saburov and Pervukhin were also demoted by the plenum, indicating they were somewhat implicated. On July 25 Pervukhin slipped still further when he was named to the secondary post of Chairman of the State Committee on

Foreign Economic Relations. As we shall see, yet other Presidium members were also involved with the anti-Party group.

For several weeks following the July 4 announcements, a tremendous propaganda campaign was held to condemn the anti-Party group before the masses and to elicit the proper pledges of support for the "Leninist" Party leadership from the population. Even seventeen days later, on July 21, *Pravda* castigated *Pravda Ukrainy, Sovetskaya Litva* and other republic newspapers for slackening the pace in "the militant task of our newspapers to continue to explain each issue in the decision of the June plenum." On July 5 *Pravda* reported that already in Moscow alone over 8,000 Party organizations had held meetings at which more than 60,000 persons had spoken.

The members and candidate members of the Party Presidium fanned out across the country to address meetings and personally hammer home the proper line. Khrushchev, Bulganin, Voroshilov, Kuusinen, Furtseva, Shvernik and, a week later, Zhukov visited Leningrad in connection with the celebrations of the 250th anniversary of the city. Printed below are excerpts from published speeches by a number of the leaders and from newspaper and journal editorials, selected because they deviate from, elaborate on, or go beyond the charges and explanations made in the Central Committee resolution. Since these materials contain important clues about the specific events of June 18 — June 29 and also about earlier differences among the leadership, careful attention should be given to variations in tone and to the specific charges by various speakers. Finally, a word of caution: Like the Central Committee resolution itself, these charges are made by the victors. They are neither objective nor complete accounts of what happened.

Kosygin (Moscow): They were not in the least guided by Party and state interests. The major motive in their anti-Party activities was personal resentment and ambition. They felt that they held little power. They had little interest in the successes of our national economy. They made efforts to discredit these successes. And they were pleased when we had failures.

Naturally, it is necessary to reveal and criticize shortcomings in economic and Party work. . . . But what kind of criticism can be given by a group of opportunists who collected data on shortcomings in order not to correct them but to discredit the Party's line?

Instead of helping the Party in radically increasing the output of livestock products, this group collected material in order to show that our country is allegedly unable to solve this task. However, it was, of course, unable to prove this for our country has every possibility of catching up with the USA in the per capita production of meat, milk, and butter during the next few years. The group attempted to contrast the rate of development of agriculture to that of heavy industry. Everyone is well aware, however, that successes in agriculture do not mean in the least that heavy industry should develop more slowly in this connection. The Party always has been and always will be concerned about the preponderant development of heavy industry. . . .

The anti-Party group had its own platform. This platform was directed against the decisions of the 20th Party Congress. . . . (*Pravda,* July 4, 1957)

K. D. Petukhov (Chairman, Moscow City Economic Council): Rather than setting an example by a Party approach to the matter and by carrying out the directives adopted by the Party, they concentrated their efforts on opposing these decisions. In particular, when Molotov held the post of Minister of State Control, he did not co-operate in carrying out the decisions of the February plenum of the Party Central Committee on reorganizing the management of industry and construction, but spent his time writing letters against these decisions. . . . (*Pravda,* July 4, 1957)

N. T. Kalchenko (Chairman, Ukrainian Council of Ministers): As is known, Kaganovich was the Secretary of the Ukrainian Communist Party Central Committee for a long time. At that time he slandered and insulted in every way Party personnel, discrediting many honest and loyal Party people and stamping on their dignity. He shamelessly hurled accusations at many administrative personnel and representatives of the esteemed Ukrainian intelligentsia. If Kaganovich had not been recalled from the Ukraine in time, he would have done tremendous damage to the Ukrainian Communist Party and the Ukrainian people. (*Pravda,* July 5, 1957)

Kuusinen (Leningrad): Not long ago, when many collective farms had already begun to carry out the important job of increasing the production of milk, butter, and meat under the slogan of catching up with and surpassing America in this respect, Malenkov, Kaganovich, and Molotov attempted to prove that this was allegedly an erroneous line, as though they were disappointed that the Soviet people would live better. . . . (*Pravda,* July 7, 1957)

Shvernik (Leningrad): It has now been established that the "Leningrad Case," in the organization of which Malenkov took an active part, was fabricated.

The Leningrad Party organization, which developed in the traditions of the Great October Socialist Revolution, was, is and will be our Party's loyal supporter. It has struggled and is now struggling for the victory of Leninism. It fought Trotskyites, right-wing opportunists, nationalists — all the enemies of Soviet power. In this it has been an example of selfless constancy and devotion to the cause of our Party and people.

The Party Control Committee has reviewed in 1957 a large number of files on former Party members rehabilitated by judicial agencies in order to rectify violations of revolutionary legality tolerated by Malenkov, Kaganovich, and Molotov during the period of mass repressions. The Party Control Committee has readmitted the majority of them to the Party. . . . (*Pravda,* July 7, 1957)

Khrushchev (Leningrad): Comrades, you have most likely already read the resolution of the Party Central Committee plenum on the anti-Party group of Malenkov, Kaganovich, and Molotov. This group was hatching treacherous schemes. It wished to take into its own hands key Party and government positions in order to change the Party's political line. . . .

In the field of foreign policy this group, and especially Comrade Molotov, obstructed in every way implementation of measures for relaxation of international tension and strengthening world peace. They preferred the policy of "tightening all the screws" which contradicts the wise Leninist policy of peaceful co-existence of the socialist and capitalist systems. . . .

Everyone now knows how their anti-Party actions ended. The Party Central Committee unanimously condemned this anti-Party group and the careerist Shepilov who joined them and who turned out to be a completely shameless double-dealer.

The Malenkov, Kaganovich, and Molotov group timed their violent attacks on the Party to coincide with the celebration of Leningrad's anniversary. Discussion of the question of which members and candidate members of the Presidium of the Central Committee were to travel to Leningrad for the celebration served as the occasion for the members of the anti-Party group to take direct action against the collective leadership of the Central Committee.

Why did it happen this way? It appears that not at all the least circumstance in this matter was that all the members of this group were especially guilty of the crudest errors and shortcomings which took place in the past, while Malenkov, who was one of the main organizers of the so-called Leningrad Case, was simply afraid to come to you here in Leningrad. . . . (*Pravda,* July 7, 1957)

Zhukov (Leningrad): With great regret due to circumstances beyond my control I did not have the opportunity of participating in your celebrations devoted to the glorious anniversary of this city and the presentation of government awards. . . .

I was in command of the troops on the Leningrad front in the fall of 1941 at the most difficult, critical time — when the Germans had broken through to the Pulkovo Heights and individual German tanks were fighting their way to the meat combine. I saw Leningraders defend their native city unstintingly alongside the Soviet Army. . . . Later, when co-ordinating the actions of the Leningrad and Volkov fronts to break through the blockade, I once again admired the heroism of the Leningraders . . .

As you know, this anti-Party group resisted measures for a decisive increase in agriculture. Its members objected especially to the slogan "catch up with the United States of America in the near future in the per capita production of meat, milk, and butter," advanced by the Central Committee on the initiative of Nikita Sergeyevich Khrushchev, a slogan which was unanimously approved by all Soviet people.

The anti-Party group opposed extending the political, economic, and legislative powers of the Union republics; it apparently did not want to give up the powers it had held for nearly 30 years. Not being familiar with the situation in the localities, they did not believe that our fraternal republics would be able, without their "wise leadership," to decide properly their own internal affairs. This was a consequence of their detachment from life. . . . Yet life has shown that members of the anti-Party group had themselves become . . . detached from the people, had seriously lagged behind politically, and had not only lost the right to claim the status of leaders of the Party and state, but even to claim the title of full-fledged members of our great Communist Party. The anti-Party group of Malenkov, Kaganovich, and Molotov stubbornly opposed measures followed by the Party to eliminate the consequences of the cult of the individual leader, especially in the sphere of unmasking and calling to account those chiefly responsible in their time for violations of legality. Now that their far from Party-like activities have been exposed, it has become clear why they were against unmasking the illegal acts that had been committed. They feared their responsibility before the Party and the people for exceeding their rights and acting illegally.

Then Comrade Zhukov cited instances of the violation of legality by the members of the anti-Party group, Malenkov, Kaganovich, and Molotov. (*Pravda,* July 15, 1957)

A. Shelepin (Secretary of the Komsomol): . . . For many years the schools provided primarily a book-learning education, and did little to develop a practical facility for independent work. . . . Following the Party's directive, the first step has been taken to alter the school program in order to bring the schools closer to life itself and to give them close ties with production.

We must note that Shepilov, who affiliated himself with the anti-Party group, opposed this trend in the schools' work and oriented the secondary schools mainly in the direction of preparation for higher schools. Such a policy could seriously harm the state and upbringing of Soviet youngsters. . . . (*Komsomolskaya Pravda,* July 16, 1957)

V. Matskevich (USSR Minister of Agriculture): As we all know, only three or four years ago a number of branches of agriculture were in a state of neglect. The country did not harvest enough grain, and the development of animal husbandry was in a very abnormal state. Malenkov, during the long period when he handled agricultural matters in the Party Central Committee, and afterwards in his capacity as Chairman of the USSR Council of Ministers, hindered the solution of basic problems of agricultural development, particularly those of increasing the material incentive of collective farmers and state farm and machine and tractor station workers in raising agricultural production. At the same time, Malenkov, in order to build himself up and gain cheap popularity, tried to take personal credit for measures of the Party Central Committee to reduce the agricultural tax and to raise procurement and purchase prices for farm products, as well as other measures to bring about a sharp advance in agriculture and raise the material well-being of the collective farm peasantry and the entire Soviet people.

Kaganovich, a member of the anti-Party group, attacked the Party's agricultural policy even though he knew nothing about agriculture; and, in this way, impeded the realization of major steps for increasing agricultural production and raising the collective farmers' material incentive. (*Pravda,* July 12, 1957)

Kommunist editorial: Shepilov, now known by the Party to be a factionalist who allied himself with the anti-Party group of Malenkov, Kaganovich and Molotov, bears a great share of the responsibility for the spread of unsound tendencies among a portion of the artistic intelligentsia. In charge of the ideological sphere, Shepilov violated the trust of the Central Committee. He retreated from the line set at the 20th Party Congress in questions of literature and the arts and took a liberal position which deviated from the Leninist adherence to principle. He was also two-faced in questions of art. In public statements and especially in his practical work he permitted the unsound tendencies of some writers and artists.

Seeking personal popularity, he began to play fast and loose with demagogues and attempted to implement a program "broader" than that of the Party. Shepilov pretended to speak from Party positions in giving free scope to the activities of the artistic intelligentsia, ignoring the fundamental demands of ideological and artistic standards in creative work and relentless opposition toward everything foreign. In this he departed radically from the line of the Party and its Central Committee. In reality, Shepilov did not stand for genuine freedom of creative work but made concessions to anarchic elements.

It is well known that the resolutions of the Party Central Committee, based on the Leninist principle of Party spirit, have emphasized fully the need for connection between literature and art on the one hand and Party policy on the other. Shepilov did not think it necessary to explain the tremendous importance of this Party requirement or to show its significance. He chose another road, that of ridiculing the simplified solution of this matter. . . .

The conference with the writers' *aktiv* of the Party Central Committee in May 1957 and the reception given for the artistic intelligentsia by Party and government leaders played a major part in improving the atmosphere in the professional unions. Comrade N. S. Khrushchev spoke for the Party Central Committee at both the conference and the reception. He told the writers about the great heroic work that our people, the builders of communism, are performing. He revealed wonderful prospects for the future and, in particular, announced even before press publication that there was a real possibility of catching up with the USA in the next few years in per capita output of milk, butter, and meat. . . .

The anti-Party group of Malenkov, Kaganovich, and Molotov and their associate Shepilov attempted to discredit and cast doubt on the importance of the conference in the Central Committee and the reception given for representatives of the artistic intelligentsia. The exposure of this group will undoubtedly have a beneficial impact on the further development of our literature and art. . . . (Editorial, *Kommunist,* No. 10, July 1957)

Party Life: The June plenum of the Party Central Committee lasted a week. It was attended by members and candidate members of the Central Committee and members of the Central Inspection Commission — 309 persons in all. The plenum took place in circumstances of the broadest and most unrestrained democracy. The speakers were not restricted by time limits. Malenkov, Kaganovich, and Molotov each spoke twice, and at the concluding session of the Plenum their written declarations were read. Two hundred and fifteen comrades signed up to speak at the plenum. Sixty spoke. All the remaining, who did not have an opportunity to speak, expressed their point of view in written form. And not a single person at the Central Committee plenum supported the anti-Party group. . . .

The participants in the anti-Party group, striving to seize the leadership of the party, were presented before the whole world as loners who do not have any kind of ties with the people. The struggle, which developed in the Central Committee against this group, bore a profoundly principled character because it was not a matter of personalities, but about the policy which they wished to fasten on the party. . . .

Comrade Molotov repeatedly came out against improving the relations of the USSR with Yugoslavia; he impeded the conclusion of a state treaty with Austria, even though that treaty with this state located in the center of Europe had important significance for relaxing international tensions. Comrade Molotov was against the normalization of relations with Japan, denied the expediency of establishing personal contacts between leading figures of the USSR and state figures of other countries. . . .

Comrade Molotov was against the business of cultivating 35 million hectares of virgin land which has gained such enormous significance in the economy of the country. The anti-Party group was against strengthening the material interests of the collective farm peasantry in widening the production of agricultural products. It expressed itself against altering the old, bureaucratic order of planning in the collective farms. . . .

Constant resistance was shown by the anti-Party group to those measures which were introduced by the Party for the liquidation of the consequences of the cult of personality, for the removal of the violations of revolutionary legality which had occurred in the past and for the creation of those conditions which make it impossible for them to be repeated. No small part was played here by the fact that Malenkov, Kaganovich, and Molotov were especially deeply guilty of the coarsest mistakes and shortcomings which had taken place in the past.

Everything done by the Party in the struggle with bureaucracy, for the reduction of the bloated state apparatus, for the restoration of Leninist norms of party life, for widening the ties of the Party with the masses of people, also encountered either open or hidden resistance of the anti-Party group. . . . To this group those methods of work are organically foreign which develop the independence of Party organizations, raise the activity and initiative of the working people. Malenkov, Kaganovich, and Molotov were long accustomed to relying only on the apparatus, to believing only in the strength of paper and administrative orders. . . .

Convinced that their incorrect statements and actions were being constantly rebuffed in the Central Committee Presidium, which is consistently carrying out the line of the 20th Party Congress, Comrades Molotov, Kaganovich, and Malenkov started on the path of group struggle against the Party leadership. If one recalls their statements at the 20th Party Congress and their speeches at the plenums of the Central Committee, the falseness of their words about unity and their oaths of loyalty to the Party becomes clear. . . . They resorted to intrigues and began a factional struggle. Not believing in collective leadership and having no respect for it, this anti-Party group organized a secret plot against the Central Committee. They counted on presenting the Central Committee with a *fait accompli* of a change in the leadership of the Party and in its policy, but they badly miscalculated. . . . (Editorial, *Party Life,* No. 13, July 1957)

The implication contained in the Central Committee resolution and later explanations that the anti-Party group had been united for some time around a broadly based platform which opposed all, or most, of the major post-Stalin policies appears highly doubtful. To a considerable degree, after mid-1957 the anti-Party group, like Beria earlier, became a scapegoat for difficulties in Soviet society and thus were charged en masse with numerous treacherous acts. A more plausible explanation would be that under the exigencies of the situation in the first half of 1957, the members of the group found common agreement for limited action on a single issue or on several key issues. It is highly unlikely, for example, that Molotov and Kaganovich agreed with Malenkov's policies during 1954 on investment priorities and the foreign policy implications of nuclear weapons. Again, Shepilov was accused of permitting "rotten liberalism" in the arts, a charge which does not fit well with Molotov's political views. Certainly, Malenkov and Shepilov could not be labelled "conservatives" in the same sense as Molotov and Kaganovich. The indictments against the various members of the group must be carefully weighed against earlier evidence about their policies and actions.

There were also variations in the vigor and depth of attacks on the anti-Party group. Bulganin and Voroshilov, for example, merely recited, in many instances verbatim, the official Central Committee resolution on the anti-Party group. As would be revealed later, these two men had pressing personal reasons for displaying reticence. On the other hand, Khrushchev, Zhukov, Kalchenko and Shvernik extended the charges from the realm of policy differences and factionalism to crimes against other Party members and violations of socialist legality. Khrushchev not only charged Malenkov in July with having a hand in the Leningrad Case, but in August connected him with Beria.

. . . Comrade Malenkov . . . fell under the complete influence of Beria and acted as his shadow and tool. Holding a high position in the Party and state, Comrade Malenkov not only failed to restrain J. V. Stalin but made skillful use of his weaknesses and habits in the last years of his life. On many occasions he urged him to take actions that deserve the strongest condemnation. . . . (*Pravda,* August 28, 1957)

The failure of *Pravda* to publish Zhukov's specific accounts of the crimes of the anti-Party group would indicate that he went further in his public accusations than the other leaders.

In view of these charges of criminal activity, it is of interest that the members of the group were not brought to trial; nor were they deprived of membership in the Party. That they retained Party membership is especially noteworthy in view of the statement in the Central Committee resolution that the plenum had "unanimously demanded" that they be expelled from the Party and Zhukov's assertion that they had "lost the right" to Party membership.

On the basis of later public denunciations of the anti-Party group, accounts by foreign communists and impromptu remarks by Khrushchev, a gross outline of events in June 1957 can be reconstructed even though there is considerable variation in details and several specific events are shrouded in uncertainty. The Presidium met on June 18, as Khrushchev publicly said, on the pretext of considering preparations for the 250th anniversary of Leningrad. In view of Khrushchev's allegations about Malenkov's involvement in the Leningrad Case, one suspects that the anniversary was not the only subject related to Leningrad that was discussed. The Presidium continued in almost constant session until the convocation of the Central Committee plenum on June 22. As the July *Party Life* editorial suggests, the anti-Party group had hoped to resolve the leadership issue in the Presidium, where, as it appears from later evidence, there was at least a temporary majority of full members against Khrushchev. While the Presidium debate undoubtedly ranged over a large number of policy issues, it apparently focused on the group's proposals in some manner "to change the composition of the Party's leading bodies."

The major unanswered question is how, and in what manner, was the issue thrown into the Central Committee, against the wishes of the group opposing Khrushchev. Khrushchev has asserted that the Central Committee members were informally told about the course of the Presidium deliberations and gathered in Moscow demanding that a plenum be convened. Several accounts state that military planes were used to fly in Central Committee members.

In the Central Committee Khrushchev received strong backing from the powerful regional Party secretaries and other Party professionals and from the military (as indicated by Zhukov's elevation to full membership in the Presidium). The unanimous vote against the anti-Party group does not indicate that every member of the Central Committee was a Khrushchev supporter; but, rather, that once the outcome of the issue began to come clear, everyone jumped on the bandwagon.

The Fall of Zhukov

The June crisis was only one of a number of instances after 1953 when the military played a part in the leadership struggle. As we have seen, the military most probably participated in the purge of Beria and was a substantial beneficiary from the decline of power of the secret police. As indicated by the *Red Star* editorial of January 27, 1955, the military gave support to those political leaders favoring continued emphasis on heavy industry. The promotion of the new Marshals in March 1955, and the elevation of Zhukov to Minister of Defense can be viewed in part as a reward for that support after Malenkov's resignation from the Premiership. Khrushchev's description of Stalin's crimes and mistakes in the Secret Speech were obviously calculated to appeal to the military and to Zhukov personally. The 20th Congress elected six full and twelve candidate members to the Central Committee from among the high-ranking professional military commanders. Zhukov was made a candidate member of the Party Presidium. In sum, whether or not the military leadership was politically inclined, given the dissension among the top political leadership, the military could not help but be involved in the leadership struggle, especially when policies were involved in which the military had a stake.

As a corollary, the more the military elite was wooed during the political in-fighting, the greater independence it could achieve. The professional assertiveness shown by the military after 1954 contrasted markedly with its submissiveness during the Stalin era. The increased prominence of the military in elite politics, displayed by the events of June 1957, even led some Western observers in the summer of 1957 to speculate on the possibility of a future military take-over of the country.

Not only was the role of the military in elite politics increasingly visible as the leadership struggle intensified, but the military – and Zhukov personally – began to express publicly some views which appeared to be contrary to interests of the Party and its leaders. The appeal for greater truthfulness in historical writing following the denunciation of Stalin led to some divergences between military and Party historians. Military journals tended to concentrate on the mistakes of Stalin during World War II and, in contrast, the professional competence and skill of the military command. Party journals, on the other hand, laid greater emphasis on the decisive role of the Party during the war. There were even differences in emphasis expressed in military and Party publications on the relative importance of military commanders – like Zhukov – and political officers – like Khrushchev – in particular battles. During late 1956 and early 1957, the credit given to the professional soldiers and to Zhukov personally for military victories appeared to increase. The reader will recall the personal credit implicitly claimed by Zhukov for defeating the Germans at Leningrad in his speech in Leningrad during July 1957. The importance attached to the nature of historical writing on World War II was demonstrated by the fact that the Party Central Committee itself deemed it necessary, in late September 1957, to commission a five-volume *History of the Great Patriotic War of the Soviet Union, 1941-1945* under the supervision of an editorial board composed of leading Party ideologists and military officers (excluding Zhukov, however). The Central Committee resolution noted that:

One of the most important tasks of this historical research is to show the role of the Communist Party as the organizer of the nationwide struggle against the enemy, its multi-faceted activity in directing the front, the partisan war behind the enemy lines and the economic and political life of the country. (*Pravda,* September 29, 1957)

At a more practical and politically explosive level, the military command, under Zhukov's leadership, began to assert the independence of military commanders vis-à-vis Party-political officers. Throughout the entire Soviet history, the Party has exercised controls over the professional military officers at all levels. The degree of political intervention through Party officials attached to units has varied from one period to another, but there has always existed some confusion and tension between the authority and responsibilities of the military commander and the political supervisor.

In 1955 the *zampolit,* or political officer, at the company level was abolished; and in general the authority of the Chief Political Administration – which is simultaneously an integral section of the Central Committee staff and a unit of the Ministry of Defense in charge of Party-political affairs – began to wane. In January 1956 Zhukov, in his speech before a Party conference of the Moscow military district, outspokenly supported the status of the professional military commanders in the following statement:

In the district, certain efforts have been made to bring under criticism the official activity of commanders at meetings. Such efforts are reprehensible. Our task is the all-round strengthening of the authority of commanders. . . . (*Red Star,* daily newspaper of the Ministry of Defense, January 25, 1956)

In other statements, Zhukov stressed that propaganda work in the armed forces should concentrate less on ideological indoctrination in Marxism–Leninism and more on practical military tasks. For officers, ideological study was placed on a voluntary rather than a mandatory basis.

At the same time, during 1956 and 1957, there were occasional criticisms in the press about lagging indoctrination efforts and the weakening of Party activities in the armed services. The Central Committee in April 1957 issued "Instructions to Party Organizations in the Soviet Army and Navy." Although these instructions were not published, they were cited and commented upon in *Red Star* and *Soviet Fleet.* They appear to have attempted to steer a middle way between the military's professional aspirations and the political leadership's concern for adequate Party controls and indoctrination in the military.

. . . The Party Central Committee has entrusted Party organizations with penetrating competently and actively into all facets of combat training, military discipline and the training of personnel; employing criticism and self-criticism to uncover shortcomings in the instruction and training of soldiers, in Party-political work and in the work of Party bureaus and political agencies; and assisting commanders to take timely action to eliminate shortcomings in increasing the combat readiness of units and ships.

Criticism and self-criticism is the tested weapon of our Party. At Party meetings Communists can and should criticize Party members and candidate members for indifference toward improving their military and political knowledge, for amoral actions which degrade the high title of Communist, and for violation of Party discipline. . . .

Criticism should be businesslike, comradely and helpful in eliminating shortcomings, improving continually the quality of military and political training and strengthening military discipline. Criticism of a commander's orders and instructions at Party meetings is not permitted. . . . (*Soviet Fleet,* May 12, 1957)

* * *

. . . In the Soviet Army the commander guides all combat and political preparations and the education of his personnel. The instructions emphasize that Party organizations must be responsible in every way for strengthening the unity of command and the authority of commanders and chiefs.

Political organs and Party organizations must actively support the orders of commanders, protect the authority of the commander, train personnel to obey and execute orders. The Party Central Committee points out in the instructions: "At Party meetings, criticism of orders and decrees of commanders is not permitted." It is necessary to execute strictly these demands of the instructions and to conduct a struggle with those who attempt to undermine the firmness of orders and decrees of a commander.

It is very important for the commanders of units and ships to participate actively in the work of Party organizations. . . . (*Red Star,* May 12, 1957)

> Not only did the power and political authority of the military establishment as a whole appear to increase, but Zhukov personally emerged from the June crisis with heightened prestige. He was made a full member of the Party Presidium and his speech attacking the anti-Party group in Leningrad was prominently reported — though not in full. His activities in Leningrad in July were also given wide coverage.
>
> On October 4 Zhukov left Moscow amid considerable fanfare for a three-week vacation and business trip which took him to the Crimea, Yugoslavia, and Albania.

On October 4 Marshal of the Soviet Union, G. K. Zhukov, left by plane from Moscow for the Crimea. He is going on a visit to the Yugoslav Federal People's Republic in response to an invitation extended on behalf of the Yugoslav government by General of the Army I. Gosnjak during his visit to the Soviet Union last summer.

At the Central Airport Marshal G. K. Zhukov was sent off by Marshal of the Soviet Union I. S. Konev, USSR Deputy Ministers of Foreign Affairs N. S. Patolichev and N. P. Firyubin, Admiral S. G. Gorshkov, Marshal of Aviation S. I. Rudenko, Generals of the Army M. S. Malinin and G. K. Malandin, Col. Generals A. V. Gerasimov, A. A. Gryzlov, N. I. Gusev, A. S. Zheltov, S. U. Rubanov, Ye. G. Trotsenko, M. A. Shalin, Commandant of the City of Moscow Maj. General I. S. Kolesnikov, and other generals and officers of the Soviet Army, acting head of the USSR Ministry of Defense's Foreign Relations Section Col. D. F. Chikin, assistant directors of departments of the USSR Ministry of Foreign Affairs P. S. Dedushkin and K. A. Kochetkov, and representatives of the press. . . . (*Pravda,* October 5, 1957)

Almost daily reports on Zhukov's trip were printed in the Soviet press. On October 27, *Pravda*'s front page carried the following bulletin:

MARSHAL G. K. ZHUKOV DEPARTS FROM ALBANIA. October 26. Today, Marshal G. K. Zhukov left Tirana for home. On the same day, Marshal G. K. Zhukov returned to Moscow.

On its last page the same issue of *Pravda* printed the following announcement:

The Presidium of the USSR Supreme Soviet has appointed Marshal of the Soviet Union Rodion Yakovlevich Malinovsky USSR Minister of Defense.

The Presidium of the USSR Supreme Soviet has removed Marshal of the Soviet Union Georgy Konstantinovich Zhukov from the post of USSR Minister of Defense.

For six days public silence cloaked the status and whereabouts of Zhukov. Western observers were uncertain at first whether he had been promoted or demoted. *Pravda* resolved the mystery on November 3.

OFFICIAL ANNOUNCEMENT — CONCERNING THE PLENUM OF THE PARTY CENTRAL COMMITTEE.

A plenum of the Party Central Committee was held at the end of October, 1957.

The plenum discussed the question of improving Party political work in the Soviet Army and Navy.

The plenum adopted a resolution on this question which is published today.

The plenum removed Comrade G. K. Zhukov from membership in the Presidium of the Central Committee and from membership in the Party Central Committee.

After paying tribute to the victory of the armed services in World War II, the fighting readiness of the military, and the loyalty of the armed services to the Motherland and the Communist Party, the Central Committee resolution went to the heart of the matter.

. . . The 20th Party Congress set for the Party and the people the job of maintaining our defenses at the level of modern military technology and science, and guaranteeing the security of our socialist state. Along with the commanders who exercise unified authority, an important role in the achievement of this task belongs to the Military Councils, political agencies and Party organizations in the army and navy. They must all resolutely and consistently carry out the policy of the Communist Party.

The main source of the might of our army and navy lies in the fact that the Communist Party, the guiding and directing force of Soviet society, is their organizer, leader and instructor. . . .

The Party Central Committee plenum notes that recently Comrade Zhukov, former Minister of Defense, had been violating the Leninist, Party principles of leadership of the armed forces and had been following a policy of restricting the work of Party organizations, political agencies and Military Councils and of eliminating the leadership and control of the Party, its Central Committee and the government over the army and navy.

The Central Committee plenum confirmed that the cult of Comrade G. K. Zhukov began to be infused in the Soviet Army with his personal participation. With the help of sycophants and flatterers, he began to be praised to the skies in lectures, reports, articles, films and pamphlets, and his personality and his role in the Great Patriotic War were excessively glorified. In order to please Comrade G. K. Zhukov, the correct history of the war was distorted, the actual state of affairs was misrepresented, and the tremendous efforts of the Soviet people, the heroism of all our armed forces, the role of commanders and political workers, the military skill of the commanders of fronts, armies and fleets, and the leading and inspiring role of the Communist Party were downgraded.

The Party and the government valued highly the services of Comrade G. K. Zhukov, bestowing on him the title of Marshal of the Soviet Union, honoring him with the title of Hero of the Soviet Union four times and awarding him many orders. He was held in great political esteem: At the 20th Party Congress he was elected a member of the Party Central Committee. The Party Central Committee elected him a candidate member of the Presidium of the Party Central Committee and later a member of the Presidium of the Party Central Committee. However, as a result of a lack of Party consciousness and a mistaken understanding of this high recognition of his services, Comrade G. K. Zhukov lost the Party modesty taught to us by V. I. Lenin, conceitedly thought that he was the only hero of all the victories scored by our people and their armed forces under the leadership of the Communist Party, and flagrantly violated Leninist, Party principles of leadership of the armed forces.

Thus, Comrade G. K. Zhukov failed to justify the confidence placed in him by the Party. He proved to be politically deficient, disposed to adventurism both in his understanding of the major tasks of the Soviet Union's foreign policy and in his leadership of the Ministry of Defense.

In light of the above, the Party Central Committee plenum decided to remove Comrade G. K. Zhukov from membership in the Presidium and the Party Central Committee and instructed the secretariat of the Party Central Committee to give Comrade Zhukov other work. . . . (Adopted unanimously by all the members of the Central Committee, candidate members of the Central Committee and members of the Central Inspection Commission and approved by all the military personnel and Party and Soviet officials present at the Central Committee plenum). (*Pravda,* November 3, 1957)

Following the familiar pattern, the mistakes and shortcomings of Zhukov were now discussed at thousands of meetings throughout the country. Newspaper editorials and reports of speeches at Party meetings enlarged upon the basic charges against him with one exception: The accusation that he was disposed to "adventurism" in foreign and military policy was not subsequently amplified or supported, and it is not clear what, if any, basis there may have been for this charge. The participation of high military officers in the denunciation of Zhukov was prominently reported in the press. In part, the publicity given to criticism of Zhukov by his fellow officers was designed to reassure the population of the justness of the charges and the continuing loyalty to the political leadership by the military high command. However, these criticisms, and especially the vicious *ad hominem* attack on Zhukov by his longstanding rival Marshal Konev (printed below), suggest that the Party leadership was successful in strengthening its controls over the armed forces in part because the officer corps itself was divided over the Zhukov issue.

The following items are some of the important press commentaries on the disgrace of Zhukov:

. . . Intensification of political work in the army and navy is the universal task of all Communists, commanders and political workers. Their job is firmly and consistently to implement in the armed services the policy of the Communist Party, to be the carriers of the great ideas of Marxism–Leninism. They have one common goal – to serve the people, each at his own post, and in close co-operation to continue relentlessly to strengthen the armed services of the Soviet state. . . .

At Party *aktiv* meetings of military districts, numerous facts were cited which indicated that the former Minister of Defense had excessively employed rule by administrative command, had treated insultingly his subordinates, and had not understood the role of educational work in the army of a socialist state or the fact that the discipline and morale of our army are maintained by the consciousness of its rank and file.

Outstanding military figures – Marshals of the Soviet Union Comrades Malinovsky, Konev, Rokossovsky, Sokolovsky, Yeremenko, Timoshenko and Biryuzov, Admiral Gorshkov and Generals of the Army Batov, Zakharov, Kazakov and others – spoke at the Party Central Committee plenum. Many of them had known Comrade Zhukov in their common work for decades. They pointed out Zhukov's serious shortcomings, sharply criticized the mistakes and distortions he had allowed, and unanimously condemned his incorrect, non-Party behavior in the position of USSR Minister of Defense. . . .

In his speech at the Party Central Committee plenum, Comrade Zhukov recognized that the criticism of his mistakes was correct and stated:

"The present plenum has been a great Party school for me. To my great regret, it is only here that I have really become aware of the importance of these mistakes I made in guiding the armed forces, especially recently, and of the political mistakes which I committed as a member of the Party Central Committee and a member of the Presidium and which have been discussed here at the plenum.

I recognize that the criticism of me here at the plenum has been correct on the whole, and I consider it comradely, Party assistance to me personally and to other military workers to understand correctly the requirements and policy of the Party on the question of proper leadership of the army and navy and on the question of correct Party political education of the armed forces' personnel.

In proposing a penalty, some comrades stated that I had already been removed from the Central Committee in 1946 during Stalin's lifetime and that I had failed to understand the need to correct those mistakes for which I was removed. At that time, comrades, I could not, and did not, admit that my removal from the Central Committee was correct. I did not admit that the charges made against me were correct. Now it is a different matter. I recognize my mistakes, I have become deeply aware of them in the course of the plenum, and I give my word to the Party Central Committee that I will completely eliminate my shortcomings." (Editorial, *Pravda,* November 3, 1957)

* * *

A meeting of the *aktiv* of the Moscow City Party organization was held in the Great Kremlin Palace on October 31. The meeting discussed the resolution of the Party Central Committee plenum "Concerning the Imrovement of Party Political Work in the Soviet Army and Navy." Comrade Ye. A. Furtseva, member of the Presidium of the Party Central Committee and Secretary of the Central Committee and the Moscow Party Committee, delivered a report. . . .

Marshal of the Soviet Union K. S. Moskalenko, Commander of the Moscow Military District, was the first to speak in the discussion. He stated that Communists in the army were deeply grateful to the Party Central Committee for having always paid great attention to the cause of further consolidating our country's armed forces and intensifying Party political work in the army and navy.

The resolution of the Party Central Committee plenum, he said, is of vital importance. It reveals quite correctly the shortcomings in Party political work in the army and navy. These shortcomings resulted from the incorrect, non-Party behavior of Comrade Zhukov. . . .

Marshal of the Soviet Union S. S. Biryuzov, commander-in-chief of the nation's anti-aircraft defense, emphasized that our Communist Party has always been, and always will continue to be, the organizer and leader of our armed forces. . . .

Zhukov . . . fostered a policy of belittling the role of Party organizations in the army and of restricting Party political work. Zhukov did not take into account the opinions of others, he did not consider it necessary to seek advice or to discuss suggestions from below, he rarely met with military personnel and tried to impress everyone with the fact that he was an exceptional person. . . .

In his speech Marshal of the Soviet Union R. Ya. Malinovsky,

USSR Minister óf Defense, discussed questions of improving further Party political work in the army and navy. . . .

Discussing Zhukov's non-Party behavior, the speaker noted that this was not accidental. It derived from his ambition and desire for glory. . . . Anyone who attempts to juxtapose himself to the Party will be deprived of the respect and confidence of the Party and the people, irrespective of his past services. . . ." (*Pravda,* November 3, 1957)

*   *   *

. . . Instead of relying on local Party organizations and mobilizing army and navy personnel for the more rapid implementation of tasks in further perfecting their military skill and for the all-round strengthening of military discipline and order, Comrade Zhukov, through his erroneous actions, lowered Party organizations to the level of purely educational agencies. As a result, the activity of Party organizations and their independent work were downgraded. . . .

The Soviet Army is a new type and its discipline is rooted in the conscious execution by the personnel of their military duty with lofty patriotism and loyalty to the homeland and with fidelity to the ideals of Marxism–Leninism. Zhukov, however, attempted to replace all educational work by purely administrative measures.

In our army and navy there existed a strong and good tradition of close ties between units and formations, on the one hand, and local Party and Komsomol organizations, enterprises and institutions, on the other. . . . Lately, however, Zhukov's tendency to separate the army and navy from the Party resulted in a violation of this good tradition. In addition, the Statutes of our Party, which require political agencies to maintain close contact with local Party committees, were violated quite frequently.

Comrade Zhukov's mistakes in guiding the armed forces were made worse by some of his groundless statements on questions of Soviet military science and the development of the armed forces. Even in such a clear question as the importance of military regulations he introduced hopeless confusion by stating that our regulations allegedly play a negative role in the education of commanding officers and do not help to develop their creative initiative. . . .

Thus, this is not a question of isolated mistakes but of a series of mistakes, of his pronounced tendency to regard the Soviet armed forces as his own domain. . . .

However, even though Comrade Zhukov proved to be wanting as a statesman, could it be that he was a general above criticism and a perfect military leader who made no mistakes in his work and had no failures on the fronts of war? This, at least, is how Comrade Zhukov tried to picture himself to the Party, the people and the armed forces. . . .

Comrade Zhukov should remember that there were many flagrant mistakes and blunders in his activities. It should not be forgotten, for example, that Comrade Zhukov occupied the high post of Chief of the General Staff in the period immediately before the war and that he bears not a small share of the responsibility for the condition and combat readiness of the Soviet armed forces in resisting fascist aggression. . . .

Grave responsibility for the fact that the troops in our frontier military districts were taken by surprise by the sudden attack of the fascist armies also rests upon the Chief of the General Staff, Comrade Zhukov, who had available unquestionable information about the real threat of attack by fascist Germany on the USSR. . . .

Comrade Zhukov undeservedly ascribes to himself a special role in formulating the plan of strategic offensive operations for routing the fascist German troops at Stalingrad. However, if one turns to the facts of history, it becomes clear that not only the idea itself but also all the basic features of the plan for routing the fascist German troops at Stalingrad originated with the front commanders and their staffs during the course of the fierce defensive battles that developed on the Stalingrad sector. . . .

Comrade Zhukov . . . showed an especially clear tendency to stress that he was the only one of the Soviet military leaders who suffered no defeats in the Great Patriotic War. This is contrary to the facts of history, above all the commonly known fact that Comrade Zhukov held the post of Chief of the General Staff and later Deputy Supreme Commander during the difficult period when the Soviet Army, suffering serious defeats, was retreating into the interior of the country.

In the course of the Great Patriotic War Comrade Zhukov also committed other grave blunders in leading the troops, which frequently resulted in the unsuccessful outcome of operations. . . . [There follow several specific examples of Zhukov's costly military blunders.]

During a period when the entire Party and people were waging a struggle against the consequences of the cult of an individual, Comrade Zhukov, as an exceptionally vain person without Party modesty, used his position as Minister of Defense to spread the cult of his personality among the armed forces. He ignored the best traditions of Party work in the army and navy, instituted blatant rule by administrative fiat and tried to decide all matters personally. Criticism and self-criticism in Party organizations of the armed forces were all but abandoned, and a halo of glory and infallibility was artifically created around Zhukov's person, with his particiation.

Sycophants and flatterers began to praise and glorify Comrade Zhukov in lectures, reports, pamphlets and films. The painter Vasily Yakovlev especially excelled in this respect. He painted Zhukov against the background of the Brandenburg Gates and the burning Reichstag, showing him on a rearing white stallion trampling the banners of defeated fascist Germany. Just like St. George the Dragon Slayer on an old icon! . . .

Comrade Zhukov also had a say in the script of the movie "The Battle of Stalingrad" which has been remade by a film studio. In the new version of this movie, which is entitled "The Great Battle," everything that propagandized the Stalin cult was removed, but, on the other hand, Zhukov occupies a completely undeserved place in it. . . . (Marshal of the Soviet Union I. S. Konev, *Pravda,* November 3, 1957)

Khrushchev Consolidates His Victories

In mid-November Khrushchev granted two far-ranging interviews with American journalists during which he made several remarks about the leadership in the Soviet Union. In an interview with Henry Shapiro, reported in the Soviet press on November 19, there was the following interchange:

Shapiro: Following the June plenum of the Party Central Committee and now in connection with the release of Marshal Zhukov from his post, speculation has arisen abroad about a lack of stability in the Soviet leadership. What can you say on this subject?

Khrushchev: We have a saying, a hungry man dreams of bread. The representatives of imperialist reaction would like very much for the leadership of the Soviet Union to be unstable and they dream of such instability. They have pursued this mirage for 40 years and they still are not able to rid themselves of it. We understand: Otherwise they would not be capitalists.

What do you mean by "unstable leadership"? Evidently this means tottering, shaky leadership. It is clear to any unbiased person that this does not describe the agencies of leadership in the Soviet Union. As regards the changes in the composition of the Soviet ruling bodies, they speak for the strength of the collective leadership of our Party's Central Committee. Indeed, could a weak, unstable leadership have adopted such decisions as the expulsion from the Central Committee of Molotov, who had been in the leadership for decades, as the expulsion of Kaganovich, Malenkov and Shepilov? Or let us take the case of Marshal Zhukov. Zhukov had actually shown himself to be an outstanding soldier and commander and had deservedly received high decorations. But he made major political mistakes and therefore the Party Central Committee expelled him from the Presidium and the Central Committee. What does this indicate? It demonstrates that the Party Central Committee corrects anyone, regardless of past services, who makes mistakes. The Central Committee expresses the will of the Party, and the people follow the Party. In this lies the strength or, as you put it, the stability of the leadership of our Party and government.

Shapiro: Would not some officers get the impression that Zhukov was unfairly treated?

Khrushchev: Like a drowning man clutching at a straw, our opponents clutch at their own suppositions. Disappointment is in store for those who would have wanted to see Zhukov's dismissal create some kind of unfavorable impression. Our Party, the Soviet people and the personnel of the Soviet army accepted this decision correctly. All Soviet people are demonstrating complete agreement and solidarity with the Communist Party and the Soviet government.

Shapiro: When you speak of the collective leadership, do you mean the Central Committee or its Presidium?

Khrushchev: I mean the Central Committee of our Party. The Presidium is an executive body of the Central Committee.

Shapiro: Does initiative come from the Presidium or from the Central Committee?

Khrushchev: The Presidium raises questions which conform to the Party's interests, and the Central Committee considers them. The Central Committee discusses and adopts such decisions as conform to the interests of the Party and the people. . . . (*Pravda,* November 19, 1957)

> Ten days later, on November 29, *Pravda* and *Izvestia* reported a second Khrushchev interview with William Randolph Hearst, Jr., Robert Considine, and Frank Conniff.

Considine: In the United States the term "adventurism in foreign policy," which was applied to Zhukov, has caused some uncertainty. I would like to ask what precisely is meant by "adventurism in foreign policy."

Khrushchev: Following an unreal foreign and domestic policy — this is adventurism. It means what it says.

Considine: Were any specific countries or specific crises in mind, as in Syria or Hungary?

Khrushchev: Syria and Hungary have no relation to the given case. That was not the policy of one man, that was the policy of the Soviet government, including Comrade Zhukov, who took the same stands. . . .

Conniff: I remember that you quoted Lenin as saying that it is necessary to retain in the Party by every means those comrades who have temporarily deviated from the Party line, if basically they remain good and honest people. . . . Tell me, could this point of view not have been applied to Zhukov?

Khrushchev: Marshal Zhukov was not expelled from the Party, he is a member of our Communist Party. He is a great military specialist, and we are certain that he will devote his efforts and knowledge to the cause of our Party, to the cause of the people. The Party has punished him, but to the degree of his political mistakes, which he himself has admitted. (*Pravda,* November 29, 1957)

At the December 1957 Central Committee plenum, still other men, whose fortunes had been closely tied to those of Khrushchev's, were appointed to the leading Party organs.

A plenum of the Party Central Committee was held December 16 and 17, 1957. . . .

The Central Committee plenum elected Comrade N. A. Mukhitdinov a member of the Presidium of the Party Central Committee.

The plenum elected Comrades N. G. Ignatov, A. I. Kirichenko and N. A. Mukhitdinov Secretaries of the Party Central Committee. (*Pravda,* December 19, 1957)

A careful reading of *Pravda* for February 2, 1958 provided the first indication that another top leader was due soon for demotion. In the ritual of naming candidates for the Supreme Soviet, it is customary for various organizations to nominate, in addition to the man who is to be elected, several members of the top leadership — for honorary purposes. Subsequently, at the end of the nomination period, the top leaders publish a statement withdrawing their names in all districts other than the one in which they are to run. Bulganin is suggestively absent from the following report of the first nomination meetings.

At the first meetings held yesterday, the following candidates for the USSR Supreme Soviet were nominated: K. Ye. Voroshilov, A. I. Mikoyan, A. I. Kirichenko, N. A. Mukhitdinov, M. A. Suslov, N. M. Shvernik, N. S. Khrushchev, the well-known innovator in railway transport, Comrade V. G. Blazhenov, . . . (*Pravda,* February 2, 1958)

> Suspicions that Bulganin was slipping were strengthened when his name was mentioned far less often than those of other top leaders in subsequent newspaper reports of nomination meetings around the country; and when it was announced that he would run from the obscure — and hence humiliating — Maikop Urban Election District of the Adighe Autonomous Oblast.
>
> At the first session of the newly elected Supreme Soviet, which convened on March 27, 1958, Khrushchev's power was dramatically displayed and his *de facto* authority was given *de jure* recognition.

. . . The USSR Supreme Soviet next took up the question of forming a USSR government — the USSR Council of Ministers. Deputy P. P. Lobanov, Chairman of the Council of the Union, read the statement addressed to the chairman of the joint meeting from Deputy N. A. Bulganin, Chairman of the USSR Council of Ministers, concerning the submission of resignation by the USSR government to the USSR Supreme Soviet in correspondence with the USSR Constitution.

On the motion of I. V. Kapitonov, who spoke for a group of Deputies from the city of Moscow, from Moscow, Leningrad, Gorky and Sverdlovsk Oblasts, and from the Ukraine and Uzbek Republics, the USSR Supreme Soviet adopted the statement of Deputy N. A. Bulganin, Chairman of the USSR Council of Ministers concerning the submission of resignation by the USSR government . . .

Speaking in accord with the instructions of the Party Central Committee and the Councils of Elders of the Council of the Union and the Council of Nationalities, Deputy K. Ye. Voroshilov, Chairman of the Presidium of the USSR Supreme Soviet, proposed that Deputy N. S. Khrushchev, First Secretary of the Party Central Committee, be appointed Chairman of the USSR Council of Ministers. . . . (*Pravda,* March 28, 1958)

*   *   *

Speech by Comrade K. Ye. Voroshilov, Chairman of the Presidium of the USSR Supreme Soviet:

"The Supreme Soviet approving N. S. Khrushchev as Premier, March, 1958." (Sovfoto)

. . . Comrades! Our entire Party and all Soviet people know Nikita Sergeyevich Khrushchev as an outstanding personality of the Communist Party and the Soviet government, as a famous son of our working class. For over 40 years Nikita Sergeyevich has served the interests of the working people, the great cause of the working class, of the whole Soviet people and of our Leninist Party, the cause of socialism and communism, with unflagging energy, firmness and according to principle. . . .

Our dear Comrade Nikita Sergeyevich Khrushchev, with his unusual creative ability and really inexhaustible, boundless energy and initiative, played an outstanding role in all this great creative work of the Communist Party and the Soviet people. . . .

The name of Comrade Khrushchev is firmly linked with outstanding successes in the conduct of the Soviet Union's peace-loving foreign policy. . . . Without exaggeration, it can be said that all the peoples of the world now know Nikita Sergeyevich Khrushchev as the staunch-est, most principled and tireless champion of peace. . . .

As head of the Soviet government, Comrade Nikita Sergeyevich Khrushchev will undoubtedly pursue continually and with greater en-ergy a principled Leninist foreign policy, a policy of peace and security of the peoples.

Dear comrade Deputies! In proposing the appointment of Com-rade Nikita Sergeyevich Khrushchev as Chairman of the USSR Coun-cil of Ministers, I would like at the same time to take note of his re-markably beneficial work as First Secretary of the Central Committee of our Communist Party. . . .

Our Party's authority has risen higher than ever before, and the unity between the Party and the people is now strong. And the Party Central Committee has decided that Comrade Nikita Sergeyevich Khrushchev is to remain in the post of First Secretary of the Party Cen-tral Committee. . . . (*Pravda,* March 28, 1958)

VII · LATER EVIDENCE

With Khrushchev's elevation to Chairman of the Council of Ministers, he acquired institutional authority to correspond with his power. After March 1958, Khrushchev held the three most powerful positions in the Soviet Union: First Secretary of the Party Central Committee, Chairman of the Council of Ministers, and Chairman of the Party Central Committee's Bureau for the Russian Republic. A cult of Khrushchev began to grow, legitimizing his power by proclaiming his great abilities and accomplishments. Top political figures and the press hailed "the Central Committee headed by Khrushchev" just as they had once saluted "the Central Committee headed by Stalin." The Stalin succession crisis had been resolved.

This is not to say, however, that Khrushchev was a new Stalin. The society he governed had changed, and his methods of rule were different. A critical difference was the decline of terror. Stalin's lieutenants feared to cross him because they knew all too well the terrible consequences of his ire. Khrushchev has often demoted his lieutenants, reshuffled them, and sometimes sent them into political retirement — but he has not killed them. For this reason, they have not been so intimidated that they might not argue against Khrushchev's proposals when they were being discussed, or even publicly hint at their dissent. Compared to Stalin's, Khrushchev's policies appear to bear a greater stamp of compromise; and not infrequently his programs have been eroded during implementation. Nevertheless, so far as we know, the final decision on policy has been Khrushchev's. Soviet politics in 1958 and thereafter is different from Soviet politics in the period 1953–1957. Therefore, we have reached a suitable cutoff point for our documentary study of the Stalin succession crisis.

The source materials in this chapter appeared after March 1958 but they pertain to the period 1953–1957. In general, materials relating to elite politics after 1958 have not been included, nor have all the statements about the "crimes" of the "anti-Party group" during the Stalin era. They are presented in the order of publication without comment. It must be remembered that they are retrospective and that they were intended not primarily to set the historical record straight, but for political purposes. In part they serve the purposes of damning Khrushchev's opponents, providing scapegoats for Soviet difficulties, or justifying a policy change. Moreover, their use as guides to events in 1953–1957 is further complicated by the possibility that later discussions of the "sins" of the "anti-Party group" might in some way be connected with post-1957 political maneuvering. For example, the reader will notice differences among the various speakers at the 21st and 22nd Party Congresses in the tone of their attacks on the anti-Party group. Some speakers appeared to be advocating that the members of the group be brought to trial, or at least be dismissed from the Party, while other speakers were more restrained in their condemnations. This might indicate that the question of the further disposition of the anti-Party group had itself become an issue which threatened some members of the post-1958 elite or at least evoked some disagreement among the leadership.

At any rate, the reader should keep in mind the satirical jest that has been current in the Soviet Union to the effect that for a Communist the future is known but the past is always changing. On the other hand, although the following statements cannot be taken at face value, they ought not to be simply rejected. They need to be carefully tested against contemporary evidence. Some statements, as for example T. A. Yurkin's explanations of leadership differences over agricultural policy, at the December 1958 Central Committee plenum, appear more reasonable and more closely attuned to the facts as we know them than do others.

The reader should pay particular attention to: the later implication of other leaders in the anti-Party group and the manner in which their implication was publicly revealed; the descriptions of the specific events in June 1957 (e.g., Ignatov's statements at the 22nd Party Congress); and hints about the involvement of the issue of the rehabilitation of purge victims in the leadership struggle. On this latter point, Furtseva's comments at the 22nd Party Congress on the recriminations in the Presidium in the spring of 1957 over responsibility for the purges could suggest a line of interpretation that Khrushchev directly provoked the actions of the anti-Party group in June 1957.

The Party Central Committee Plenum on Agriculture, December 15–19, 1958

Khrushchev (December 15, 1958): . . . Now, when we analyze the development of agriculture over the past five years, we must once again talk about the anti-Party group of Malenkov, Kaganovich, Molotov, Bulganin and Shepilov. The tongue rebels against calling such people comrades — even though they remain members of the Party — when one stops to think where they sought to push the Party by their factional work, trying to frustrate realization of the decisions of the September Central Committee plenum [1953] and the 20th Party Congress and to revise the Leninist general line of the Party on fundamental questions of our country's development. . . .

The opposition of the anti-Party group to the Party's very important measures for strengthening the collective farms and raising the well-being of the collective farmers attests to the fact that Molotov, Kaganovich, Malenkov and the others showed no understanding of agriculture; they regarded the peasantry incorrectly, considering it as a force which resisted socialist construction. It was this fallacious line toward the collective farms and collective farmers, which contradicted Lenin's views, that led in practice to the difficult position in agriculture which we had in 1953. . . .

Or, let us take another proposal of Molotov's — to increase the amount of the state loan in the countryside. His reason for this proposal was that the collective farmers were taking too small a part in subscriptions for the loan, were subscribing small sums, less than in the cities. And Molotov also succeeded in having this proposal adopted. Increasing the size of the loan could not, of course, resolve the task of finding the means, but it did worsen the political mood of the collective farmers. . . . (*Stenographic Report,* pp. 10-12)

Bulganin (December 18, 1958): . . . Comrades, my Party duty obligates me, especially in these conditions, repeatedly to return to the question of the activities of the anti-Party group, of my relationship to it; it obligates me to define my relationship toward what has been said about the anti-Party group in the report, to speak out once more about myself, about those mistakes which I committed before the Party, linking myself with this group. . . .

Everything that Comrade Khrushchev said in his report about the anti-Party group — about Molotov, Malenkov, Kaganovich, about me, and Shepilov — and everything that has been said here by the comrades is correct, everything fully corresponds with reality. It is known that after Comrade Khrushchev became a member of the Central Committee, Malenkov, Kaganovich, and Molotov always took their own special line, which disagreed with the position of the Central Committee, on all basic questions of domestic and international life that the Party Central Committee had to decide.

Comrades, about my own position. For the sake of objectivity, I must honestly declare that before the events of June 1957, I was not with Malenkov, Kaganovich, and Molotov on questions of reorganizing the administration of industry and construction, on the question of the virgin lands and their development, and on other questions. I was with the majority of the Presidium of the Central Committee, I was with the Central Committee, I spoke out and fought for the line of the Party and implemented it in my practical work. But, no matter how regrettable it is for me, a fact remains a fact: when in 1957 the anti-Party activity of Malenkov, Kaganovich, Molotov and Shepilov actively developed, I joined them, supported them and became their partner and accomplice. Being then the Chairman of the Council of Ministers, I became not only their accomplice, but also nominally their leader. The anti-Party group met in my office to arrange their anti-Party factional work. In such a way, if at a certain stage I conducted myself correctly and in a Party manner, I later in essence shared with them all the anti-Party filth.

At the June 1957 Central Committee plenum I sincerely voted for the plenum's resolution on the anti-Party group and fully agreed, and agree now, with that resolution and also with everything that has been said at this plenum. All subsequent decisions with regard to me personally I understand as correct and proper for me and necessary for the Party. The stern, sharp and principled evaluation of the criminal activities of Malenkov, Kaganovich and Molotov, and the entire anti-Party group and my participation in this group has revealed to me and helped me to understand all the harmfulness of the anti-Party group, and has helped me see all the rot and dankness of the anti-Party swamp in which I found myself. The party uncovered and exposed the political significance of the activities of the anti-Party group and precisely my mistakes. I sincerely acknowledged my mistake and asked the Central Committee to help me again return to the Party road. Today I am honestly trying to fulfill the obligations which the Central Committee has entrusted to me, the obligations of Chairman of the Stavropol Economic Council. In my practical work I see all the genius and wisdom of the policy of our Party and our Central Committee. . . .

I well remember the fierce struggle conducted by Molotov, Kaganovich, Malenkov and Shepilov against the reorganization of the management of industry and construction, against widening the rights of the Union republics and local Party and soviet organs. These questions were raised in the Central Committee by Comrade Khrushchev. Was this not the reason that Molotov, Malenkov, Kaganovich and Shepilov opposed these proposals? It was just this reason that they had no desire even to hear about these proposals. At the time Molotov, Malenkov, Kaganovich and Shepilov declared that we would have anarchy in the administration of industry and construction and that widening the powers of the Union republics and local Party and soviet agencies and, in particular, granting planning powers to the Union republics and transferring to them certain of the functions of the USSR State Planning Committee would even contradict Lenin. Now there is no need to prove the complete absurdity of these assertions. . . .

I well remember the situation in the Presidium of the Central Committee when Comrade Khrushchev presented the question about the virgin lands and their cultivation and when he introduced, almost at the same time, the proposal about the new order of planning in agriculture. "This is adventurism," said Molotov. "We will be left without grain," said Molotov, Malenkov and Kaganovich. "It is necessary to stifle the movement for the slogan — to overtake the USA in per capita output of livestock products; we do not have enough fodder," they said. . . .

What a danger would have threatened the Party and the Soviet people had Molotov, Malenkov and Kaganovich come to power. . . . (*Ibid.,* pp. 338-40)

K. G. Pysin (Secretary of the Altai Krai Party Committee — December 18, 1957): . . . Malenkov and others of the anti-Party group, who were opposed to opening up the virgin lands in Altai, have suffered final defeat. You will remember, Nikita Sergeyevich, when you visited us in the summer of 1954 in Altai and saw grain growing on the state farms already set up by us in the virgin lands. Malenkov, at that time Chairman of the Council of Ministers, signed a resolution censuring us for organizing virgin land state farms, and we were forbidden to organize any more and we were subsequently compelled to organize only ten state farms in 1955.

I speak about this because Malenkov did not simply disagree with developing the virgin lands, he interferred with this nationwide business. . . . (*Ibid.,* p. 318)

S. D. Ignatiev (Secretary of the Tatar Party Oblast Committee in 1958 and at the time of Stalin's death, Minister of State Security — December 18, 1958): . . . Bulganin's address today sounded just as weak and unconvincing as his earlier speeches.

Voice from the Audience: Correct.

He describes this business as if he has only now seen the true face of the anti-Party group of Malenkov, Kaganovich, Molotov, and Shepilov, and that, allegedly, this was not visible to him during those days of ruthless, malicious assaults on the Leninist part of the Central Committee Presidium and on the policy of the Party, during those days when they raised even the question of the leadership of the Central Committee and of the Party. Bulganin is not a schoolboy so that he could not detect the aims of the anti-Party group. At any rate, now even our schoolboys are capable of understanding politics. No, Nikita Sergeyevich spoke correctly when he said: Bulganin chased after the gingerbread which the anti-Party group offered him. Although the gingerbread was poisonous, nevertheless, Bulganin, being dissatisfied with his position in the Party, chased after it when it was promised to him. . . . (*Ibid.,* p. 350)

A. Yu. Snechkus (Secretary of the Lithuanian Party Central Committee — December 18, 1958): . . . Comrade Ignatiev expressed his attitude toward Comrade Bulganin's speech. I fully agree with Comrade Ignatiev's speech, and would only add that, as Bulganin's speech at an earlier plenum showed, he himself has not revealed all his connections with the anti-Party grouping, and in particular with Malenkov. You will remember, at that time a whole series of members of the Party Control Committee spoke, Comrade Shvernik spoke, and it was clear to everyone how close Bulganin's relations were with Malenkov and that Bulganin tried in every way to protect Malenkov. At that Plenum Bulganin did not admit this, and even now, in today's speech, he also has said nothing about it, he has not given an explanation of what he was accused of by the Party Control Committee. It seems to me that Bulganin's speech today cannot satisfy us. . . . (*Ibid.*, p. 365)

Ye. P. Kolushchinsky (Secretary of the Omsk Oblast Party Committee — December 18, 1958): . . . And what would be the situation now if the Central Committee Presidium and the Central Committee plenum had not defeated the evil group of conspirators? Bulganin here, at the Central Committee Plenum, again speaking of this conspiratorial group, gave his following evaluation: Molotov — divorced from life, knowing absolutely nothing of industry or agriculture; Kaganovich — a phrasemonger, confusing work with his empty talk; Malenkov — an intriguer, capable of all kinds of vileness; but about himself he was silent and said nothing. But Molotov, Kaganovich and Malenkov are not merely windbags and intriguers knowing nothing of industry and agriculture. The Party has given a true characterization and evaluation of the base, treacherous, conspiratorial group of fractionists and splitters. And in this group Bulganin secreted himself; he would assign to himself the designation of a seduced "joiner." No, you were a participant in this mean, treacherous group, so you shall be designated properly.

It seems to me it is necessary once again to think over and to investigate . . . the monstrous provocation when Malenkov at the 19th Party Congress talked about the fact that the grain problem had been solved. This was a foul provocation perpetrated on our people: the grain problem had been solved but there was not sufficient bread. . . . (*Ibid.*, pp. 398-99)

T. A. Yurkin (Deputy Minister of Agriculture for the Russian Republic — December 19, 1958): . . . The anti-Party group of Malenkov, Molotov, Kaganovich, Bulganin and Shepilov furiously fought against the policy of the Party in the sphere of developing the virgin lands, it threatened that this would lead to a reduction of the grain harvest per hectare, that therefore the supply of bread would not increase, and state expenditures on the virgin lands would not pay off.

And to what tricks didn't this contemptuous group have recourse! The apparatus of the State Planning Committee of that time declared that for the virgin lands there were no funds, no material supplies, and came out against allocating funds for tractors, dwellings, metal and so forth. They categorically refused supplies, they said that there were no resourses. Kaganovich led this business. . . .

At that time I was closely involved in working out measures for the virgin lands. I saw what tremendous work, what a strong will, patience and resoluteness Nikita Sergeyevich Khrushchev displayed when he carried on the struggle with the anti-Party group . . .

Yesterday Comrade Bulganin gave an explanation to the Plenum about his anti-Party activities and presented the case as if he had all along supported the general line of the Party and that only in June 1957 the devil had confused him and he jumped into the anti-Party group.

Such a naïve explanation, of course, convinces no one. I, for example, and other members of the Central Committee were present several times at sessions of the Central Committee Presidium during discussions of questions about plowing up the virgin and waste lands, about agricultural planning, and about organizing state farms on the virgin lands. We saw how Nikita Sergeyevich conducted a desperate struggle with Molotov, Malenkov, Kaganovich, and Shepilov. However, Bulganin was silent as a rule. He may say that silence is a sign of agreement. But, with whom he was agreeing was shown in June of last year when the office of the Chairman of the Council of Ministers became a place of conspiracy. . . . (*Ibid.*, pp. 408-09)

V. V. Matskevich (USSR Minister of Agriculture — December 19, 1958): . . . It is necessary to say that when the question of preparing materials for the reorganization of the Machine Tractor Stations arose as a practical matter, Molotov and Kaganovich literally tried to terrorize the apparatus of the Ministry of Agriculture in order to dig up, or more truthfully cook up, materials which would condemn this measure. And Shepilov and his assistants, such as academician Laptev, attempted "theoretically" to prove the "mistakes" of the worked-out proposals. . . . (*Ibid.*, p. 422)

The 21st Party Congress,
January 27 to February 5, 1959

I. V. Spiridonov (First Secretary, Leningrad Oblast Party Committee): . . . You are all familiar with Bulganin's speech at the December plenary session of the Party Central Committee. . . . Who is he himself, if not an accomplice, rather than merely one who went along with the anti-Party group? After all, the explanation that it was an accident and the machinations of the devil (Bulganin explained that the devil had enmeshed him with the anti-Party group) can be applied to Gogol's characters but not to people who possess an understanding of Party affairs, of political affairs. But, whether badly or well (rather badly), Bulganin at least spoke up before the Party and the people with a condemnation of his anti-Party position. But in a year and a half Comrade Pervukhin, candidate member of the Central Committee Presidium, and Comrade Saburov, member of the Central Committee, have not once condemned the anti-Party group and their role in it. What meaning are we to place on this silence, Comrades Pervukhin and Saburov, and may we not ask you to answer to the Congress for your mistakes? . . . (*Pravda,* January 30, 1959)

A. I. Kirichenko (Secretary of the Central Committee and Member of the Presidium): . . . The anti-Party group removed its mask and took an organized stand against the policy outlined by the 20th Congress; this was on June 18, 1957, when the members of the group had tallied their forces in the Central Committee Presidium and had concluded that they had sufficient strength to change the Party and government policy. We know how this ended. . . . (*Pravda,* February 1, 1959)

R. Ya. Malinovsky (USSR Minister of Defense): . . . The decree of the October [1957] plenary session of the Party Central Committee, "On Improving Party Political Work in the Soviet Army and Navy," was of enormous assistance in accomplishing the latest tasks of the Armed Forces. It contained a comprehensive program for the further development and consolidation of the Armed Forces in the spirit of the 20th Party Congress decisions and the Leninist principles of armed forces leadership. With the greatest promptness, the Party Central Committee detected the efforts of Marshal Zhukov, former Defense Minister, to divorce the Army from the Party and gave this new "Bonaparte" his come-uppance. . . . (*Pravda,* February 4, 1959)

M. G. Pervukhin (USSR Ambassador to East Germany): . . . I consider it my Party duty to discuss, as Comrade Spiridonov said, my mistake and my attitude to the anti-Party group and to do so here, before the Party's supreme organ, the Congress.

First of all, let me say that, together with the entire Party, I have condemned and do condemn the factional, schismatic activity of the anti-Party group. At the June plenary session of the Central Committee I voted in favor of the plenary session resolution on the anti-Party group . . .

I shall now relate the circumstances of my mistake. When the Central Committee discussed the reorganization of the management of industry and construction, I expressed doubts and objections concerning some of the proposals for the contemplated reorganization. My erroneous position in this extremely important matter and the dissatisfaction associated therewith led me to commit a major political mistake: At sessions of the Central Committee's Presidium held just before the June plenary session, I supported the anti-Party group's attacks on Comrade Khrushchev and consequently, as I later realized, on his policy on many domestic and foreign questions.

The anti-Party group evidently came into being long before the June plenary session of the Central Committee and was waiting for a suitable moment to take its stand against the Central Committee leadership. My erroneous position prior to the June plenary session to a certain extent helped them to do this. This is my chief offense against the Party.

I must say, however, that when the anti-Party group openly put the question of removing the Central Committee leadership, I disagreed and did not support this demand. Realizing that they had planned an inadmissible, anti-Party move which could have far-reaching harmful consequences, I spoke up at the June plenary session of the Central Committee, telling everything I knew about the group's factional anti-Party activities. As the decision of the Central Committee's plenary session states, I thereby admitted my mistakes and condemned them at the plenary session, helping the plenary session of the Central Committee to expose the factional activities of the group.

I am profoundly aware of my guilt before the Party and I am trying to prove this in the work that has been entrusted to me. Until this lamentable occurrence I had never taken a stand in opposition to the line of the Central Committee Presidium. Specifically, I was in complete agreement with Comrade Khrushchev's proposal to develop the virgin lands and other measures for achieving gains in agriculture. My position on foreign policy likewise did not differ from that of the Central Committee Presidium. When the question of normalizing relations with Yugoslavia was discussed at the July plenary session of the Central Committee, I took my stand in favor of the decisions of the Central Committee Presidium and, together with others, I criticized Molotov's incorrect position. . . .

I must express my ardent and sincere gratitude to the Central Committee and to the Central Committee Presidium, which, guided by Leninist standards of Party life, have given me a chance to show by deeds in important state work that I can atone for my guilt before the Party and be of use to it. I shall do everything in my power to justify this high trust of the Party. . . . (*Pravda,* February 4, 1959)

I. I. Kuzmin (Deputy Chairman of the USSR Council of Ministers and Chairman of the USSR State Planning Committee): . . . In referring to the guidance of the Party Central Committee in the drafting of the fundamental tasks of the seven-year plan as a whole and of its basic lines, I cannot help but recall that the members of the anti-Party group of Malenkov, Kaganovich, Molotov, Bulganin and Shepilov accused our party's Central Committee and Comrade N. S. Khrushchev of emphasizing practice at the expense of theory in the approach to the tasks of economic construction. The Yugoslav revisionists, as you know, have made similar charges. . . .

Comrades! Comrade Pervukhin spoke at the morning session of the Congress. There was essentially nothing in his speech about his anti-Party activity. I think this is not because he had nothing to say but because, from the moment the anti-Party group was exposed, Comrade Pervukhin has been hiding his face in the apparent hope that his activity in the anti-Party group and inactivity in major state posts entrusted to him by the Party would go unnoticed. . . .

Comrade Pervukhin, why do you distort the real situation so grossly? Since you lacked the courage to confess your errors, I shall take the liberty of reminding you of certain facts of your activity.

As you know, Comrade Pervukhin was for a long time Minister of Power Plants and in his capacity of Deputy Chairman of the USSR Council of Ministers supervised the Ministry of Power Plants. In this time

Comrade Pervukhin systematically followed a policy of preponderant construction of hydroelectric stations. As a result, enormous sums were unnecessarily diverted to this construction. The country's electrification was retarded and the national economy harmed. In addition, Comrade Pervukhin understated the country's need for expanded electric power capacity. He tried to justify this line in his speech at the first session of the USSR Supreme Soviet in 1954.

In his report before this Congress Comrade N. S. Khrushchev clearly showed that if this line had been maintained the national economy would be unable to maintain the high rate of development of the seven-year plan.

Against the dictates of common sense and totally ignoring the question of economic efficiency, Comrade Pervukhin sought to have liquid and gas fuel at the electric power stations replaced with coal, often brought in over long distances. This did serious damage to establishment of the most economical fuel balance structure in the country.

Incidentally, when Comrade Saburov, another member of the anti-Party group, introduced a proposal to reduce the rate of development of the oil industry and the construction of oil refineries, Comrade Pervukhin supported him. As a result the structure of the fuel balance received an improper orientation.

In the development of power capacity Comrade Pervukhin followed a policy of limiting the capacity of thermal power plants to 300,000 or 400,000 kw., although we know, and you, Comrade Pervukhin, were perfectly well aware, that much larger stations are economically far more advisable. Such acts also restricted the development of electric power capacity. The Central Committee was forced to intervene. In the interests of justice I must say that Nikita Sergeyevich Khrushchev intervened in this matter and a correct orientation was given to the development of electric power production and to the structuring of the fuel balance. . . .

Another fact. You know that Comrade Pervukhin for a long time was in charge of the Ministry of the Chemical Industry. Here, too, he committed grave errors. . . . Even the production of mineral fertilizers, which, as you know, is not something new, failed to receive maximum possible development, considering the availability of raw materials and funds, in the time that you, Comrade Pervukhin, were in charge of the Ministry of the Chemical Industry. Here, too, the Central Committee was forced to intervene. Nikita Sergeyevich Khrushchev intervened in this matter. The question was brought up for consideration at the

May plenary session of the Party Central Committee and, as you know, received the solution that was required.

After this, Comrade Pervukhin, how can you say that you had no differences with the Party Central Committee?

In his speech before the Party Congress Comrade Pervukhin stated that when the reorganization of the management of industry and construction was under way he merely expressed doubts concerning individual provisions of the reorganization program. How can you so grossly distort what happened only a short time ago, the witnesses to which are present in this hall? After all, it was you, together with Molotov and Shepilov, who made up that same triumvirate in the anti-Party group which actively campaigned against the reorganization of the management of industry and construction. It was you who spoke of an "organizational itch," it was you who spoke of some kind of "biases" in the idea of reorganization. You took an open and patently hostile attitude to the Party Central Committee's line on the reorganization of the management of industry and construction. . . . (*Pravda,* February 5, 1959)

M. Z. Saburov: . . . As you know, comrades, I committed a mistake and displayed political instability in the Party Central Committee's struggle with the anti-Party group in June, 1957. I therefore consider it my duty to answer to the 21st Congress for this mistake.

What was my mistake, and what role did I play in the period when the Party was combating the anti-Party group?

I had long known, as had all the members of the Presidium of the Party Central Committee, that the group of members of the Presidium of the Central Committee that included Malenkov, Molotov and Kaganovich, and later Bulganin and Shepilov, had taken their own special position within the Central Committee Presidium on all basic problems of domestic and foreign policy and were endeavoring, on one pretext or another, to block the taking of decisions on these crucial matters. At almost every session of the Presidium of the Party Central Committee this group advanced its opinions, comments and "amendments." Furthermore, the Central Committee Presidium for a very long time showed forbearance toward it and frequently put off final decisions on problems under discussion.

Among the major questions on which the anti-Party group waged a struggle inside the Central Committee Presidium were the plowing up of the virgin lands; the new planning procedure in agriculture; the slogan for catching up with the United States in per capita output of milk, butter and meat; the raising of the prices of several agricultural products delivered to the state; the cancellation of arrears for economically weak collective farms; the exemption of individual farms from milk deliveries, and a number of other matters concerning agriculture that were raised in the Presidium of the Central Committee, particularly by Comrade Khrushchev.

The participants in the anti-Party group also opposed expanding the rights of the Union republics, reorganizing the management of industry and construction and the work of the State Planning Committee, abolishing loans, etc. I could enumerate a number of other problems whose resolution this anti-Party group systematically opposed in the Central Committee.

This group also either opposed or tried in every way to obstruct the adoption of decisions on important problems of foreign policy. In particular, it opposed the Party Central Committee's policy in such important problems as the necessity of developing our economic ties with the people's democracies and extending aid to these countries, to say nothing of our helping the poorly developed and dependent countries of Asia and the Near East. The participants in the group behaved like people blinded by narrow-minded national insularism, evincing failure to understand the Party's policy in problems of the utmost importance.

Comrades! Neither on all these nor on other critical problems of Communist Party policy did I ever partake of the views of these anti-Party elements who had become divorced from life. On the contrary, throughout the period of my membership in the Presidium of the Party Central Committee I firmly and consistently supported the line pursued by the healthy part of the Presidium members, headed by Comrade Khrushchev. . . .

My mistake, comrades, was that at a meeting of the Presidium of the Central Committee preceding the June plenary session of the Party Central Committee, I criticized shortcomings in the work of the Central Committee Presidium not from the standpoint of the healthy part of the Presidium of the Party Central Committee but from the standpoint of the anti-Party group, which, using trivial and easily eliminated shortcomings as a cloak, attacked Comrade Khrushchev in an effort to effect a change in the Central Committee's leadership and, consequently, in the policy of the Central Committee, which was hewing to Leninist positions, the positions of the decisions of the 20th Party Congress.

Even at the meeting of the Presidium of the Party Central Committee before the June plenary session I nevertheless adopted a different

stand, protesting the filthy attempts of Kaganovich and the other participants in the anti-Party group to besmirch the name of N. S. Khrushchev
and stating that the line of the Central Committee Presidium was correct and that collective leadership was in effect in the Central Committee
Presidium, that ill will should be renounced and a policy of revenge
abjured, and that we should end by taking cognizance of and eliminating
the shortcomings noted, which were not of a fundamental character. . . .

Committed to correct positions on the basic questions of Party
policy and having discerned the anti-Party group's real purposes, which
amounted to a change in the leadership of the Central Committee and
in the Leninist policy being pursued by the Central Committee Presidium and by N. S. Khrushchev personally, I – with the help of several
comrades in the healthy part of the Central Committee Presidium's
members, Comrades Mikoyan and Kirichenko – quickly broke with the
anti-Party group and, at the plenary session of the Central Committee
in June 1957, truthfully told all I knew of its designs, thereby helping
the plenary session and the Party as a whole to expose this group's plans
and intentions.

The June plenary session of the Party Central Committee noted
my political instability at that moment, and taking into consideration
that I had helped the plenary session in exposing the anti-Party group,
removed me from membership in the Presidium of the Central Committee but left me a member of the Central Committee. At the decision
of the Party Central Committee, I was later appointed director of a
plant in the city of Syzran. I acknowledged the correctness of this decision, and in my work at the plant I have been exerting myself to the
utmost to atone for my error through work and to vindicate the confidence of the Party Central Committee and of my people. . . . (*Stenographic Report,* pp. 290-92)

G. A. Denisov (First Secretary, Saratov Oblast Party Committee):
. . . Comrade Pervukhin's speech at the present Congress cannot be
passed over in silence, comrades. Comrade Pervukhin declared that he
had helped the Party Central Committee to unmask the anti-Party
group; he represented himself to the Congress as a hero. Is it so, Comrade Pervukhin?

We members of the Central Committee all remember how it really
was and remember your behavior. Didn't you come out against the reorganization of the management of industry and construction? Didn't
you disagree with Nikita Sergeyevich Khrushchev's proposals on major

questions of foreign policy? Didn't you swing into the camp of the conspirators? And how can you say after this that you helped the Party to unmask the anti-Party group of conspirators? Your speech before the Congress was insincere. After all, Comrades Pervukhin and Saburov, you felt compelled to tell the June plenary session of the Party Central Committee about the activity of the anti-Party group only after the members and candidates of the Party Central Committee had unanimously condemned the anti-Party group. Only then did you speak up, and even then not at once. That is not helping the Party Central Committee to unmask the anti-Party group; it is your confession. . . . (*Pravda,* February 6, 1959)

The 22nd Party Congress, October 17–31, 1961

N. S. Khrushchev (October 17): . . . The Leninist course expressed by the 20th Congress was at first carried out against the fierce resistance of anti-Party elements, zealous partisans of the methods and practices prevailing under the cult of the individual, revisionists and dogmatists. The factionalist anti-Party group consisting of Molotov, Kaganovich, Malenkov, Voroshilov, Bulganin, Pervukhin and Saburov, and Shepilov, who joined them, came out against the Party's Leninist course.

At first the strong resistance to the Party's line on condemning the cult of the individual, fostering inner-Party democracy, condemning and rectifying all abuses of power, and exposing the individuals guilty of repression was rejected by Molotov, Kaganovich, Malenkov and Voroshilov. Their stand in this matter was no accident. They bear personal responsibility for many mass repressions against Party, soviet, economic, military and Y.C.L. cadres and for other similar manifestations that took place during the period of the cult of the individual. At first this group was only an insignificant minority in the Presidium of the Central Committee.

But when the Party launched the struggle to restore Leninist norms of Party and state life, when it set about such urgent tasks as developing the virgin lands, reorganizing the management of industry and construction, enlarging the rights of the Union republics, improving the well-being of Soviet people, and restoring revolutionary legality, the factional group activized its anti-Party subversive work and began to recruit supporters in the Central Committee Presidium. It added Bulganin, Pervukhin and Saburov, and Shepilov joined them. Realizing that they had succeeded in throwing together an arithmetical majority in the Presidium, the participants in the anti-Party group went into open attack, seeking to change the policy in the Party and the country — the policy set forth by the 20th Party Congress.

Having reached agreement at their secret gatherings, the factionalists demanded an extraordinary meeting of the Presidium. They counted on carrying out their anti-Party designs, on seizing the leadership of the Party and country. The anti-Party group wanted to confront the members of the Central Committee and the whole Party with a *fait accompli*.

But the factionalists miscalculated. Members of the Central Committee who were then in Moscow, learning of the factional actions of the anti-Party group within the Presidium, demanded the immediate calling of a Central Committee plenary session.

The Central Committee plenary session, held in June 1957, resolutely exposed the anti-Party group and routed it ideologically. The June plenary session demonstrated the political maturity, monolithic unity and close cohesion of the Central Committee on the basis of the Leninist line of the 20th Congress. Ideologically routed in the course of the plenary session and faced with unanimous condemnation by the Central Committee session, the participants in the anti-Party group came forth with the confession that they had conspired and with an admission of the harmfulness of their anti-Party activity. Comrade Voroshilov came forth at the plenary session with an admission of his mistakes, saying that "the factionalists misled" him and that he fully recognized his errors and firmly condemned them, together with the whole subversive work of the anti-Party group.

As you know, the resolution of the Central Committee plenary session on the anti-Party group was adopted unanimously; the participants in the anti-Party group also voted for it, except Molotov, who abstained from voting. Later, at a primary Party organization's discussion of the results of the plenary session, Molotov too declared that he considered the plenary session's decision correct and accepted it. . . . (*Pravda*, October 18, 1961)

N. V. Podgorny (First Secretary of the Ukrainian Party Central Committee — October 19): . . . One cannot but tell of Kaganovich's provocational activities in the Ukraine. After becoming Secretary of the Ukraine Communist Party Central Committee in 1947, he surrounded himself with a pack of unprincipled people and toadies, betrayed cadres devoted to the Party, and trampled upon and terrorized leading officials of the republic. Like a true sadist, Kaganovich found satisfaction in mocking activists and the intelligentsia, belittled their human dignity and threatened them with arrests and imprisonment. It is no accident that many Party, soviet and professional workers still call the period of Kaganovich's tenure the "black days" of the Soviet Ukraine.

Kaganovich inflated the cult of Stalin, pandered to him, exploited his weak sides for his own careerist purposes and at the same time created his own cult of the individual, representing himself as the "leader" of the Ukrainian people. To this end the press carried articles extolling his activities in the Ukraine in the 1930's, although it is known that even at that time he was recalled from the Ukraine for serious mistakes. Matters reached a point where he demanded, for example, that artists add his portrait to already completed paintings representing the liberation of the Ukraine from the German occupiers, although he had nothing to do with these events.

Considering himself infallible, Kaganovich personally, bypassing the Central Committee, decided major questions of the life of the republic, and very frequently decided them incorrectly. Being a master of intrigues and provocations, he accused leading writers of the republic, as well as a number of executive Party officials, of nationalism, literally without any grounds. Upon Kaganovich's instructions, abusive articles against a number of writers devoted to the Party and the people appeared in the press.

However, this did not satisfy Kaganovich. He began working to convene a plenary session of the Central Committee with the agenda: "The struggle against nationalism as the chief danger in the Ukraine Communist Party (Bolsheviks)," although in reality there was not even a trace of such a danger. There couldn't be, since, to our good fortune, the Central Committee of the Ukraine Communist Party was for many years headed by the staunch Leninist Nikita Sergeyevich Khrushchev, who instilled in Communists and the Ukrainian people a spirit of internationalism, friendship of peoples and selfless devotion to the great ideas of Leninism.

Comrade N. S. Khrushchev enjoyed enormous prestige among the Communists and all the working people of the Ukraine and, relying on them, disrupted by every means the provocations of Kaganovich. And if today the remarkable poet-Communist and Lenin Prize Winner Maxim Faddeyevich Rylsky is among us delegates to the 22nd Congress, and if many other figures in Ukrainian literature continue to fight actively for the cause of the Party, they owe this above all to the courage and inflexible will of our Nikita Sergeyevich Khrushchev.

In the conditions of the prevalence of the Stalin cult, this was truly a heroic struggle, particularly since in the end Kaganovich pursued the aim of compromising and making short work of executive cadres of the Ukraine Communist Party, and above all he set out to compromise Comrade N. S. Khrushchev. This is now totally clear to us. . . .

I believe, comrades, that Kaganovich did the Party and the people a great deal of harm. He is a degenerate, in whom there has been nothing communist for a long time. We think his actions are incompatible with the title of member of the great Party of Communists. . . . (*Pravda*, October 20, 1961)

Ye. A. Furtseva (USSR Minister of Culture — October 20) : . . . The factionalists opposed the re-establishment of Leninist norms because they themselves had at the time been involved in their violation. They were against rehabilitation of innocent victims because they themselves were to blame for the mass repression and gross infringements of legality that had cost our people so tragic a price. . . .

The comrades will recall the augmented session of the Central Committee Presidium in 1954, which was attended by all the Ministers of the Soviet Union and by representatives of public organizations. At that time, on Comrade Khrushchev's initiative, the Presidium was discussing the question of amalgamating Moscow's construction organizations into a single system under the Chief Moscow Construction Administration; heretofore these organizations had been scattered among 60 departments. This amalgamation was essential if we were to get moving on housing construction and establish an industrial base for construction work. Furthermore, the dispersal of construction work affected the distribution of housing accommodations, because in many instances the departments had neglected to supervise this matter and permitted violations of the prescribed procedure. You should have seen the fury with which Molotov opposed this proposal. What arguments did he give? Only one, that the administration of construction must not be concentrated in a single chief administration under the Moscow Soviet, but that all the departments should concern themselves with this matter. Is any comment needed? . . .

And finally, there was the question of reorganizing the management of industry. The Central Committee spent a long time in 1957 studying this acute matter, thoroughly and from all sides. It was plain that the organizational forms of management then existing had begun to hamper the further development of productive forces. The ministries had to be abolished and economic regions formed. Conferences on this question were held in the republics, provinces and cities. Then the Central Committee of the CPSU convened an augmented conference in which all members and candidate members of the Central Committee's Presidium took part. At this conference no one, not even Molotov, objected to the reorganization of the management of industry. The Presidium of the Central Committee twice discussed the report that was to be submitted to the plenary session of the Central Committee. There were no objections from Molotov on these occasions either. But the night before the plenary session, at 3 A.M., the members of the Central Committee's Presidium received from Molotov a half-page note in which he informed the Presidium that he disapproved of the reorganization of industry, giving absolutely no reasons and merely alleging that the time had not yet come for such a reform in our country. Is there any need to comment on this? Life has shown who was right. . . .

Not long before the June plenary session of the Central Committee there was a meeting of the Central Committee's Presidium, which was attended by many members and candidate members of the present Presidium. I think that they can all clearly recall the situation at that meeting. The meeting was discussing the complete rehabilitation, including rehabilitation in the Party, of persons who had at one time been prominent in our army's leadership — Tukhachevsky, Yakir, Uborevich, Yegorov, Eideman, Kork and others. So obvious was their innocence that even Molotov, Malenkov, Kaganovich and others declared for their rehabilitation, although they had had a hand in their tragic deaths. And at that point in the discussion Nikita Sergeyevich very calmly but bluntly asked them: "When were you right, then? When you voted to doom them, and that doom was so tragically sealed, or now that you are for completely rehabilitating them? Tell us, when were you right?" This blunt and honest question infuriated and flustered them. It had become plain from their conduct at that meeting that they were afraid that the truth would come out, that the flagrant violations of Soviet legality committed by them would become known to the whole Party and to the people. And at that point these dissidents resorted to conspiracy, with the purpose of turning the Party back from the new policy of re-establishing Leninist norms of Party life to the old practices of the days of the cult of the individual. It was this that united them. . . . (*Pravda,* October 22, 1961)

A. I. Mikoyan (October 20): . . . The factionalist anti-Party group, of which Molotov became the chief ideologist, was later joined by Bulganin, Pervukhin, Saburov and Shepilov. . . .

Just before the 20th Congress of the CPSU Molotov, in a report at a session of the USSR Supreme Soviet, openly questioned whether a socialist society had been built in the USSR. His statement was: "Along with the Soviet Union, in which the foundations of socialist society have already been built, there are those people's democracies that have taken only the first, but extremely important, steps in the direction of socialism." According to Molotov, it appeared that, first, socialism had not yet been built in the USSR; second, the first steps toward socialism were being taken by only some of the people's democracies; and, third, there were people's democracies in which even these steps had not been taken.

You yourselves appreciate that with premises like these there could be no thought of a plan for building communism.

Influenced by criticism in the Central Committee, Molotov was forced to excuse himself in the pages of the magazine *Kommunist*; he tried to reduce the issue to one of erroneous formulation. But it was not an erroneous formulation that was involved. If only the foundations of socialism had been built, it was clearly impossible to pose the question of transition to the full-scale building of communism. If only some of the people's democracies had taken the first steps in the direction of socialism, it meant that the world socialist system had not formed and there could be no talk, therefore, of its growing influence on the course of social development. This was a fundamentally wrong, non-Leninist assessment of the line-up of class and political forces in the world of today.

The result of his underestimating the forces of socialism and, consequently, overestimating the forces of imperialism was that Molotov made serious mistakes on questions of international development — on peaceful co-existence and the possibility of preventing a world war, and on the multiplicity of the forms of transition to socialism in various countries.

In general, Molotov rejects the line of peaceful co-existence, reducing the concept to nothing more than a state of peace, or rather the absence of war at a given moment, and denying the possibility of preventing a world war. In its substance this view approximates that of the foreign adversaries of peaceful co-existence, who interpret it as a variant of the "cold war," as a state of "armed peace." . . .

When the Party decided to abolish the industrial ministries and set up economic councils, and also to reorganize the Machine and Tractor Stations,* the factionalists considered the moment had come for seizing power and changing the Party's policy by a coup at the top. They had held their peace at the Congress, but now, at their clandestine meetings, they began to hatch a plot against the Party. And then in June 1957, the members of the group, having tallied the votes against the Party leadership that they could muster from the members of the Central Committee's Presidium, went over to the direct attack. But they miscalculated.

The plenary session of the Central Committee measured up to Leninist requirements and administered the anti-Party oppositionist group a crushing ideological and organizational defeat. The group's members made appropriate statements at the plenary session, and afterwards, a year to a year and a half later, wrote letters to the Central Committee in which they acknowledged and condemned their mistakes. Molotov was the only one who did not vote for the resolution of the Central Committee's plenary session or anywhere in any form repudiate his anti-Party activity or his views, which had inflicted great harm on the Party. What he had said in the primary organization about agreeing with the decision of the plenary session had been insincere, prompted by tactical considerations. To this day he clings bullheadedly to his conservative–dogmatic views.

The Central Committee consistently bases its activity on Leninist norms of Party life. This has shown itself in the fact that the fight against the conservative–dogmatic group was waged by the methods of inner-Party democracy, without resort to repressive state measures, as had been the case under the cult of the individual. But the victory of the anti-Party group would have led to reprisals against all the active supporters of the 20th Congress, by methods that the Party can never forget. . . . (*Pravda,* October 22, 1961)

D. S. Polyansky (Chairman of the Russian Republic Council of Ministers — October 23): . . . It is also necessary to refer to Comrade Voroshilov's conduct as a participant in the anti-Party group. The

---

* The MTS were abolished in early 1958 at Khrushchev's initiative.

Party Central Committee was very lenient with you, Comrade Voroshilov. After all, you played an active role in this group, although you do say that you were "confused by the devil." We don't believe the devil has anything to do with this. You wanted to cover up the traces of your participation in the repressions against completely innocent people, especially against the cadres of military leaders, repressions known to the whole country. As a member of the anti-Party group, and an active participant in it, Comrade Voroshilov behaved insolently, rudely and defiantly. At a critical moment he even refused to meet with members of the Party Central Committee who demanded the convening of a plenary session of the Central Committee. He forgot that he had been elected to the Presidium of the Central Committee and consequently could be deprived of this high trust. And how did he behave at the Central Committee plenary session? I will recall only one incident. When Kaganovich was accused of mass repressions in the Kuban, which were carried out on his instructions and with his personal participation, Voroshilov came to Kaganovich's defense; he jumped up from his seat and, shaking his fists, cried: "You are still young and we'll fix your brains." We then answered his remark: "Calm down, the Central Committee will look into the matter of whose brains should be fixed!" So, Comrade Voroshilov, don't pretend to be an innocent Ivan. You must bear full responsibility for your anti-Party deeds, like the anti-Party group. . . . (*Pravda*, October 24, 1961)

N. G. Ignatov (Deputy Chairman of the USSR Council of Ministers — October 23): . . . This group of factionalists has now been rendered harmless. As our colloquial expression has it, the serpents have had their fangs pulled. Some of them are now crawling and others hissing, but none of them can bite any longer. If we talk about them, it is not because they constitute any danger to the Party but in order that the Party and the Soviet people will know the nature of these renegades who had lost touch with life and will know what they were out to do.

What aims had the anti-Party group set for itself? To render the Party leaderless, to change the membership of the Presidium when the Central Committee's back was turned, to seize the leadership of the Party, to turn the Party off the Leninist path and revive the practices that had obtained under the cult of the individual. Molotov, Kaganovich, Malenkov and Voroshilov were guided in this disgusting business not only by thirst for power but also by dread of being called to account for the unlawful and arbitrary acts they had committed, from which many innocent Party members and non-Party people had suffered.

After Comrade Khrushchev's truthful report to the 20th Congress on the cult of the individual, the Party learned about cases of the most flagrant violations of socialist legality, abuse of power and unjustified persecution. And when the Party set about eliminating the effects of the cult of the individual, the factionalists realized that the time would come sooner or later when they would have to answer for their villainous deeds. As you know from the speeches of the delegates to the Congress, the factionalists made long and painstaking preparations for accomplishing their designs; they gradually, one by one, recruited their supporters and with Jesuitical refinement created an intolerable situation in the work of the Presidium of the Central Committee. These were experienced plotters and double-dealers. . . .

But it is a well known fact that Molotov was and remains muddleheaded in his understanding of international relations and the country's internal development. He had a great many things all wrong on the question of ways and means of building communism in our country, in his assessment of the forces of socialism and imperialism, on the questions of the co-existence of states with different social systems, the possibility of preventing a world war, and the forms of transition to socialism in different countries. And no wonder. Molotov was and remains a hopeless dogmatist who has lost all notion of reality. He was out of step with our Party.

As we know, when the anti-Party group had knocked together its so-called arithmetical majority in the Central Committee Presidium, it set about the practical realization of its plans to seize the leadership of the Party and the country. But its members made a big mistake; they forgot that, besides them, there was the Central Committee, whose members had implicit faith in Comrade Nikita Sergeyevich Khrushchev and stood with him for the consistent pursuit of the Leninist course mapped by the 20th Congress.

You have learned from the Central Committee's report that the members of the Central Committee who were in Moscow demanded that a plenary session of the Central Committee be called at once. They were vigorously supported by Comrade Khrushchev and other comrades who upheld the Leninist line. And the plenary session was called. . . .

The members of the Central Committee sent their representatives to the session of the Presidium with a statement on the need for convening a plenary session of the Central Committee. Let me read this statement to you:

"To the Presidium of the Central Committee: We, members of the CPSU Central Committee, have learned that the Central Committee Presidium is in continuous session. We are also aware that you are discussing the question of the leadership of the Central Committee and of the Secretariat. Matters of such importance for our whole Party cannot be concealed from the members of the Plenum of the Central Committee. In view of this fact we, members of the CPSU Central Committee, urgently request that a plenary session of the Central Committee be called and this matter submitted to it for discussion. We, as members of the Central Committee, may not stand aloof from the question of our party's leadership."

When this request was reported to the Presidium, the factionalists kicked up a terrible fuss.

Comrades! It is not fitting that I recount to you from this lofty rostrum the vile things they said to the Central Committee's members when they arrived. And what do you think it was all about? Why, how dare the members of the Central Committee approach them?! Comrade Khrushchev and the other comrades who supported him flatly insisted that the members of the Central Committee be received. Then this so-called arithmetical majority — the factionalists — proposed that the members of the Central Committee be received not by the Presidium but by one of their supporters — Bulganin or Voroshilov. Seeing what this group was up to, Nikita Sergeyevich Khrushchev stated that he too would go to the meeting with the members of the Central Committee, and he stood his ground. And what a lucky thing that was for the fortunes of our party!

N. S. Khrushchev: They wanted to keep me from meeting with the members of the Central Committee, and they singled out Voroshilov for the job. I told them that the Plenum had elected me First Secretary of the Central Committee and no one could deprive me of the right to meet with the members of the Central Committee of the Communist Party. It was the Plenum of the Central Committee that had elected me, and it should therefore be the Plenum that took the decision. It would be as the Plenum of the Central Committee decided.

N. G. Ignatov: Then the Presidium authorized Comrades Khrushchev and Mikoyan, as well as Voroshilov and Bulganin, to meet with the members of the Central Committee.

N. S. Khrushchev: Two against two, as you see.

N. G. Ignatov: As you see, the factionalists were unwilling to meet the members of the Central Committee, as Nikita Sergeyevich has told us so truthfully and vividly. More than that, instructions were given not to admit the members of the Central Committee to the Kremlin, and many of them had to use literally illegal means in making their way to where the Central Committee's Presidium was in session. This is something unheard of, comrades, a disgrace! . . . (*Pravda,* October 25, 1961)

L. F. Ilyichev (Director of the Central Committee's Department of Propaganda and Agitation for the Union Republics — October 24): . . . Presumably many of you will remember Comrade N. S. Khrushchev's article in a March 1951 issue of *Pravda* on the urgent tasks of developing the collective farm countryside. The article contained new basic propositions on the development of agriculture; it boldly and openly raised painful questions of collective farm development and was permeated with deep humaneness and concern for the needs of the collective farm peasantry.

But this article brought down "wrath from on high." What happened? It seemed that Stalin "did not like" the article. He reacted to it very intolerantly and morbidly. I, who was editor-in-chief of *Pravda* at that time, was blamed for political immaturity. The very next day the editors were advised to publish a so-called "correction." This correction is worth repeating in full at the 22nd Party Congress.

"Editor's note: Correction of an error.

Through an oversight of the editorial office, in printing Comrade N. S. Khrushchev's article 'On Building and Improvements on the Collective Farms' in yesterday's *Pravda,* an editorial note was omitted in which it was pointed out that Comrade N. S. Khrushchev's article was published as material for discussion. This statement is to correct this error."

No, comrades, the article was absolutely correct, and was imbued with a spirit of Leninist creativity and concern for the flourishing of the collective farm system. There had of course been no thought of an editor's note. Therefore there had been no omission. What was "omitted" was simply common sense on the part of those who did not know life, were isolated from it and interpreted every creative thought as an insult, as an encroachment on their personal authority.

How did events develop subsequently?

The draft of a private letter of the Central Committee was prepared which in a raucous, extremely irritable tone literally annihilated the article. But Malenkov, the inspirer of this disgraceful document, overdid it. It was clear where the initiators of the document were leading the matter. Instead of proof, which of course did not exist, this entire so-called document consisted of outcries against the article, such as "condemn as anti-Marxist," "condemn as harmful," "condemn as erroneous," etc. . . .

Molotov considered himself the chief "theoretician" among them. It is necessary to recall the events of 1957, when the anti-Party group shifted to an open attack on the Central Committee. Precisely at that time Molotov published the pretentious article "On Lenin" in the central press. The article deliberately represents the author as a "monopolist" on Leninism, a Leninist, a friend and companion-in-arms of our leader. The author was lecturing the Party on Leninism — and this at a time when Molotov had clearly broken with Leninism.

On April 18, 1960, Molotov sent the editors of the magazine *Kommunist* an article devoted to the 90th anniversary of V. I. Lenin. The article was entitled "On Vladimir Ilyich Lenin." Note that the article was written after the ideological, political and organizational rout of the anti-Party factionalist group. The editors did not publish the article. They were right in not publishing it, because it bore the stamp of a dogmatic position not only on many political and economic questions but also on questions of theory, a position condemned by the 20th Congress of our party. Not a single word was said in it about the subversive actions of the anti-Party factionalist group. It is as if it had never existed. . . .

Take Kaganovich. His speeches as a rule abounded in elementary errors, but he, too, tried to picture himself as a theoretician. His zeal to extol the Stalin cult knew no bounds. It was he who pushed the proposal to introduce the concept "Stalinism" in place of Marxism–Leninism "to mark a new stage in theory." And the would-be economist Malenkov made the anti-Leninist assertion that the preponderant development of heavy industry was not obligatory. Fawning and playing the toady, Shepilov reached the point of outright and gross falsification of Marxism. He credited Stalin with discovering the law of the mandatory correspondence of production relations to the nature of production forces, although every student knows the name of the author of this law. Stalin was obliged to state that not he but Marx had discovered this law. . . .
(*Pravda,* October 26, 1961)

N. M. Shvernik (Chairman of the Central Committee's Party Control Committee — October 24) : . . . In the course of the work done by the Party Control Committee to rehabilitate Communists condemned without reason, we constantly encountered the grievous consequences of the high-handed deeds and lawless acts perpetrated personally by Malenkov, Kaganovich and Molotov. It developed that in the period of the ascendancy of the cult of the individual, they had taken the lead in building up an atmosphere of suspicion and mistrust. Holding positions of authority, Malenkov, Kaganovich and Molotov committed the most flagrant violations of revolutionary legality and the Leninist norms of Party life. . . .

It has now been established that Malenkov, bent on taking a leading position in the Party and the state, entered into close collusion with Yezhov and later on with Beria, and under the pretense of displaying "vigilance" arranged the mass fabrication of cases against Party and Soviet officials, who were charged with being enemies of the people. In so doing he resorted to the foulest devices: intrigues, frame-ups, lies.

When visiting Byelorussia in 1937 Malenkov, working with Yezhov, concocted a story that there was a large anti-Soviet underground in the republic, allegedly headed by the Party and Soviet leadership. Pursuing this monstrous frame-up, Malenkov arranged for summary justice to be meted out to Byelorussia's Party, soviet, trade union and Young Communist League cadres. . . .

That same year, using the same methods to frame people, Malenkov effected the destruction of devoted Party cadres in Armenia. On his way to Yerevan, Malenkov paid a call on Beria in Tbilisi and arranged with him the procedure for the so-called "inquiry" that was supposed to confirm their story that a widely ramified anti-Soviet organization existed in Armenia. The result of this frame-up was that, on Malenkov's personal instructions, almost the entire leadership of Armenia's Central Committee and Council of People's Commissars was illegally arrested. Malenkov personally interrogated the prisoners, using proscribed methods in the process.

Malenkov's trips to a number of provinces in the Russian Republic were equally ill-omened. Each trip was followed by the arrest of secretaries of province Party committees and many other officials. . . .

Malenkov bears a very substantial share of the blame for extremely flagrant violations of the Party Statutes and revolutionary legality committed with respect to the Leningrad Party organization in 1949 and 1952.

Equally great crimes against the Party and the Soviet people were committed by another member of the anti-Party group — Kaganovich. . . .

Under Kaganovich arrests of railroad officials were made by lists. His deputies, nearly all road chiefs and political-section chiefs, and other executive officials in transport were arrested without any grounds whatever. They have now been rehabilitated, many of them posthumously.

The Party Control Committee has in its possession 32 personal letters from Kaganovich to the NKVD demanding the arrest of 83 transport executives. . . .

Especially heavy blame for the violation of socialist legality must be laid at the doorstep of Molotov, who for a long time was Chairman of the Council of People's Commissars and in that capacity himself flouted Soviet laws in the most flagrant manner.

Thus in 1937, when the internal situation in the country was marked by great strides in economic construction and cultural development and by the strengthened moral and political unity of Soviet society, Molotov advanced "theoretical" arguments for the need to step up the effort against so-called "enemies of the people" and had a personal hand in the mass repressions. At the February–March, 1937, plenary session of the Central Committee, Molotov said: "The present subversive–sabotage organizations are especially dangerous in that these saboteurs, subversives and spies pretend to be Communists, ardent supporters of the Soviet regime."

Making cruel sport of those who sought to caution Stalin and Molotov against conjuring up all sorts of conspiracies and sabotage and espionage centers, Molotov called on the Party to annihilate the "enemies of the people" alleged to be hiding behind Party cards.

The documents show that it was under Molotov that so illegal a method as condemning people by lists was introduced. . . . (*Pravda,* October 26, 1961)

B. N. Ponomarev (Director of the Central Committee's International Department — October 24): . . . The Congress criticized the Party history "Short Course" because it was permeated with the spirit of the Stalin cult, treated many fundamental questions incorrectly and belittled the role of V. I. Lenin, the Party and the masses. It was decided to create a scientific Marxist textbook on the history of the CPSU. The necessary directives were worked out in order to give this book the correct, Leninist orientation. During discussion of the directives at a meeting of the Presidium of the Party Central Committee, Molotov and Kaganovich zealously, literally foaming at the mouth, opposed the very idea of producing a new textbook on Party history that would meet the requirements of Leninism. They thereby worked for the confirmation, contrary to the decisions of the 20th Congress, of the correctness of everything that had been done earlier, including the period 1937–1938. They also strove to see to it that Communists should continue to be reared on the basis of the "Short Course," which was imbued with the cult of the individual. Although they were rebuffed at the Presidium meeting, they continued their line. In April 1957, not long before the anti-Party group acted openly, Molotov lauded the "Short Course" in the pages of the press without even mentioning the harmful consequences of the cult of the individual. Furthermore, he tried to erect his own type of "theoretical" basis for justifying the mistakes and lawlessness that characterized the period of the Stalin cult. In this article Molotov wrote: "We know that individual mistakes, and sometimes serious mistakes, are inevitable in solving such big and complex historical tasks. No one has or can have a guarantee on this score." In other words, Molotov tried to argue: "As it was under the cult of the individual, so it will continue to be." But the Party and its Central Committee said: "No, it must not and never again will be this way!" . . . (*Pravda,* October 26, 1961)

P. A. Satyukov (Editor-in-Chief of *Pravda* — October 25): . . . What need, they asked, for these trips around the country, what was the point of all these conferences and meetings on collective farms, at construction projects and factories? Kaganovich went so far as cynically to call the trips being made by Party leaders to the localities needless "knocking about the country." We got along without them, he said, and we shall continue to do so. The Party dealt a crushing blow to these anti-Party views and these champions of the cult of the individual. . . .

Molotov did work under Lenin. But the plain truth of the matter is that he had no grounds for making excessive claims. As we know, in not one of Lenin's speeches or in his "Testament" addressed to the regular Party Congress in 1922 is Molotov mentioned at all among the prominent Party figures of the period. Nowhere and at no time did Lenin say anything about Molotov's "services in the area of theory," either. He said nothing because there were no such services. But Lenin did have something to say about Molotov's penchant for bureaucracy. . . .

This is how Vladimir Ilyich rated Molotov's work in the Central

Committee post that had been entrusted to him: *". . . gigantic communist task is being thoroughly bungled as a result of obtuse bureaucracy!"*

The partiality for bureaucracy that Lenin had noticed proved to be the determinant feature of all Molotov's work. He never did manage to make the grade as a political leader of the Leninist type, though he held high positions for a long time. . . . (*Pravda,* October 27, 1961)

A. N. Shelepin (Chairman of the KGB [Committee on State Security] — October 26): . . . Stalin and his intimates Molotov and Kaganovich used the murder of Sergei Mironovich Kirov as an excuse for organizing reprisals against people who were objectionable to them, prominent state figures.

This was the time when the emergency criminal laws were adopted that made it possible to expose to public dishonor and to exterminate honest leaders who were devoted to the Party and the people. A whole series of extrajudiciary bodies made their appearance in this period. It has been established that the proposal for instituting them was personally drafted by Kaganovich. The draft of this document, in his writing, is in the archives.

Flagrantly abusing their high positions in the Party and state, Molotov, Kaganovich and Malenkov sealed the fates of many people with a stroke of the pen. One is simply amazed at the criminal thoughtlessness with which all this was done.

I want to give the delegates a few more facts to supplement what has already been said at our Congress. In November 1937, Stalin, Molotov and Kaganovich sanctioned the arraignment (their signatures are preserved on this document) before a court of the Military Collegium of a large group of comrades from the ranks of prominent Party, state and military workers. Most of them were shot. Those innocently shot and posthumously rehabilitated include such prominent Party and state figures as Comrades Postyshev, Kossior, Eikhe, Rudzutak and Chubar; People's Commissar of Justice Krylenko; Unshlikht, Secretary of the USSR Central Executive Committee; People's Commissar of Education Bubnov, and others.

The brutal attitude that was shown to people, to executive comrades who found themselves under investigation, is evidenced by a number of cynical notations written by Stalin, Kaganovich, Molotov, Malenkov and Voroshilov on letters and petitions from the prisoners. Yakir, for example, a former commander of a military district, had sent a letter to Stalin assuring him of his complete innocence.

Here is what he wrote: ". . . I am the honest fighting man, devoted to the Party, state and people, that I have been for many years. My entire conscious life has been spent working selflessly and honestly in full view of the Party and its leaders. . . . Every word I say is honest, and I shall die with words of love for you, the Party and the country, with boundless faith in the victory of communism."

Stalin wrote on this letter: "Scoundrel and prostitute." Voroshilov added "A perfectly accurate description," Molotov put his name to this and Kaganovich appended: "For the traitor, scum and . . . (next comes a scurrilous, obscene word) one punishment — the death sentence."

The day before he was shot, Yakir sent Voroshilov the following letter: "To K. Ye. Voroshilov. I ask you, in memory of my many years of honest service in the Red Army in the past, to give instructions that my family, helpless and quite innocent, shall be looked after and given assistance. I have addressed the same plea to N. I. Yezhov. Yakir, June 9, 1937."

On this letter from a man with whom he had worked for many years, who as he well knew had time and again looked death in the face while defending the Soviet regime, Voroshilov wrote his conclusion: "In general I doubt the honesty of a dishonest person. K. Voroshilov. June 10, 1937."

Isn't it a good thing that Comrade Voroshilov saw his mistakes in time! . . .

As has already been stated here, Malenkov has on his conscience the so-called "Leningrad Case," which brought grievous tragedy into the families of many Communists of that glorious city so dear to us. For careerist ends, Malenkov by means of intrigue compromised Comrade Kuznetsov, former Secretary of the Party Central Committee; Comrade Voznesensky, member of the Politburo, and other prominent Party workers.

Crying out to Malenkov's conscience is the memory of a number of workers of the Armenian Party and Soviet apparatus who were arrested on his instructions in connection with the murder of Comrade Khandzhyan, First Secretary of the Armenian Party Central Committee, who, as it later developed, had been killed in his office by Beria personally. By thus destroying quite innocent people, Malenkov helped his associate Beria to cover up his crime. . . .

Comrades! I want to tell you about still another case. In the June days of 1957, when the factionalists had gone over to an open attack on the Central Committee, Bulganin, abusing his official position, posted his bodyguard in the Kremlin and stationed additional guards — who allowed no one in without his instructions — at the government building in which the Presidium of the CPSU Central Committee was holding its session. This shows that the conspirators were prepared to take the most extreme steps to achieve their filthy purposes.

Happily for us, the Central Committee saw the danger of the anti-Party group in time and rendered it harmless.

I must declare at this Congress, with a full sense of responsibility for the statement, that several members of the anti-Party group, and above all Molotov, have thus far failed to draw the proper conclusions from this grim lesson, are behaving badly, double-dealing with the Party and holding to their old views.

The time has therefore come for the Party Central Committee's Party Control Committee to consider calling the members of the anti-Party group to the strictest account. And in this matter I fully support the proposals made by the delegates who have spoken before me. . . .

The anti-Party group is not being talked about at our Congress because it represents a danger to the Party today. It does not! The members of the anti-Party group are political corpses, who, far from representing any danger, do not even represent a shadow of a danger. We are talking about these factionalists with the purpose of once more laying bare their true complexion, of once more underlining the full extent of their nothingness as compared with the greatest of what the Party and people have accomplished since the 20th Congress, with the truly breath-taking horizons being opened up to us by the magnificent new program of the CPSU! . . . (*Pravda,* October 27, 1961)

N. S. Khrushchev (Concluding speech — October 27): . . . Comrade delegates! I wish to tell the Congress how the anti-Party group reacted to the proposal that the question of abuses of power in the period of the cult of the individual be placed before the 20th Party Congress.

Molotov, Kaganovich, Malenkov, Voroshilov and others categorically objected to this proposal. In answer to their objections they were told that if they continued to oppose the raising of this question, the delegates to the Party Congress would be asked to decide the matter. We had no doubt that the Congress would favor discussion of the question. Only then did they agree, and the question of the cult of the individual was presented to the 20th Party Congress. But even after the Congress, the factionalists continued their struggle and obstructed in every possible way the clarification of the question of abuses of power, fearing that their role as accomplices in the mass repressions would come to light. . . .

The participants in the anti-Party factionalist group hoped to seize leadership in the Party and the country and to remove the comrades who were exposing the criminal actions committed in the period of the cult of the individual. The anti-Party group wanted to place Molotov in the leadership. Then, of course, there would have been no exposures of these abuses of power.

Even after the 20th Congress had condemned the cult of the individual, the anti-Party group did all in its power to prevent the exposure from going any further. Molotov said that in large matters there may be bad things and good. He justified the actions that had taken place in the period of the cult of the individual and claimed that such actions are possible and that their repetition in the future is possible. Such was the course of the anti-Party factionalist group. This is not a simple aberration. It is a calculated, criminal and adventurist position. They wanted to divert the Party and the country from the Leninist path, they wanted to return to the policy and methods of leadership of the period of the cult of the individual. . . .

I knew Comrade Yakir well. I knew Tukhachevsky too, but not as well as Yakir. In 1961, during a conference in Alma-Ata, his son, who works in Kazakhstan, came to see me. He asked me about his father. What could I tell him? When we investigated these cases in the Presidium of the Central Committee and received a report that neither Tukhachevsky nor Yakir nor Uborevich had been guilty of any crime against the Party and the state, we asked Molotov, Kaganovich and Voroshilov:

"Are you for rehabilitating them?"

"Yes, we are for it," they answered.

"But it was you who executed these people," we told them indignantly. "When were you acting according to your conscience, then or now?"

But they did not answer this question. And they will not answer it. You have heard the notations they wrote on letters received by Stalin. What can they say? . . .

Let us recall Sergo Ordzhonikidze. I attended Ordzhonikidze's funeral. I believed what was said at the time, that he had died suddenly, because we knew he had a weak heart. Much later, after the war, I learned quite by accident that he had committed suicide. Sergo's brother had been arrested and shot. Comrade Ordzhonikidze saw that he could no longer work with Stalin, although previously he had been one of his closest friends. Ordzhonikidze held a high Party post. Lenin had known and valued him, but circumstances had become such that Ordzhonikidze could no longer work normally, and in order to avoid clashing with Stalin and sharing the responsibility for his abuse of power, he decided to take his life. . . .

When the anti-Party group was smashed, its participants expected that they would be treated in the same way they had dealt with people at the time of the cult of the individual and in the way they hoped to deal with those who favored the restoration of Leninist norms of Party life.

I had a typical conversation with Kaganovich. This was two days after the end of the June plenary session of the Party Central Committee, which expelled the anti-Party group from the Central Committee. Kaganovich called me on the telephone and said:

"Comrade Khrushchev, I have known you for many years. I ask you not to let them treat me in the vindictive way people were treated under Stalin."

And Kaganovich knew how people had been treated because he himself had been a participant in these reprisals.

I answered him:

"Comrade Kaganovich! Your words once more confirm the methods you intended to use to achieve your disgusting ends. You wanted to return the country to the state of affairs that existed under the cult of the individual, you wanted to indulge in reprisals against people. And you measure other people by your own yardstick. But you are mistaken. We firmly observe and we shall adhere to Leninist principles. You will be given a job," I said to Kaganovich, "you will be able to work and live in tranquillity if you labor honestly, as all Soviet people labor."

Such is the conversation I had with Kaganovich. This conversation shows that when the factionalists failed, they thought they would be dealt with in the same way they intended to deal with the Party cadres if they had succeeded in realizing their wicked designs. But we Communists–Leninists cannot embark on the path of abuse of power. . . .

I want to talk particularly about Comrade Voroshilov. He has been approaching me and telling me about his tribulations. His state of mind is understandable, of course. But we are political leaders and we cannot be guided by feelings alone. Feelings may differ, and they can be deceptive. Here at the Congress Voroshilov listens to the criticism directed against him and walks around like a beaten man. But you should have seen him at the time when the anti-Party group raised its hand against the Party. Then Voroshilov was a man of action; he came forth, if not on horseback, at least in his full regalia, in battle dress, so to speak.

The anti-Party group used Comrade Voroshilov in its struggle against the Central Committee. It is no accident that the factionalists singled out Voroshilov to meet with the Central Committee members who were working to convene a plenary session of the Central Committee. The anti-Party group calculated that with his prestige Voroshilov could influence the Central Committee members and shake their resolve in the struggle against the anti-Party group. The anti-Party group also named Bulganin for the meeting with the Central Committee members. But Bulganin did not enjoy the same prestige as Voroshilov. They placed great hopes on Voroshilov, as one of the oldest Party leaders. But this too was of no help to the factionalists.

The question arises: How did Comrade Voroshilov get into this group? Some comrades know about the strained personal relations between Voroshilov and Molotov, between Voroshilov and Kaganovich and between Malenkov and Voroshilov.

And yet, despite these relations, they nevertheless joined forces. Why, on what basis? Because after the 20th Congress they were afraid of further exposures of their illegal actions in the period of the cult of the individual, they were afraid they would have to answer to the Party. It is known, after all, that all the abuses of that time were committed not only with their support but with their active participation. Fear of responsibility and a desire to restore the state of affairs that existed in the period of the cult of the individual — these are what united the participants in the anti-Party group despite the personal animosity they felt toward one another.

Comrade Voroshilov committed grave errors. But I believe, comrades, that he must be treated differently than the other active participants in the anti-Party group — than Molotov, Kaganovich and Malenkov, for instance. It must be said that in the course of the bitter struggle with the factionalists during the early part of the June plenary session of the Central Committee, when Comrade Voroshilov saw the monolithic unity of the Central Committee members in the struggle against the anti-Party group, he apparently became aware that he had gone too far. Voroshilov understood that he had joined with men who were fighting against the Party, and he condemned the actions of the anti-Party group and admitted his mistakes. He thereby in some measure helped the Central Committee. We cannot underestimate this step on his part, comrades, because at the time this was a support for the Party.

The name of Kliment Yefremovich Voroshilov is widely known among the people. Therefore his participation in the anti-Party group along with Molotov, Kaganovich, Malenkov and the others strengthened this group, as it were, and made a certain impression on people inexperienced in politics. By leaving this group, Comrade Voroshilov helped the Central Committee in its struggle against the factionalists. Let us answer him in kind for this good deed and make his situation easier.

Comrade Voroshilov has been sharply criticized; this criticism was just, for he committed grave mistakes and Communists cannot forget them. But I believe that our approach to Comrade Voroshilov should be considerate, that we should show magnanimity. I believe that he sincerely condemns his actions and repents them. . . .

Here at the Congress much has been said, for instance, about the furious energy displayed by the anti-Party factionalists Molotov, Kaganovich, Malenkov and others against the Leninist Party Central Committee and against me personally. Speaking against the course set forth by the 20th Congress, the schismatics concentrated their main fire against Khrushchev, who did not suit them. Why against Khrushchev? Well, because Khrushchev had been promoted by the will of the Party to the post of First Secretary of the Central Committee. The factionalists badly miscalculated. The Party smashed them both ideologically and organizationally.

The Central Committee of our Party has displayed an exceptionally high political maturity and a truly Leninist understanding of the situation. It is characteristic that literally not one member or candidate member of the Central Committee and not one member of the Inspection Commission supported the miserable handful of schismatics. . . . (*Pravda,* October 29, 1961)

K. Ye. Voroshilov (Statement to the 22nd Party Congress — October 26): . . . Dear comrade delegates! Being unable, for reasons of health, to speak at this historic 22nd Congress of our great Leninist party, I consider it my Party duty to state the following: . . .

The Central Committee's report to the 22nd Party Congress, delivered by Comrade N. S. Khrushchev, contains a just appraisal of the factionalist activity of the anti-Party group of Molotov, Kaganovich, Malenkov, Bulganin and others, and my name is mentioned among the factionalists.

Yes, I admitted and admit that at the beginning of the struggle against this group I supported certain erroneous, harmful statements by some of its members, but I had no idea of its factionalist activities until their true face was exposed and they themselves admitted their factionalist activity in the course of examination of the conduct of these "cliquists" at the June 1957 plenary session of the Party Central Committee. After this I immediately stated that I had never known about this, had never joined any group and had never had any dealings or associations with this sort of people.

Having deeply realized the enormous harm that could have been done our Party and country by the anti-Party group of Molotov, Kaganovich, Malenkov and others, I resolutely condemn its factionalist activity, which was aimed at diverting the Party from the Leninist path. I fully understand the gravity of the mistake I made when I supported the harmful statements of the members of the anti-Party group.

My attitude toward our Leninist Party, toward its executive bodies and toward its policy in all domestic and foreign policy questions was clearly and definitely set forth in my speeches at the 20th and 21st Party Congresses. This attitude is determined by my deep devotion to the interests of the Party and the people, and I have no other interests but these. I am in full accord with the important work done by the Party to restore the Leninist norms of Party life and eliminate the violations of revolutionary legality of the period of the cult of the individual, and I deeply regret that in this situation I, too, made mistakes.

Throughout my 58 years in the ranks of our glorious Communist Party I have never, nowhere and under no circumstances, retreated from the Statute and Program requirements and norms for the members of our Party, have never betrayed the great principles of Marxism–Leninism, have never participated and will never participate in anti-Party — whatever they may be called — groupings. — K. VOROSHILOV, delegate to the 22nd Party Congress and Party member since 1903."
(*Pravda,* October 29, 1961)

APPENDICES

I · Presidium of the Party Central Committee, 1953 to 1957

	Central Committee Secretariat	Provincial Secretaries	Other
March 1953	Khrushchev	Melnikov* Bagirov*	
July 1953	Khrushchev	Kirichenko*	
July 1955	Khrushchev Suslov	Kirichenko	
Feb. 1956	Khrushchev Suslov Brezhnev* Furtseva* Shepilov*	Kirichenko Mukhitdinov*	Shvernik* (Control Com.)
Feb. 1957	Khrushchev Suslov Brezhnev* Furtseva* Shepilov*	Kirichenko Mukhitdinov* Kozlov*	Shvernik* (Control Com.)
June 1957	Khrushchev Suslov Brezhnev Furtseva Aristov Belyayev Kuusinen Pospelov*	Ignatov Kirichenko Kozlov Kalnberzin* Kirilenko* Mazurov* Mukhitdinov* Mzhavanadze*	Shvernik (Control Com.)
Dec. 1957	Khrushchev Suslov Brezhnev Furtseva Aristov Pospelov* Kuusinen Kirichenko Ignatov Mukhitdinov	Kozlov Kalnberzin* Kirilenko* Mazurov* Mzhavanadze*	Shvernik (Control Com.)

GOVERNMENT FUNCTIONARIES

Date	Central Government	Other
March 1953	Beria, Bulganin, Kaganovich, Malenkov, Mikoyan, Molotov, Pervukhin, Saburov, Voroshilov, Ponomarenko*	Shvernik* (trade unions)
July 1953	Bulganin, Kaganovich, Malenkov, Mikoyan, Molotov, Pervukhin, Saburov, Voroshilov, Ponomarenko*	Shvernik* (trade unions)
July 1955	Bulganin, Kaganovich, Malenkov, Mikoyan, Molotov, Pervukhin, Saburov, Voroshilov	Shvernik* (trade unions), Ponomarenko* (Ambass., Poland)
Feb. 1956	Bulganin, Kaganovich, Malenkov, Mikoyan, Molotov, Pervukhin, Saburov, Voroshilov	Zhukov* (Defense Min.)
Feb. 1957	Bulganin, Kaganovich, Malenkov, Mikoyan, Molotov, Pervukhin, Saburov, Voroshilov	Zhukov* (Defense Min.)
June 1957	Bulganin, Mikoyan, Voroshilov, Kosygin*, Pervukhin*	Zhukov (Defense Min.), Korotchenko* (Ch., Ukraine Council of Min.)
Dec. 1957	Bulganin, Mikoyan, Voroshilov, Kosygin*, Pervukhin*	Korotchenko (Ch., Ukraine Council of Min.)

* Candidate member

II · Secretariat of the Party Central Committee, 1952 to 1957

Oct. '52	Mar. 7 '53	Mar. 14 '53	Apr. 7 '53	Mar. '55	July '55	Feb. '56	Dec. '56	Feb. '57	July '57	Dec. '57
Stalin°										
Malenkov°	Malenkov°									
Khrushchev°	Khrushchev°	Khrushchev°	Khrushchev°	Khrushchev°	Khrushchev°	Khrushchev°	Khrushchev°	Khrushchev°	Khrushchev°	Khrushchev°
Suslov°	Suslov	Suslov	Suslov	Suslov	Suslov°	Suslov°	Suslov°	Suslov°	Suslov°	Suslov°
Mikhailov°	Mikhailov									
Aristov°	Aristov				Aristov	Aristov	Aristov	Aristov	Aristov°	Aristov°
Ponomarenko°										
Pegov†										
Brezhnev†						Brezhnev†	Brezhnev†	Brezhnev†	Brezhnev°	Brezhnev°
Ignatov†										Ignatov°
	Ignatiev	Ignatiev								
	Pospelov	Pospelov	Pospelov	Pospelov	Pospelov	Pospelov	Pospelov	Pospelov	Pospelov†	Pospelov†
	Shatalin	Shatalin	Shatalin							
					Shepilov	Shepilov†		Shepilov†		
					Belyayev	Belyayev	Belyayev	Belyayev	Belyayev°	
						Furtseva†	Furtseva†	Furtseva†	Furtseva°	Furtseva°
									Kuusinen°	Kuusinen°
										Kirichenko°
										Mukhitdinov°

° Member, Central Committee Presidium
† Candidate, Central Committee Presidium

III · Presidium of the Council of Ministers, 1953 to 1958

	Mar. '53	July '53	Dec. '53	Feb. '55	Mar. '55	Dec. '56	May '57	June '57	Dec. '57	Mar. '58
CHAIRMAN	Malenkov°	Malenkov°	Malenkov°	Bulganin°	Bulganin°	Bulganin°	Bulganin°	Bulganin°	Bulganin°	Khrushchev°
FIRST DEPUTY CHAIRMEN	Beria° Molotov° Bulganin° Kaganovich°	Molotov° Bulganin° Kaganovich°	Molotov° Bulganin° Kaganovich°	Molotov° Kaganovich°	Molotov° Kaganovich° Mikoyan° Pervukhin° Saburov°	Molotov° Kaganovich° Mikoyan° Pervukhin° Saburov°	Molotov° Kaganovich° Mikoyan° Pervukhin° Saburov° Kuzmin	Mikoyan° Kuzmin		Mikoyan° Kozlov°
DEPUTY CHAIRMEN	Mikoyan°	Mikoyan°	Mikoyan° Saburov° Pervukhin° Tevosyan Malyshev Kosygin	Mikoyan° Saburov° Pervukhin° Malenkov° Tevosyan Malyshev Kosygin	Malenkov° Tevosyan Malyshev Kosygin Zavenyagin Kucherenko Lobanov Khrunichev	Malenkov° Tevosyan Zavenyagin	Malenkov°	Kosygin†	Mikoyan° Kuzmin Kosygin† Ustinov	Kosygin† Zasyadko Kuzmin Ustinov

° Member, Central Committee Presidium
† Candidate, Central Committee Presidium

NOTE: Technically speaking, according to the decree of March 7, 1953, the Presidium of the Council of Ministers was composed only of the Chairman and First Deputy Chairmen. However, the Deputy Chairmen apparently soon were also considered Presidium members.

Mikoyan was apparently a Deputy Chairman of the Council of Ministers following Stalin's death even though he was not mentioned as such in the March 7, 1953 decree. His official biography in the *Large Soviet Encyclopedia's* supplement for 1962 notes that he was a Deputy Chairman from 1946 to 1955. It also indicated that for a period in 1957 and 1958 he was demoted from First Deputy Chairman to Deputy Chairman. Although there was no official announcement of this action at the time, references to Mikoyan (and Kuzmin, the other First Deputy Chairman in July 1957) after the late summer 1957 identified him simply as a Deputy Chairman.

IV · Party Congresses, Central Committee Plenums, and Important Sessions of the Supreme Soviet, 1953 to 1958

Date	Event	Proceedings
5–14 Oct. '52	19th Party Congress	
7 March '53	CC Plenum (Joint session with Council of Ministers and Presidium, Supreme Soviet)	Leadership and institutional arrangements after Stalin's death.
14 March '53	CC Plenum	Changes in membership and reduction in size of the Secretariat. Possibly discussed the new economic course and repudiation of the Doctor's Plot.
15 March '53	First Post-Stalin session of the Supreme Soviet	Ratified governmental reorganization and promised more consumers' goods.
June '53	CC Plenum	Purge of Beria.
8 August '53	Supreme Soviet session	Malenkov's report disclosed agricultural deficiencies and revealed plans for increasing production, and announced the new course in economic policy.
3–7 Sept. '53	CC Plenum	Khrushchev designated First Secretary. Khrushchev's report on agriculture.
Feb. 23–Mar. 2 '54	CC Plenum	Resolution on grain production and the Virgin Lands based on Khrushchev's report.
June '54	CC Plenum	Agriculture. Criticisms of ministries for slighting Virgin Lands.

25–31 Jan. '55	CC Plenum	Livestock production. Industrial priorities. Decision to demote Malenkov.
3–9 Feb. '55	Supreme Soviet session	Bulganin replaced Malenkov as Chairman, Council of Ministers. Zhukov named Defense Minister.
4–12 July '55	CC Plenum	Khrushchev's report on Yugoslavia. Bulganin's report on industry and technology. Discussion of harvest preparations. Announcement of 20th Party Congress. Kirichenko and Suslov promoted to Presidium; and Aristov, Belyayev and Shepilov named to Secretariat.
14–25 Feb. '56	20th Party Congress	Khrushchev's ideological pronouncements about peaceful co-existence, noninevitability of war, etc. The Secret Speech condemning Stalin. Creation of the Central Committee Bureau for the RSFSR.
27 Feb. '56	CC Plenum	Election of new Presidium and Secretariat. Zhukov, Shepilov, Brezhnev, Furtseva, and Mukhitdinov named candidate members, Presidium and Ponomarenko dropped as candidate member. Furtseva and Brezhnev added to Secretariat.
20–24 Dec. '56	CC Plenum	Amendment of 6th Five-Year Plan. Reorganization of State Economic Commission. Shepilov released from Secretariat.

5–12 Feb. '57	Supreme Soviet session	Pervukhin's report on the revised economic plan.
13–14 Feb. '57	CC Plenum	Announcement of plans for industrial reorganization and call for public discussion of Khrushchev's Theses. Shepilov appointed to Secretariat. Kozlov named candidate member, Presidium.
7–10 May '57	Supreme Soviet session	Ratification of plans for industrial reorganization.
22–29 June '57	CC Plenum	Expulsion of anti-Party Group. Widespread changes in leading government and Party organs.
28–31 Oct. '57	CC Plenum	Expulsion of Zhukov and resolution on Party-political work in armed forces.
16–17 Dec. '57	CC Plenum	Trade unions. Report on conferences of world communist parties. Kirichenko, Ignatov, and Mukhitdinov appointed to Secretariat. Mukhitdinov promoted to full member, Presidium.
25–26 Feb. '58	CC Plenum	Dissolution of the MTS. Decision to name Khrushchev Chairman, Council of Ministers (?).
27–31 Mar. '58	Supreme Soviet session	Khrushchev replaced Bulganin as Chairman, Council of Ministers.

V · The Power Elite, 1953 to 1958

The following biographical information about the Soviet political elite between 1953 and 1958 has been abridged from the official biographical notes in the 1962 Yearbook *of the* Large Soviet Encyclopedia *unless otherwise indicated.*

ARISTOV, A. B.   Born in 1903. Joined the CPSU in 1921. Began his working career as a fisherman. Graduated from the Leningrad Metallurgical Institute in 1932. Taught from 1934 to 1939 and subsequently held leading Party and government jobs. Secretary of the Party Central Committee, 1952–53 and 1955–60. Member of the Party Presidium 1952–53 and 1957–61. Deputy Chairman, Central Committee Bureau for the RSFSR, 1957–61.

BELYAYEV, N. I.   Born in 1909. Joined the CPSU in 1921. Graduated from the Moscow Institute of People's Economy in 1925. After 1940 was engaged in leading Party work. Member of the Party Central Committee after 1952. First Secretary, Kazakh Party Central Committee, December 1957. Became a member of the Party Presidium in 1957. (*1958 Yearbook*)

BERIA, L. P.   Born in 1899 to a poor peasant family in Georgia. Joined the CPSU in 1917. Graduated from the Baku Mechanical–Technical Institute in 1919. From 1921 to 1931 held leading positions in the CHEKA. In 1931 became First Secretary of the Georgian Party Central Committee and Secretary of the Transcaucasian Regional Committee. Became a member of the Party Central Committee in 1934. People's Commissar of Internal Affairs, 1938–45. After 1941 was a member of the State Defense Committee and after May 1941 was Deputy Chairman of this Committee. In July 1945 was designated Marshal of the Soviet Union. (*Large Soviet Encyclopedia*, Vol. 5, 1950).

BREZHNEV, L. I.   Born in 1906. Joined the CPSU in 1931. Graduated from the Kursk Technicum for Land Utilization and Reclamation in 1927 and from the Dneprodzherzhinsk Institute in 1935. In the late 1920's worked as a land specialist in Kursk Oblast and as a deputy chairman of a raion executive committee. In 1935–36 served in the Red Army.

In 1937–38 was director of a technicum and then was deputy chairman of the Dneprodzherzhinsk City Executive Committee. After 1938 held responsible Party jobs. In 1939–41 was Secretary of the Dneprodzherzhinsk Oblast Party Committee. During World War II, was head of the Political Commissariat of the Army and later Chairman of the Military Council. Between 1946 and 1950 was First Secretary of the Zaporozhe Oblast Party Committee and then First Secretary of the Dnepropetrovsk Oblast Party Committee. In 1950–52 was First Secretary of the Moldavian Republic Party Central Committee. Secretary of the Party Central Committee, 1952–53 and 1956–60. Deputy Chief of the Main Political Administration of the Soviet Army and Navy, 1953–54. Second Secretary (February–August, 1954) and then First Secretary of the Kazakh Republic Central Committee, until 1956. Candidate member, Party Presidium, 1956–57, and full member after 1957.

BULGANIN, N. A.   Born in 1895 to a working-class family in Nizhny Novgorod (Gorky). Joined the CPSU in 1917. In 1918–22 worked in the apparatus of the CHEKA. Between 1922 and 1927 held leading positions in the Supreme Council of National Economy. In 1937 named Chairman of the Council of People's Commissars for the Russian Republic. From 1938 to 1941 was Deputy Chairman of the USSR Council of People's Commissars and Director of the USSR State Bank. Member of the Military Council for the Western Front, 1941–43. In 1944 was elected a member of the State Defense Committee and Chairman of the USSR People's Commissariat for Defense. In February, 1948 was elected a member of the Party Politburo. (*Large Soviet Encyclopedia*, Vol. 6, 1951).

FURTSEVA, YE. A.   Born in 1910. Joined the CPSU in 1930. Graduated from the Moscow Institute of Chemical Technology in 1942 and from the Higher Party School through correspondence courses in 1948. Instructor of the All-Union Komsomol, 1936–37. Secretary of Moscow's Frunze Borough Party Committee, 1942–50. Second Secretary (1950–54) and First Secretary (1954–57) of the Moscow City Party Committee. Secretary of the Central Committee, 1956–60. Candidate member, Party Central Committee, 1952–56 and full member of the Central Committee, 1956. Candidate member of the Party Presidium, 1956 and full member, 1957–61.

IGNATOV, N. G.   Born in 1901. Joined the CPSU in 1924. Between 1917 and 1932 served in the Red Army and in the OGPU (secret police). After completing courses on Marxism–Leninism in Party schools in 1934, held Party jobs. Second and then First Secretary of Kuibyshev Oblast and City Party Committees, Second and then First Secretary of Orlov Oblast and City Party Committees, First Secretary of Krasnodar Krai and City Party Committees, 1937–52. Minister of Procurements, 1952–53. Secretary of the Party Central Committee, 1952–53 and 1957–60. Candidate member, Party Presidium, 1952–53 and full member, 1957–61. Member of the Central Committee Bureau for the RSFSR, 1956–57.

KAGANOVICH, L. M.   Born in 1893 to a poor Jewish family in Kiev Gubernia. At 14 worked in a shoe factory. During World War I was a member of the Kiev Bolshevik committee. Was in the army after 1917. After January 1918 worked in Leningrad and later in Moscow as Commissar of the Agitation Department of the Red Army. In 1922 became candidate member of the Party Central Committee and in 1924 full member. Secretary of the Central Committee, 1924–25. Named candidate member of the Politburo in 1926 and full member in 1930. First Secretary of the Ukrainian Party Central Committee, 1925–28. First Secretary of the Moscow Party Committee, 1930–35. People's Commissar of Transportation, 1935–44. First Secretary and member of the Politburo of the Ukrainian Party Central Committee, in 1947. In 1947 returned to Moscow as a member of the Politburo and from March 1953 First Deputy Chairman of the USSR Council of Ministers. (*Large Soviet Encyclopedia*, Vol. 19, 1953).

KALNBERZIN, YA. E.   Born in 1893. Joined the CPSU in 1917. In 1931–33 studied in the Institute of Red Professors. First Secretary of the Latvian Party Central Committee, 1940–59. Candidate member of the Party Central Committee, 1941–52 and full member after 1952. Candidate member of the Party Central Committee, 1941–52 and full member after 1952. Candidate member, Party Presidium, 1957–61.

KHRUSHCHEV, N. S.   Born in 1894 to a coal miner's family. Joined the CPSU in 1918. From his early years worked as a shepherd and later as a blacksmith in the Donbas region. An active participant in the civil war. After finishing the Workers' Faculty at the Donbas Industrial Institute in 1925, he held leading Party jobs in the Donbas and Kiev. In 1929 entered the Moscow Industrial Academy. From 1931 was Secretary of the Bauman and then Krasnopresnensky Borough Party Committees in Moscow. In 1932–34 was Second Secretary of the Moscow Oblast Party Committee and later First Secretary of the Moscow City Party Committee. From 1935 to 1938 was First Secretary of the Moscow Oblast and City Party Committee. From January 1938 was First Secretary of the Ukrainian Party Central Committee. From March to December 1947 was Chairman of the Ukrainian Council of Ministers and was afterward re-elected First Secretary of the Ukrainian Party Central Committee, where he remained until 1949. During World War II was in active military service and a member of the Kiev Special Military Council. Performed great organizational work for the partisan movement against the German Fascist aggressors. From December 1949 to March 1953 was a Secretary of the Party Central Committee and First Secretary of the Moscow Oblast Party Committee. From March to September 1953, Secretary of the Party Central Committee. From September 1953, First Secretary of the Party Central Committee. From March 1958, Chairman of the USSR Council of Ministers. From 1956, Chairman of the Central Committee Bureau for the RSFSR. Candidate member of the Politburo, 1938–39 and full member after 1939.

KIRICHENKO, A. I.   Born in 1908. Joined the CPSU in 1930. Graduated from the Azov Black Sea Institute for Engineers and Mechanics of Socialist Agriculture. After 1938 held leading Party jobs. First Secretary of the Ukrainian Central Committee, 1953–57. Member of Presidium of the Ukrainian Supreme Soviet, 1951. Member of the Party Central Committee from 1952. Candidate member, Party Presidium, 1953–55 and full member after 1955. Secretary of the Party Central Committee after 1957. (*1958 Yearbook*).

KIRILENKO, A. P.   Born in 1906. Joined the CPSU in 1934. In 1929–30 engaged in Komsomol, Soviet, and co-operative work. In 1936 graduated from the Ryibinsk Aviation Institute. In 1936–38 worked as a construction engineer. In 1938–41 was second secretary of a raion Party committee, and the Secretary and later Second Secretary of Zaporozhe Oblast Party Committee. Served in the army in 1941–43. Second Secretary of Zaporozhe Oblast Party Committee, 1943–47. First Secretary, Nikolaev Oblast and City Party Committees, 1947–50. First Secretary, Dnepropetrovsk Oblast Party Committee, 1950–55. First Secretary, Sverdlovsk Oblast Party Committee, 1955–62. Member, Party Central Committee from 1956. Member, Central Committee Bureau for the RSFSR, 1956–57. Candidate member, Party Presidium, 1957–61.

KOSYGIN, A. N.   Born in 1904. Joined the CPSU in 1927. Graduated from the Leningrad Co-operative Technicum in 1924 and the Leningrad Textile Institute in 1936. Worked in the consumer co-operative system of the Siberian Krai, 1924–30. Director of a Leningrad textile factory, 1935-38. Head of a department of Leningrad Oblast Party Committee, 1938. USSR Commissar of Textile Industry, 1939–40. Deputy Chairman, Council of People's Commissars, 1940–46. Deputy Chairman of USSR Council of Ministers, March 1946 to March 1953. Minister of Light Industry, 1948–53 and Minister of Light and Food Industry, March to August 1953. Minister of Consumers' Goods Industry, August 1953 to February 1954. Deputy Chairman, USSR Council of Ministers, December 1953 to December 1956 and 1957–60. First Deputy Chairman, State Economic Commission for Current Planning and afterward First Deputy Chairman of USSR Gosplan, 1956–57. Candidate member (1946–48) and full member (1948–52), Party Politburo. Candidate member, Party Presidium, 1952–53 and 1957–60. Member of Party Central Committee from 1939.

KOZLOV, F. R.   Born in 1908. Joined the CPSU in 1926. Began working in a textile factory in 1923. Komsomol functionary in Ryazan Oblast, 1926–28. Graduated from the Leningrad Politechnical Institute in 1936. Director of a blooming mill at the Izhevsk Metallurgical Plant. After 1939, held leading Party and government jobs. Secretary of the Izhevsk City Party Committee, 1940–44. Worked in the Party Central Committee apparatus, 1944–47 and 1949. Second Secretary, Kuibyshev Oblast Party Committee, 1947–49. In 1949–52 Party organizer for the Party Central Committee at the Leningrad Kirov Plant; and then Second and later First Secretary of the Leningrad City Party Committee. Chairman, RSFSR Council of Ministers, 1957–58. Member of the Central Committee Bureau for the RSFSR, 1956–57 and from January to November 1958. Candidate member, Party Presidium (February to June 1957) and full member after June 1957.

KUUSINEN, O. V.   Born in 1881. Joined the Party in 1904. Graduated from the Historical–Philosophical Faculty of Helsinki in 1905. Editor of socialist newspapers in Finland, 1907–16. Member of the revolutionary government of Finland in 1918 and one of the founders of the

Finnish Communist Party. Secretary of the Executive Committee of the Comintern, 1921–39. Deputy Chairman of the Presidium of the USSR Supreme Soviet and Chairman of the Presidium of the Karelo-Finnish Republic Supreme Soviet, 1940–58. Member of the Party Central Committee from 1941. Member of the Party Presidium, 1952–53 and after 1957. Secretary of the Party Central Committee, from 1957.

MALENKOV, G. M.   Born in 1902 to the family of a civil servant in Orenburg. Joined the CPSU in April 1920 at the front. Studied at the Moscow Higher Technical School, 1921–25. Worked in the apparatus of the Party Central Committee, 1925–30. Held leading posts in the Moscow Party Committee, 1930–34. In 1939 elected member of the Party Central Committee and a Secretary of the Central Committee and a member of the Orgburo. Candidate member, Politburo, 1941. During World War II, member of the State Defense Committee. Full member, Politburo, 1946. (*Large Soviet Encyclopedia,* Vol. 26, April 1954).

MALINOVSKY, R. YA.   Born in 1898. Joined the CPSU in 1926. Participated in the civil war. Graduated from the Frunze Military Academy, 1930. During World War II was a commander at Stalingrad, on the Southern, South-Western, the 3rd and 2nd Ukrainian fronts and in 1945 was commander of the Transbaikal Front. After the war was commander of military districts and Commander-in-Chief of the Far Eastern Military Districts. Commander-in-Chief of the Soviet Army Ground Forces from March 1956, and from May 1, 1956 Deputy Minister of Defense. Minister of Defense from October 1957. Candidate member of the Party Central Committee, 1952–56 and full member, 1956.

MAZUROV, K. T.   Born in 1914. Joined the CPSU in 1940. Graduated from the Gomel' Highway Technicum in 1933 and the Higher Party School in 1947. Worked in a raion road department, 1933–36. Served in the army, 1936–38. An official of the Komsomol in Byelorussia in 1940. Worked in the army and partisan activity, 1941–43. Second Secretary, Minsk City Party Committee, 1949–50, and then First Secretary of Minsk Oblast Party Committee, 1950–53. First Secretary of the Byelorussian Party Central Committee after 1956. Member of the Party Central Committee, 1956. Candidate member of the Party Presidium, 1957.

MIKOYAN, A. I.   Born in 1895. Joined the CPSU in 1915. In 1917 on Party assignments in Baku and Tiflis. In mid-1918 appointed Commissar of the Red Army brigades during Baku's defense against German–Turkish imperialist armies. Led underground work in late 1918 during British occupation of Baku. In 1919–20, head of Bolshevik underground organization in Baku. In 1921–22, Secretary of Nizhny Novgorod Gubernia Party organization. Secretary of the South-Eastern Bureau of the Rostov Party Central Committee, 1922–24 and then until 1926 Secretary of the North-Caucasian Krai Party Committee. USSR People's Commissar for Internal Trade, 1926–30. USSR People's Commissar for Food Industry, 1934–38. Deputy Chairman, Council of People's Commissars, 1937–1946 and People's Commissar of Internal Trade, 1938–46. Member, State Defense Committee, 1942–45. Deputy Chairman, Council of Ministers, 1946–55 and 1957–58. Minister of Internal Trade, 1946–49. Minister of Trade, 1953–55. First Deputy Chairman, Council of Ministers, 1955–57 and after 1958. Candidate member, Politburo, 1926–35 and full member, 1935–52. Member of Party Presidium from 1952. Member of Party Central Committee from 1923.

MOLOTOV, V. M.   Born in 1890 to the family of a shop assistant. Joined the Bolshevik Party in Kazan in 1906. In 1912 worked for the Bolshevik newspaper, *Zvezda,* and had an active part in founding *Pravda.* During the February 1917 bourgeois revolution was head of the Central Committee's Russian Bureau. Elected candidate member of the Party Central Committee in 1920. In November 1920, named Secretary of the Party Central Committee of the Ukraine. Elected to the Politburo in 1926. In 1928–30, Secretary of the Central Committee and also Secretary of the Moscow Party Committee. Became Chairman, Council of People's Commissars, in December 1930. Deputy Chairman, State Defense Committee, 1941–45. Deputy Chairman, Council of Ministers and Minister of Foreign Affairs, 1946. In 1949 was relieved of his duties as Minister of Foreign Affairs. In March 1953 appointed First Deputy Chairman, Council of Ministers and Minister of Foreign Affairs. (*Large Soviet Encyclopedia,* Vol. 28, August 1954).

MUKHITDINOV, N. A.   Born in 1917. Joined the CPSU in 1942. Graduated from the All-Union Co-operative Institute in 1938. Party and Soviet work in the Uzbek Republic, 1947–55. First Secretary of the Uzbek

Party Central Committee, 1955–57. Secretary of the Party Central Committee, 1957–61. Member of the Party Central Committee, from 1952. Candidate member of the Party Presidium, 1956–57 and full member, 1957–61.

MZHAVANADZE, V. P.   Born in 1902. Joined the CPSU in 1927. Graduated from the Lenin Military Political Academy in 1937. Between 1915 and 1924 was a worker. In the Red Army after 1924. Military Commissar of an Infantry Regiment and then member of the Military Council of the army, 1939–45. Member of the Military Council for Military Districts and held political posts in the army, 1945–53. First Secretary of the Georgian Party Central Committee, after 1953. Candidate member, Party Central Committee after 1956.

POSPELOV, P. N.   Born in 1898. Joined the CPSU in 1916. Graduated from the Institute of Red Professors in 1930. Worked in the Tver Party organization in 1917–18 and in Siberia in 1918–20. Held responsible Party jobs in Tver in 1920–23. Worked in the apparatus of the Party Central Committee, 1924–26. Held leading Party jobs in Moscow, 1930–39. Chief editor of *Pravda,* 1940–49. Director of the Marx-Lenin Institute, 1949–52 and after 1961. Secretary of the Party Central Committee, 1953–60. Candidate member of the Party Presidium, 1957–61.

PERVUKHIN, M. G.   Born in 1904. Joined the CPSU in 1919. Graduated from Moscow's Institute of People's Economy in 1929. Engaged in leading economic work, 1937–38. Commissar of Electrical Industry and Power Stations, 1939–42. Commissar and then Minister of Chemical Industry, 1942–50. Deputy Chairman, Council of Ministers, 1950–55. Minister of Power Stations and Electrical Industry, 1953–55. First Deputy Chairman of the Council of Ministers, 1955–57. Minister of Medium Machine Building, 1957. Chairman, State Committee for Foreign Economic Relations, 1957–58. In February 1958, named Ambassador to the German Democratic Republic. Member of the Party Central Committee, 1939. Member of the Party Presidium, 1952–57. Candidate member of the Party Presidium, 1957. (*1958 Yearbook*).

SABUROV, M. Z.   Born in 1900 to a working-class family in the Donbas. Joined the CPSU in 1920. In his youth, worked on the railroads, in the fields, as a coal miner, etc. Studied in the Communist University named after Sverdlov in Moscow, 1923–26. Propagandist for the Party Central Committee in several cities of the Donbas, 1926–28. Studied in the Moscow Mechanical–Machine Building Institute, 1928. In charge of technology in a factory, 1933. Head engineer of a main administration of the Commissariat of Heavy Machine Construction, 1937–38. Head of the section for machine construction of Gosplan and then First Deputy Chairman of Gosplan, 1938. Chairman of Gosplan, 1941. Engaged in special jobs in the State Defense Committee, 1944–46. Named Deputy Chairman, Council of Ministers in February 1947. Chairman of Gosplan, 1949. Member of Party Presidium, from 1952. First Deputy Chairman, Council of Ministers, March 1955. Chairman of State Economic Commission for Current Planning, May 1955. (*Large Soviet Encyclopedia,* Vol. 37, October 1955).

SHVERNIK, N. M.   Born in 1888. Joined the Party in 1905, and became a member of the Petersburg Party Committee. Was imprisoned for a period by the Tsarist Government. In October 1917 became Chairman of the All-Russian Committee of Artillery Plant Workers, and later Chairman of the Samara City Soviet. Served in the Red Army during the civil war, and later became a Political Commissar on the Western and Southern Fronts. Presidium member of the Party Central Control Commission and the People's Commissariat of Workers' and Peasants' Inspection, RSFSR, 1923–25. Secretary of the Leningrad Oblast Party Committee, 1925. Secretary of the Party Central Committee, 1926. Secretary of the Ural Oblast Party Committee, 1927–28. Chairman, Metal Workers' Trade Union, 1929. Secretary of the All-Union Central Trade Union Council, 1930–44. First Deputy Chairman of the Presidium of the USSR Supreme Soviet, and Chairman of the Presidium of the RSFSR Supreme Soviet, 1944–46. Chairman, Presidium of USSR Supreme Soviet, 1946–53. Chairman, All-Union Central Trade Union Council, 1953–56. Chairman, Party Control Commission from 1956. Member of the Party Central Committee from 1925. Candidate member of the Politburo, 1939–52. Candidate member of Presidium, 1952–57 and thereafter full member.

SUSLOV, M. A.   Born in 1902. Joined the CPSU in 1921. Graduated from the Moscow Institute of People's Economy in 1928. Aspirant at the Economic Institute of the Communist Academy and teacher at the Moscow Institute and the Industrial Academy, 1929–31. Member of the Central Control Commission and Workers' and Peasants' Inspectorate, 1929–34. Member of Soviet Control Commission, 1936. Studied at the Economic Institute of Red Professors, 1936–37. Secretary, Rostov Oblast Party Committee, 1937–39. First Secretary of the Stavropol Krai and City Party Committees, 1939–44. Chairman, Party Central Committee Bureau for the Lithuanian Republic, 1944–46. Secretary of the Party Central Committee from 1947 and simultaneously Editor-in-Chief of *Pravda,* 1949–51. Member of the Party Central Committee from 1941. Member of the Party Presidium from 1955.

Voroshilov, K. Ye.   Born in 1881. Joined the Party in 1903. Participant in the revolutions of 1905, February 1917, and October 1917. One of the organizers of the Red Army. Member of the Party Central Committee, from 1921. People's Commissar of Military and Naval Affairs and Chairman of the Revolutionary Military Council, 1925–34. Member of the Politburo, 1926–52 and Presidium, from 1952. People's Commissar for Defense, 1934–40. Named Marshal of the Soviet Union, 1935. Chairman of the State Control Commission in Hungary, 1945–47. Deputy Chairman of the Council of Ministers, 1946–53. Chairman of the Presidium of the USSR Supreme Soviet, after 1953. (*1958 Yearbook*).

Zhukov, G. K.   Born in 1896 to a peasant family. Served in the Soviet army since October 1918. Chief-of-Staff of the Soviet Army and Chairman of the People's Commissariat for Defense during World War II. Co-ordinated the activities of the Volkhovsk and Leningrad fronts in 1943. Co-ordinated the activities of the First and Second Ukrainian and the First and Second Byelorussian fronts in 1943–44. (*Large Soviet Encyclopedia,* Vol. 16, October 1952).

INDEX TO PERSONS